SO NOW YOU'RE A LEADER

10 precepts of practical leadership

PETER STOKES
JOHN JAMES

McGRAW-HILL BOOK COMPANY Sydney

New York   San Francisco   Auckland   Bogotá
Caracas   Lisbon   London   Madrid   Mexico City
Milan   New Delhi   San Juan   Singapore
Toronto   Kuala Lumpur

To the memory of Bob Hennessy, a fine leader, and a visionary who may well have written this book—and possibly have done it better.

McGraw-Hill books are available at special quantity discounts to use as premiums and sales promotions, or for use in corporate training programs. For more information, please write to the Director of Special Sales, McGraw-Hill, 4 Barcoo Street, East Roseville, NSW 2069. Or contact your local bookstore.

National Library of Australia Cataloguing-in-Publication data:
Stokes, Peter
So now you're a leader: ten precepts of practical leadership.

Includes index.
ISBN 0 07 470321 8.

1. Management. 2. Leadership. I. James, John. II. Title.

658.4

Published in Australia by
McGraw-Hill Book Company Australia Pty Limited
4 Barcoo Street, Roseville NSW 2069, Australia
Acquisitions editor: John Rowe
Production editors: Annabel Adair, Carolyn Pike
Designer: Lesley Brown
Cartoonist: Greg Gaul
Cover designer: Steve Miller
Typeset in Berkeley Book, in Australia by Post Typesetters
Printed in Australia by McPherson's Printing Group

CONTENTS

Preface

Every advance made in this world, whether technological, philosophical or social, has been as a result of human endeavour. The quality of human endeavour is very much dependent on the quality of leadership in a society. The latter years of this century have seen the advance of theories such as economic rationalism, experiments with various social and political systems, huge advances in technology and communications, and equally huge human and natural disasters. Solutions—and theories relating to solutions—abound. This is also the case with leadership theories.

Leadership is hardly a new topic. It has received fairly detailed attention over many years from philosophers as well as from leaders themselves and in more recent decades from academics. This book does not purport to replace the many excellent works already available. What we are endeavouring to provide for the reader is more of a 'how to' manual, which provides essentially a list of do's and don'ts that have worked for ourselves and others for over half a lifetime.

The idea for this book emerged from a series of discussions during which it became clear that the issue of leadership was a passion of the authors, both of whom have experienced good and bad leadership at the hands of others and both of whom no doubt have provided either good or indifferent leadership to others over the same period. Conversations, peppered with a wide variety of anecdotal material from our experience, slowly grew into a manuscript; at the same time we both drew on a mountain of reading undertaken over many years. Although we hadn't worked together previously we had both practised leadership at middle, senior and community levels even though our careers have taken widely divergent paths.

The book aims to bring the lessons of leadership home to the average man and woman at frontline, or junior, and middle level management. If you accept what has been written and find your workplace lacking in relation to the principles espoused, do not despair. It is for this very reason the book has been written—so that you may help to *change* your workplace. If your reading of our book indicates a modus operandi at your workplace in sharp contrast to the propositions it contains, then at least consider the possibility that the book may be right and your workplace and even your boss (perish the thought) wrong.

We hope the book is easy to read. It should be capable of being read and digested in five uninterrupted hours. To ensure that there are few interruptions there are few footnotes and no lengthy references to other perhaps more erudite works. A bibliography of further reading is included. Also included is an appendix, which simply asks some questions that may help you to see where you fit in the leadership stakes. It is not a statistical instrument and it measures nothing objectively, but it does act as a sort of summary and you may get some idea of how far you have to go. You may care to give it to your boss and your subordinates.

The word *precepts* has been deliberately used. These represent very clear directions a leader should take but they contain no element suggesting coercion and no threat of dire consequences if disregarded. However, even free-flowing leadership is based upon certain inviolable principles which, if disregarded, *can* lead to disaster. The precepts are really a pathway to those principles and may not always be easy to obey or follow.

ACKNOWLEDGMENTS

Thank you to all the friends who offered encouragement, and not a few who pointed out glaring anomalies in the early drafts. Special thanks to those who proofread the drafts and offered very constructive comments. Most especially are thanks due to Anna Stokes, who went through a late draft like a whirlwind and lent a more youthful perspective to the seasoned wisdom of experience.

Figure 5.2 has been adapted from *Motivation and Personality* by Abraham H. Maslow. Copyright © 1954, © 1987 by Harper & Row, Publishers Inc. Copyright © 1970 by Abraham H. Maslow. Reprinted by permission of Harper & Row, Publishers Inc.

Introduction

There have been stories about leaders and the led since the serpent led Adam and Eve astray in the Garden of Eden. There can be little argument that that story is the earliest example in our culture (and there are numerous parallels in other cultures) of a leader not leading from correct principles and the followers getting it wrong. Since that time, the concept of leadership has undergone some study and ultimate sophistication but there are still numerous examples of people being led up the garden path (no pun intended) by questionable leaders.

We want to use this Introduction to give some historical background, explain some of our definitions, and to indicate to the reader why the study of leadership is neither incidental nor accidental. You will not need to know anything more of the theories than is contained in this brief Introduction.

For generations, the term *leader* seemed to have heroic connotations and was often used in conjunction with power or authority. Leadership was almost invariably perceived to be power-based. In fact, the word did not have its origins in heroism; it probably started out its life as a word meaning 'guide' rather than anything more directive. We probably all have some preconceived idea of what the words leader and leadership mean today. There are many definitions, some of which we think are well wide of the mark.

For our purposes:

Leadership is the art of consistently influencing or directing people towards the achievement of a clear common goal, in such a way as to engender loyalty, respect and willing co-operation.

The definition is fairly descriptive but you will understand why, as the book progresses. It's very important to explain the definition because of the preconceptions some people have. Even today many people view leadership as being very visible and leaders being very powerful and obvious. That preconception is historical itself. Therefore it is necessary that everyone remembers some key factors about true leadership.

- The word *art* has been carefully chosen. Leadership is not a science; it cannot be graphed, quantified or performed by rote. It is not the sole province of the academic.
- It has to be *consistent,* in terms of quantity, quality and timeliness. By timeliness we mean it cannot be allowed to diminish over a period.
- We use the word *influence* because coercion or driving is not leadership, it is normally a manifestation of power, and while power is an aspect of leadership, we want to look at it in a different way.
- *Directing* in our definition doesn't mean ordering; it means showing people the way, as we would direct a stranger to a railway station. That in itself is predicated upon someone wanting to go to the railway station. This raises the next point.
- Achieving a *clear common goal* means that **everyone** must know where it is they are being influenced or directed to go and must be enrolled in that goal by the leader.

If the goal is leader-selected then the last part of the definition becomes more problematical and the leader's task will include the responsibility of making the selected goal common to all. In any event, achieving a worthwhile goal needs to be done with a sense of harmony, otherwise its effects will be only ephemeral. Manipulation is not leadership. We cannot stress highly enough the need to maintain respect, loyalty and willing co-operation, because if these qualities are absent the leadership will break down under stress.

A leader is best when people barely know that he exists, not so good when people obey and acclaim him, worst when they despise him. Fail to honour people they fail to honour you! But of a good leader who talks little; when his work is done, his aim fulfilled—they will all say, We did this ourselves!

Lao-Tzu (c. 600 BC)

Over the years there seem to have been four approaches, or maybe we should call them insights, to leadership. The emergence of a new approach didn't necessarily lead to the demise of the previous approaches, so all retain some validity even today. And, as will be explained, the approaches were not all discrete so that there were combinations of several as well as adaptations.

They were generally accepted as:
- the *qualities* approach
- the *situational* approach
- the *functional* approach
- the *styles* approach

QUALITIES APPROACH

The first thing that people studied in leadership were the characteristics or qualities that perceived good leaders possessed. Examples of good leadership were chosen by a process of sifting through history. The study of some of the great heroes was in itself motivational enough to further produce some quite good leaders.

The qualities were many and they varied but they were generally based on character—such attributes as integrity, moral courage, physical courage, trust and so on. Many of these qualities are still important today but qualities such as moral courage would in most cases these days be more important than physical courage. Closer to our own generation we have added to them such things as enthusiasm, warmth, calmness, and the ubiquitous *fair, firm and friendly*. It is very easy to convince ourselves that we have those qualities.

The qualities weren't wrong, it's just that too many people thought that if one had the correct breeding then that was all that mattered. People misunderstood qualities or, at the very least, over-estimated them. After all, many of the leaders over time, especially in the 'stiff upper lip brigade', had those qualities in abundance—and look at some of the disastrous legacies we have inherited.

By observing a number of good leaders over centuries and determining the characteristics that they had in common, it seemed easy to come up with a formula that may have been valid in heroic times. These qualities came from legend and from role models. Qualities are still important, but there are now new understandings.

SITUATIONAL APPROACH

The original terminology 'situational leadership' applied in a much more generic sense than it does now as that term has since become a commercial product, which has confused things somewhat. Theorists have postulated three 'situational' theories. The first is that of the *'contingency'* theory. The theory proposes that a situation is controlled by three elements: the structure of the task; the position power of the leader; and the leader/team relationship. The theory suggests that in a given situation, with a given team relationship, a particular type of leader is going to be the most appropriate.

Historically it could be seen in the characters of Joan of Arc, George Washington or King Arthur—or even the great Cincinattus from classical times—though these examples are perhaps somewhat heroic. The emphasis is really on the person having the appropriate technical competence or knowledge for a given situation at a given time.

There was a school of thought that advocated this in practice. If you were in a plane crash and were stranded in the jungle for instance, maybe the best leader would be a navigator rather than the aircraft captain. There is also no doubt that this theory has worked at a higher level in recent political history, as a response to the saying: 'Cometh the hour—cometh the man'. Take the example of Nelson Mandela, for instance. Therefore, leadership becomes of consequence when the opportunity and environment, or situation, are right. You could call this fate or luck. But Mandela didn't only have the *qualities*, the *situation*, and the expert knowledge on his side; there was a dire *need* on the part of the people of South Africa to be led, which helped to create that environment.

The *contingency* theory received impetus through the work of Frederick Fiedler who went so far as to suggest, with a series of tests, that a leader's style or approach didn't change. So when the situation changes maybe you needed to change the leader!

On the other hand, the *path-goal* theory of *situational leadership* suggests that leader behaviour can change on a continuum, from directive to simply one of setting goals for subordinates. This was eventually refined into the commercial product (see below).

Finally, there is a model that suggests that the way leadership decisions are best made will depend on the degree of acceptance by followers. This model suggests five different decision styles determined by the degree of acceptance.

FUNCTIONAL APPROACH

Professor John Adair, who is probably England's foremost leadership academic, helps us to formalise the example of someone like Mandela.[1] He postulated that there are those same three ingredients in any situation where people have to work together: a leader with a personality and character (*qualities*); where and in what circumstances the leadership need is occurring (*situation*); and the group, with *needs* of its own. It is the *group needs* that form the basis of the type of leadership which is often quoted among trainers today, especially in the military sphere. It is commonly referred to as *functional leadership*.

This group has three fundamental needs, often depicted as three interlocking circles:

1. The need to be held together as a team.
2. The need to achieve a common task.
3. The needs of the individuals in the team.

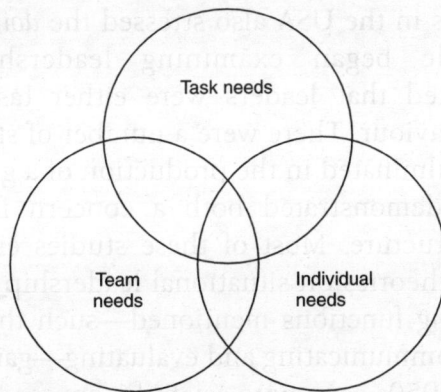

Fig. IN.1 *The elements of functional leadership*

A leader has to satisfy those needs. We will need to look at that in detail later. The concept of the three circles forms the basis of functional leadership.

By the eighteenth century, or even earlier, it had become clear that many of the attributes of good leaders had nothing to do with character. Some good leaders were scoundrels. They were good leaders because they had vision (not necessarily good either) and they could communicate that vision. Many leaders in the last century—such as Isambard Brunel, the great ship designer and bridge builder, and George Stephenson, the father of the steam train—were not necessarily heroic. However, they were not only visionary, they were incredibly competent planners. What's more, they were engineers and artisans, not politicians or soldiers. They were leaders as much because of what they *did* as because of what they *were*.

You could say that the functional approach began to make leadership more measurable, because these functions could be defined and taught more readily. There used to be an acronym for it: PLOC—planning, leading, organising, and controlling. John Adair again suggested that a good leader needed to plan, set objectives, communicate, control and evaluate.[2]

> Functional leadership says that what a person *does* is as important as what a person *is*.

Studies in the 1940s in the USA also stressed the *doing* nature of leadership and people began examining leadership 'behaviours'. Researchers suggested that leaders were either task- or employee-centred in their behaviour. There were a number of studies done at the same time, which culminated in the production of a grid that suggested that good leaders demonstrated both a concern for people and a concern for task structure. Most of these studies either preceded or coincided with the theories on situational leadership.

Many of the *doing* functions mentioned—such things as planning, setting objectives, communicating and evaluating—gained impetus during the 1940s and 1950s as a more scientific approach to management was being taught. This had grown apace as a result of World War II, when studies began to stress these more teachable functional aspects.

> Some leadership functions depend to a degree on innate traits or qualities, others can be learned from role models and through experience.

Another thing World War II gave us was an understanding of the *cross-functional* nature of leadership. Huge numbers of professional engineers, scientists, logisticians and others took their skills into the forces during the war and contributed hugely to the ultimate Allied success. Likewise, leaders from the services became well-known and successful political and corporate leaders when they emerged from the forces.

The best known were men like George Marshall, US Chief of Staff during the war. He became Secretary of State, and was credited with the economic salvation of Western Europe in the late 1940s with the

Marshall Plan. Eisenhower was another, who commanded the Allied Forces in Europe and became President of the USA from 1952 to 1960. These men were leaders whatever the situation. These factors simply reinforced the *functional* aspects of leadership. Leaders were now not only men with certain qualities, they had to be competent at carrying out functions at every level in any environment. While they may not have been experts in the particular field, they were able to harness the expertise of others.

STYLES APPROACH

By the 1950s the conventional wisdom was that leadership was becoming more democratic as the focus on leadership drifted away from the politico-military sphere of influence and became more commercially oriented. The US studies referred to above, which focused on behaviour, eventually culminated in 1960 when Douglas McGregor, an American sociologist, created his *Theory X* and *Theory Y* styles in relation to management. This, of course, was reflected in leadership thinking. *Styles* eventually became represented on a sliding scale. (See Fig. IN.2.)

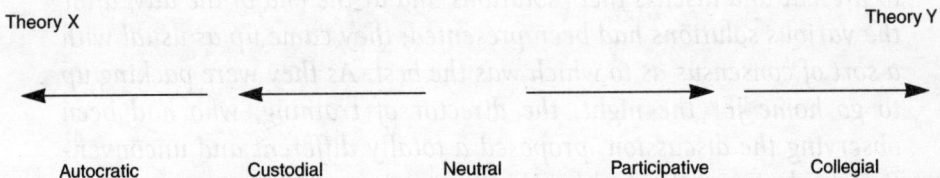

Theory X   Theory Y

Autocratic   Custodial   Neutral   Participative   Collegial

Fig. IN.2 *Styles continuum*

Whereas McGregor concentrated on styles in relation to employee–leader behaviour, he didn't necessarily suggest that X was 'task centred', and Y was 'employee centred', although that is the implication. It is hard to recall whether in the days when styles were first being taught, one style was being recommended over another, but the study of leadership 'styles' became very popular in the 1960s and early 1970s.

SITUATIONAL CONTROL

In the examination of styles in the 1970s, Hersey and Blanchard, both American psychologists and academics working together and separately, refined the characteristics of Theory X and Theory Y together with elements of the path-goal theory, but they also took into account a combination of the level of development and commitment of a subordinate. This has been further refined in recent years into the commercial product known as *situational leadership 2*.[3]

This is a narrow view of leadership but nevertheless it is excellent as a tool of functional leadership and it certainly needs to be understood by anyone interested in practical leadership.

We have to be careful of suggesting that there is a right way of doing something. It not only depends on where a subordinate, follower or worker is psychologically, or what their skill level may be, but on the changing nature of the task itself and the environmental circumstances.

Consider the following as an indication of theory and practice; and it certainly concerns situational leadership.

> *There was a true story told by a colleague years ago. He was at the British Command and Staff College Camberley doing a twelve-month military management (staff) course. This is where middle level leaders (majors) do their post-tertiary study to qualify for higher command.*
>
> *They were visiting the Normandy Battlefields in France and were given tactical combat problems to solve. The students were all asked to present and discuss their solutions and at the end of the day, after the various solutions had been presented, they came up as usual with a sort of consensus as to which was the best. As they were packing up to go home for the night, the director of training, who had been observing the discussion, proposed a totally different and unconventional solution and asked for the students' comments.*
>
> *He was howled down and he offered no more to the discussion. On the way home that evening a couple of the students questioned him on his proposed solution and asked what had possessed him to offer something so preposterous. He replied that the problem was based on an actual situation that he had found himself in on that spot some fifteen years before, that was the solution he had used and that was how he had won the battle and been decorated with the Distinguished Service Order (DSO)!*

A right way in one situation one day, could be the wrong way the next.

The way a leader needs to respond or act will also depend on how much control a leader has or needs in a given situation—not surprisingly referred to as *situational control*. This can be related in a manner to the leadership situation of the three needs: *task, team,* and *individual.*

Frederick Fiedler (who developed the *contingency* theory) and Martin Chemers sum this up very well in their book *Increasing Leadership in Action.*[4] As we explained earlier, the theory says that the control a leader has, depends on his or her relationship with the team, the nature and complexity of the task (task structure), and the sanctioning or position power of the leader over the team and the individual.

Whereas Fiedler may seem to suggest that a leader's style won't change with the changing of a situation, few practitioners would agree, because everyone has seen successful leaders modify their style as necessary. Presumably he would also disagree with cross-functional leadership except in particular 'situations'. Even so, the idea of *situational control* is helpful to train leaders to understand the necessity of flexibility.

For certain professionals, such as police or firemen, in *emergencies* the tasks are very unstructured so there is need for quite a lot of position power on the part of a leader. In *training*, however, the tasks are normally more structured and the outcomes more predictable, thus position power can be reduced and high situational control still maintained. Accordingly, police and military position powers can be lessened in non-threatening situations but may need to be increased in a crisis.

Of the three components of situational control the most important is the relationship with the team, which includes the relationship of the members of the team with each other. It follows that with a given task structure, the need for position power is reduced as the relationship with the team improves. If leaders genuinely want to create an optimum team relationship they will divest themselves of as much power and authority as they can. This distribution or devolution of both authority and responsibility has been given a number of names over recent years. We shall call it *PowerSharing* and refer to it thus through the rest of the book.

PowerSharing is the devolution to followers, or subordinates, of the responsibility for outcomes associated with any relevant task within a common vision. This includes all the resources and authority necessary to achieve the outcome without the diminution of the leader's ultimate responsibility.

PowerSharing ensures that the workforce really shares in the 'coal-face' decision making. It's really democracy at work in the workplace. In some excellent examples such as The Body Shop retail chain, or the legendary Brazilian firm, Semco (about which you will hear more), the workers seem to have far more power in the workplace than we have in our day-to-day dealing with government. There are many other examples.

Many factors have had a bearing on the recent understanding of leadership, most of which seemed to have occurred during the twentieth century. Not the least of these has been the rapid growth in electronic communication and the special qualities being demanded of corporate leaders as a result of the changing nature of the political and economic world. Unfortunately, as in so many other areas, there has been a tendency to complicate leadership teaching. In reality anyone who has a modicum of intelligence, a grain of commonsense and an average capacity for getting on with others can be a leader in given circumstances. *If they want to be!* Colour, gender and shape make no difference.

BORN LEADERS?

This doesn't mean that leadership is so easy anyone can be a leader. Some people just don't seem to relate to other people—and relating to people is a prime requisite. If someone would rather be solving the latest problems in the balance sheet than communing with his or her fellows then he or she would be best advised to stick to that role. Some people don't want to lead, some people shouldn't try to lead.

On the other hand, charm and social skills are not automatic entrees into the leadership world. Charm can be helpful as a quality, but of itself it is of no consequence in the leadership stakes. In fact, it can be a hindrance, because it can lead others to make assumptions about a person's other skill levels. In a similar way, skilled articulation or public presentation is no indicator of leadership. It doesn't even mean that the presenter is a skilled communicator in other than a very narrow field. Not everyone is an extravert[a] and introverts are by no means precluded from leadership.

There is a well-known saying that 'Leaders are made, not born'. While this may be so in the majority of cases there is nevertheless little doubt that some people are born with certain natural aptitudes which make the process of learning to be a leader in certain circumstances

(a) The spelling 'extravert' is used throughout this text based on the original spelling used by Carl Jung.

easier than it is for others. For instance, some people are born with natural aptitudes like hand-eye co-ordination. Somebody born with a natural sporting aptitude has a head start to become the captain of a sporting team over someone who can't walk and chew gum at the same time. Similarly, we will learn later that people are also born with certain psychological preferences that make it easier for them to do certain things or learn certain things. Some people have a natural advantage in the skill area, others have to work at it.

Even expert sportspeople have to learn leadership like anyone else, but unless they are decidedly anti-social they can become leaders. But they have to learn—they can't be taught. By this we mean that as leadership is an art, it is learned by experience, through role modelling and contact. It can't be learned from a book. You might ask why we are writing this book then. Well, if you want to learn to paint you will go to an art school. Your initial teachers and motivators will be artists or experts. You can also pick some things up through books—but you turn to books to give your experience the final touches. Even then most books would be written by artists or at least continually refer to the works of artists.

Having learned about art and painting, have you become a painter or artist? Not unless you have volumes of natural talent or until you have practised and been advised and critiqued over many years. But no matter what your natural talent, you become an artist when people like your work, not when you have a diploma with the word 'painter' on it. Thus it is with leadership. And a leader improves with practice.

Imagine a circus clown who has an act which involves juggling while riding a unicycle along a tightrope. Ask him to write down what he does and more than likely he couldn't. Bring in a task analysis expert and he or she could no doubt write a full length description or even a book. He or she may even be able to teach the theory better than the expert. But where does the next generation of unicyclists learn their trade? At a university or in the circus?

Now, once the unicyclist has mastered the technique he may get better by learning something about aerodynamics or the theory of moments or whatever. Even so, he would be better learning that from someone who understood the application of balance to unicycling and was capable of both theory and practice. He could also find inspiration from reading about heroic unicyclists or about people in similar roles, like Blondin for example.

> Leadership is an art—not a science.

Therefore, a budding leader needs to have seen and experienced good leadership. He or she needs to learn first-hand from people who have been leaders. Even negative experiences can teach us how not to do something. All learners need to be able to develop discernment, because unpopular leadership decisions are not necessarily bad decisions and popular decisions are not always wise decisions.

Consulting relevant books helps to fine-tune relevant skills. You can't go to school and be taught *character;* that comes from a life experience, a learned experience. You can be taught what elements go to make up *character*; in the same way you can learn the principles of ethics, but that doesn't make you ethical. We can even advise you to be ethical, but unless you have been drawn to ethical practice by inner conviction or conditioning or you have seen and appreciated ethical practice in another, the chances are that you will not understand what is being said.

> Good leadership is essentially learned behaviour and comes from role models.

ROLE MODELS

Much of what we learn about leadership will come from role models. Unfortunately, many of the most accessible and visible role models don't necessarily demonstrate a lot in the way of real leadership in this day and age. Many are held up to us as examples of leadership in one skill or another, be it political, social or even cultural. Often they only have a demonstrated skill and no pretensions to leadership. Such people as our sporting heroes and heroines, our film stars, even some of our high profile journalists, and other high profile 'personalities' are paraded as leadership models by an adoring media on the basis that they are very visible. However, this situation is not necessarily bad. It just means those people should realise what a responsibility they have and what an opportunity to influence. We are not saying that they don't make good leaders either; some obviously do.

People are easy to lead—essentially, most people respond positively to good leadership. This doesn't mean that they are easily manipulated or gullible—because the term 'easily led' generally has a pejorative sense to it. The human endeavour has shown us that people have a lot of initiative and they are generally very tolerant. Leading or being part of a good leadership environment under another is immensely rewarding and a great privilege. It is also fun.

If you would understand virtue, observe the conduct of virtuous men.

Aristotle

One thing of great importance has yet to be mentioned. Most people these days are appointed into positions of responsibility and ergo authority by virtue of their skills, knowledge or education. Rarely are people appointed because of their sheer leadership skills. There is therefore all the more reason for people to study and learn leadership.

You can't become a leader by appointment, no matter how long you stay in the position. More can be said about that later, but like the painter who only becomes an artist when people admire his or her work, a leader only becomes so when he or she is affirmed by those who are being led. You can be the boss, you can even have power and authority, but you aren't a leader until you have followers. Some of our community 'leaders' would do well to sometimes reflect on this.

Leadership cannot be mandated.

We have now covered the history and development of leadership theory. The object of the book from now on is to look at those elements and to bring them together in the concept of PowerSharing. Hopefully the ten precepts we have chosen will draw those threads together and will encourage readers to adopt a more pro-active approach to leadership.

You will find that the more you read about leadership, the more you will realise that you have been observing successful leaders leading, and in many cases you have yourselves been abiding by most of the formal principles without deliberately doing so in a planned sense. That's where a lot of the theories came from anyway—from practitioners who found what worked for them and passed it on. In this way 'theory in use' became 'espoused theory'. The background is helpful and it is interesting to see that the rise of new understandings and insights in no way lessens the validity of the old.

This book is being written to provide a 'hands on' tool to help the young, the busy, the frustrated or the aspiring leader. Because new insights have been added, there are perhaps new and unique ways of looking at things. Technology has also altered many of our perspectives and perceptions. PowerSharing enables us to clarify these new issues together with the old, in a 'user-friendly' set of ten principles, which will hopefully help the aspiring leaders to find enjoyable, fulfilling and productive careers.

Accept responsibility for all your actions and those of your followers

Accountability begins and ends with the appointed or elected leader. An enormous amount of heartache and angst could be obviated if everyone understood that—starting at the top! The difficulty with this concept is that it seems to be endemic throughout Western society that we try to avoid responsibility for our actions. Why then should aspiring leaders be any different? Let us try to put the issue of leadership accountability in its true perspective.

There will be many who will suggest that there must be times when a leader just cannot have control of what is going on, especially in a large organisation. The span is too great. Suppose the office manager of a large firm absconds with the petty cash; the chief executive surely cannot be held to account. He or she can't help it if one of the staff is dishonest. Nor should the chief executive be held responsible if the financial controller held up a bank. But he or she could be held responsible for having chosen the office manager badly, for being a poor judge of character, or for not having foolproof audit procedures; any one of which factors has a profound effect on the ultimate outcome. What we are saying is that accountability for outcomes is not divisible at any level where outcomes are produced. To illustrate this point we need a simple explanation of the input–process–outcome of any activity in a management sense.

Any activity in any enterprise can be broken down diagrammatically, as shown in Figure 1.1. This is true whether the business is making cars, designing widgets or assessing insurance claims. Every activity has inputs, a process, and outcomes—even when it comes to making morning tea. What is often forgotten is that every process itself has inputs, processes and outcomes. This Process box is represented in Figure 1.2.

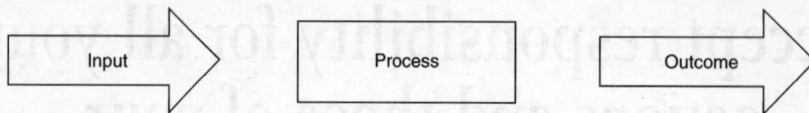

Fig. 1.1   *Elements of activity (1)*

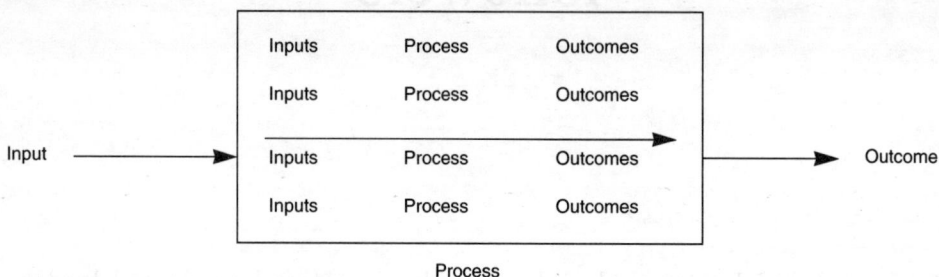

Fig. 1.2   *Elements of activity (2)*

Every input involves a number of resources, as does every process and every outcome. Those resources are: personnel, material, equipment, method, and environment. Therefore a whole operation would resemble the outline in Figure 1.3. Any reader familiar with total quality management (TQM) will recognise the components in this figure. Nothing we have to say in this book about modern-day leadership is in conflict with TQM, or any other workable managerial philosophy. What has this got to do with accountability?

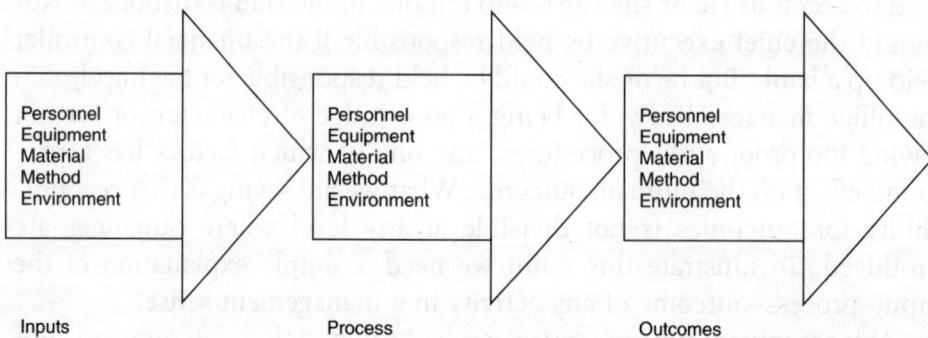

Fig. 1.3   *Components of activity*

POINT OF IMPACT

Let's look at what we will call the 'outcome interface'. The outcome interface is where the outcome relates to the next input, or where the outcome ends. In Figure 1.3 it would be represented by the point of the right-hand outcome arrow. That is similar to what Jan Carlzon, ex-chief executive of Scandinavian Airlines, calls the moments of truth in his book of the same name.[1]

In this book we shall call it the *point of impact* (POI), because this label suits our purposes better and is slightly more descriptive (See Fig. 1.4).

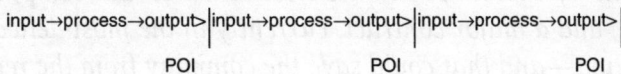

input→process→output>|input→process→output>|input→process→output>|

POI   POI   POI

Fig. 1.4   *Point of impact occurrence*

In any organisation, everyone has a customer who has to avail of an outcome. For a shop assistant the customer is very clear, and so is the outcome—a successful transaction with a shopper. The POI is obvious—the moment of contact with the customer.

However, the outcomes for the buyers or accountants are related to internal customers; they rarely have contact with the shopper. In fact, the people who have to face the most important POIs are often the most junior and inexperienced—and possibly the most poorly paid as well. Yet they are often the people who have to face the customer, who is the recipient of the outcome at the final POI.

> Every worker has a point of impact for which he or she is responsible. Some POIs are combinations of others' POIs.

This might suggest that the shop assistant is ultimately responsible because he or she is in control of the ultimate interface. That is hardly fair—nor is it true. He or she may be responsible for the final POI but the responsibility for the full POI belongs well up the chain of command. The shop assistant is responsible for the last tiny outcome in the whole process box, while the total outcome probably belongs to the store manager or even the managing director (depending on the outcome).

Picture an old-fashioned organisation where morning tea is still provided by a 'tea lady'. The 'tea lady' has an outcome—she provides tea and biscuits for jaded office workers. There are many inputs, such as coffee and tea, and many processes, such as boiling water, wheeling trolleys and so on. The outcome is tea and biscuits for the staff.

Imagine a Pythonesque situation where the tea trolley gets out of control. It careers down the stairs and overturns. Gallons of boiling tea pour down the stairs and through an unrepaired crack in the floor onto the floor below and into the electrical circuit, which short circuits, blowing all the fuses. The power goes off and the computer goes down. None of the staff who are networked to the computer have backed up, and a major contract, currently in the most delicate stage of negotiation—and that could save the company from the receiver— is suddenly without information that should have been backed up. What is more, the information technology manager only last year recommended that the company buy a series of stand-alone PCs in the next year's budget. The company faces disaster and **it is all the 'tea lady's' fault**! Or is it?

Let's look at the sequence:

- *Tea lady'*. Outcome: tea for the workers.
- *Maintenance person*. Outcome: waterproof ceilings.
- *Electrical contractor*. Outcome: emergency power.
- *Information technology manager*. Outcome: accurate data for all levels.
- *Computer operators*. Outcome: up-to-date information.

It seems as though all the people involved are responsible, because an achieved outcome at any level could have stopped the chain reaction. But in reality each person is accountable only for the outcomes over which they have direct control, no matter where the inputs might originate. Whoever is responsible for the ultimate outcome of the company must bear the final responsibility. The interface between the outcome and any customer is the POI. *While each person is responsible for their own POI, the total POI responsibility is in no way diminished or divided.*

A leader is responsible for everything in an organisation which goes into his or her POI.

This may sound overly harsh. What if a leader is on a business trip over-seas? Can someone be responsible if he or she wasn't even there? Well, that is what the leader is paid for—accepting the extra responsibility. There will, of course, be times when whoever is formally deputised has respon-sibility for overseeing the operation—for instance, when someone is on a prolonged absence. When that deputised person makes a mistake or error of judgment they must be held accountable. However, even then the origi-nal leader must bear some responsibility, perhaps for having chosen the deputy poorly or for not providing them with sufficient information.

John: I was once an operations manager for a particularly forthright boss. He took me aside early in the piece and said that if ever he was absent and a decision had to be made, then I was to make the decision. If it was wrong and his higher authority chastised him for it then that was his fault for being absent.

From this I knew three things: first, that he expected me to make decisions and not to wait for his return; second, that he would support my decision; and third, that if he disagreed with my action only he and I would know. He saw it as his responsibility to make sure that I was aware of what he wanted in all circum-stances. In other words, I had authority to act.

Any responsibility for a POI or process must be accompanied by all the authority necessary to complete the process or address the POI.

What we are saying here is that accountability lies at the feet of the per-son responsible for that outcome interface or POI. The 'tea lady' was responsible for spilling the tea, nothing more—because her outcome was providing refreshment and her customers were her fellow workers. In fact, the boss in that case was clearly accountable, because if *any one person* had been doing their job the disastrous chain of events would have been interrupted.

A colleague had an experience recently which might illustrate this more clearly. She took her car in to have a routine service one morn-ing. It was an authorised agent so they knew their business and said the car would be ready by 4.30 pm. She returned at 4.45 pm. She waited for ten minutes and inquired where her car was. The counter clerk went off and returned a minute or so later saying that it was just being tidied up and would only be a few minutes.

By 5.30 pm she was becoming agitated and gave the counter clerk a piece of her mind. She finally drove the car out of there at 6.05 pm!

When she questioned the service manager he said the clerk shouldn't have told her that the car was nearly ready when it wasn't. She pointed out that getting the car ready was not his job, and in fact she had found the clerk to be very courteous.

The service manager then blamed the service department for being overloaded. That was the fault of the scheduling clerk and the colleague was promised that it was being addressed. Then she found that the bill was twice what she expected. That was the fault of the mechanic who went beyond his authorisation in repair. However, the part had been faulty and he should have had the accounts department call her to authorise the fitting. The accounts department should have picked up the fact that there was no customer authorisation, so it was also their fault.

The next day she wrote to the general manager. She received a quick response stating that she was right; it was the fault of the service manager and it wouldn't happen next time. She gave up in disgust and still talks about it even now. They'll never have her custom again. Who was accountable for the whole mess?

Clearly, the general manager was responsible, because he is accountable for the total outcome. He obviously couldn't be responsible for all the individual outcomes, or internal POIs as we call them, but they are all just separate equations in the whole process for which he is responsible. All the people responsible for outcomes are responsible internally, not to the external customer. The only person responsible to an external customer in this instance was the counter clerk—and he was only responsible for the outcomes relating to his particular processes, which he seemed to handle courteously. He could not be responsible for the information that suggested the car was nearly ready (unless of course he was deliberately lying) because that information was someone else's outcome, or POI, which in fact became one of his inputs.

> A customer should only have to be concerned with the final POI and should not be brought into discussions about internal POIs.

One of the unknowns, of course, was whether the general manager knew he was responsible. Ignorance is no defence, but these days there is such a lack of understanding regarding responsibility that it is quite possible that he was ignorant. This is all the more reason for people to start concentrating on understanding the meaning of leadership.

CORPORATE RESPONSIBILITY

One of the great conundrums facing the world today is the question of corporate responsibility. This is a particular problem in the case of the multinational giants where the boards of directors are interconnected globally and where neither country of origin nor shareholding can satisfactorily point to a particular responsibility or POI for either an individual or a group of individuals.

The existence of massive insurance covers and complex lines of responsibility is often an excuse for people in senior positions to act irresponsibly and to plead ignorance when things go seriously wrong. Issues in the last twenty years, such as the Bhopal tragedy, the Agent Orange controversy and even the more recent problems with silicone implants all point to a tendency for large corporations to substitute profit for responsibility. That similar problems persist can be seen with the mining problems in Ok Tedi and Bougainville in Papua New Guinea.

While the handling and subsequent clean-up of recent supertanker disasters are often cited as examples of corporate responsibility actually working, there is the 'green' counter-argument that suggests that if there had been corporate responsibility in the first instance there need have been no disasters. These issues have been heightened when it is seen that in many cases, governments colluded in either the breaking of laws—or at least codes of practice—and then, to make things worse, colluded in the subsequent cover-ups or withholding of information, and sometimes even in the distribution of misinformation.

WHERE THE BUCK STOPS

When we say that accountability for outcomes is not divisible, the outcomes of which we speak are the myriad of POIs in each person's, and ultimately in each organisation's, working day for which they must account. Every process has its own set of inputs, processes and outcomes and every outcome has its own POI interface along the line. That

POI is where your output becomes someone else's input. Some giant corporations face difficulty in this area because of the enormous numbers involved. A team can perform all the activities for a particular task and may even, as a team, be accountable for an outcome. But someone has to be responsible for the team; even a democracy has a first minister. While there are some obviously structured tasks where no specific leader is necessary, there still needs to be a point of contact, even if it is a rotating one. In the case of a multinational company often with a rotating chair, clearly the board of directors must accept ultimate responsibility. This situation will be discussed in more detail later in the book.

> Every team needs a leader in some form or other.

Harry Truman, the President of the United States from 1945 to 1952, had a little plaque on his desk which said, 'The buck stops here'. The statement is not new. However, he had the moral courage to accept responsibility for his actions, the results of which, in the light of history, were enormous—among them being the decision to drop the atom bomb on Japan and the decision to dismiss General Macarthur, one of the country's greatest heroes. And Truman was only a small-town haberdasher from rural Missouri. Unfortunately, these days the buck gets passed down as well as up, and often stops with somebody who is either vulnerable or junior, or perhaps even naive or slow-witted.

The ill-preparedness of people to accept responsibility for their own actions, let alone the actions of others, is surely one of the major problems in society today. One may even wonder what has happened to the system of ultimate ministerial responsibility among politicians. It sets a bad example and destroys their credibility entirely when they blame their departments and accept no responsibility for themselves. By way of an extreme, but true example, there is an Australian case of fraud, which occurred in the 1990s, where a state premier signed documents and then tried to blame his underlings for not telling him he was helping himself to the contents of the public purse! And of course there are the now famous (or infamous) inabilities of politicians in several countries to recall circumstances of various happenings. Not knowing that you are personally misusing public money because you have neglected to find out is nearly as bad as deliberately doing it.

When George Washington admitted chopping down the cherry tree, his unwillingness to tell a lie was not the real issue. The real issue was his readiness to accept responsibility (and the consequences) for his actions.

However, it takes a lot of moral courage and character on the part of a leader to assume responsibility for outcomes that are so complex that they can at best only have a marginal input into the many processes involved in them. That is where real leadership comes in. Leadership and responsibility are connected. Part of responsibility is to have an overall awareness of what is going on. (This is such an important factor that it is the subject of a chapter in its own right.) To attain this overall awareness means divesting oneself of *executive activity* in order to overview *all activity*.

By this is meant that the more a leader *does* or spends time *doing* (executive activity) the less he or she can overview others (viewing all activity). A good leader *does* as little as possible in order to *overview* as much as possible.

> Leaders have a responsibility to acquaint themselves with the whole picture. This often means divesting themselves of executive activity.

Overviewing doesn't mean looking over your followers' shoulders all the time. Some people do just that; they seem to think that interfering is keeping abreast.

Allowing others to get on with the job sometimes involves risk taking. This is not the same as delegation, which will be covered later in the book. The risk taking we are discussing here concerns protecting followers from prying or irate superiors. That often means interposing yourself between your own superiors, who may be prone to interfere, and your own followers in order that they can get on with the job. Sometimes this involves more than just risk taking, it involves moral courage. One should consider the concept that 'my' boss has no part in the day-to-day direction of 'my' workers other than through 'me'.

> Supporting followers often takes moral courage.

Accepting the wrath of superiors for the mistakes or shortcomings of subordinates while still shielding them, and accepting the ire of your subordinates for what they perceive is the incompetence of 'management', are both examples of loyalty and a preparedness to accept that 'the buck stops here'. Moral courage sometimes just involves simply providing that sort of loyalty downwards—and also upwards if it is necessary.

Nevertheless, it can be unwise to continually hide the inadequacy of superiors. 'Blind loyalty' is a two-edged sword. Sometimes it is necessary to ensure that followers do understand whence the incompetence emanates, otherwise it may undermine confidence in the good leader and place false confidence in the perpetrator of the incompetence. Likewise, incompetence from a follower need not always be shielded from superiors. Genuine mistakes of inexperience or judgment are one thing; however, repeated mistakes are often a sign of incompetence and should be treated accordingly.

AUTHORITY AND RESPONSIBILITY

If we are to give people a sense of responsibility we cannot do so without giving the authority and resources that go with it. You cannot expect responsibility from someone without that person having the means to exercise that responsibility. We often see this situation happening in society; we tend to give people, schoolteachers for example, a great deal of responsibility with little authority—and the inevitable happens.

These days teachers are often held responsible for the behaviour of their students even after school hours, when they travel to and from school for instance. Because of our social structure, society is often more inclined to blame the teachers than the students themselves, or even the parents, when a student misbehaves. Teachers are even expected to act as social and welfare workers as well as counsellors and yet their position of power, or their authority to act responsibly, is often severely curtailed by state and school regulations. Understandably they blame someone else. The whole structure of leadership totters because no one seems to be responsible and, more importantly, no one has any authority.

On that same principle a considerable number of political leaders could be held to account. We prosecute businesspeople and board members for poor or questionable business decisions; why can't we do the same with politicians when they make poor political decisions and bankrupt whole communities? Not too many years ago politicians were seriously held to account for their actions and often suffered dire consequences. These days all we can do is vote them out every few years, often with a handsome payout.

The issue of accountability and responsibility is addressed well in PowerSharing, which we mentioned in the Introduction. While accountability is still retained at the highest or ultimate level, authority—or *power down*—is allocated with sufficient resources to the appropriate level downwards. So, PowerSharing doesn't only mean sharing authority and responsibility; it means still retaining ultimate accountability while giving followers sufficient information and resources to make their own decisions and even mistakes. That is why good leaders need training, nurturing and recognition.

PowerSharing encourages initiative to such a degree that there is an acceptance that mistakes will occur and are inevitable. What is more, if the mistakes are made in good faith and in furtherance of the ultimate outcome, then they come to be regarded as part of the leadership learning process. PowerSharing operates on the basis that forgiveness is easier to get than permission, and formalises that concept. The same mistake made too often, however, cannot be called a mistake in good faith—it is more than likely to be incompetence, as suggested previously, and needs to be addressed accordingly.

PowerSharing has been a success wherever it has been practised; commercially, industrially, politically and in conflict. PowerSharing is a philosophy not a technique—as leadership is an art not a science. One of the techniques that will help us implement PowerSharing, is devolution of authority.

Where does that leave the zero defects concept, beloved of some TQM advocates? This concept embodies the idea that in a quality organisation with the correct managerial philosophies and practices no defects, especially in manufacturing, are acceptable. People have often said that in an area such as engineering or manufacture you can aim for zero defects, because so much is dependent on machines, tolerances and the like and the human factor can be accurately predicted within certain limits. Therefore, if you know that a process is in statistical control, you can expect certain outcomes. To expect zero defects statistically is one thing, but to expect human behaviour to be so consistent that it is perfect, is utter nonsense, at least from a leadership point of view.

In the purely human dimension, if you can't make a mistake you won't make anything. There is a well-known cartoon of a tortoise that says: 'I only make progress when I stick my neck out'. When you stick out your neck there are bound to be mistakes. That doesn't mean that you don't *aim* for the highest standard possible, even for perfection if there is such a thing. However, let's remember that we are talking about an art—not a science.

> PowerSharing suggests that mistakes made in good faith are inevitable and part of the leadership process.

But what if people are too frightened to accept responsibility or make mistakes? Some people are beyond training and just do not have the character to accept responsibility or even exercise authority. Training these people is sometimes easier said than done. If this is the case then it may be advisable to cut losses.

John: *A friend told a rather salutary tale about someone working for him who would avoid accountability whenever he could and spend the rest of his time trying to compensate for it. The tragedy was that it appeared that he was in a senior position. Everyone could see through him—so you can imagine the respect level he earned from people. He compensated by being irritable with everyone, which was his way of demonstrating his authority.*

Once someone who worked for him made a fairly fundamental error of judgment, which called for dismissal. This man knew about it for days before he came to my friend and asked what he should do. When he was firmly told that the transgressor should be dismissed, the man asked my friend if he would mind doing it!

Such occurrences are more common than you would suspect. This refers to what was discussed earlier. People can learn to be leaders but they must possess certain qualities in the first place. Even those qualities can be learned if you know what they are and you are motivated. The plain fact is that many people are not motivated to develop the personal character needed for the acceptance of authority and responsibility, in which case they should never aspire to leadership.

There are many reasons why someone won't take a risk. It could be due to upbringing, environment, conditioning, personality or just plain fear. It would need a psychologist to uncover the real reason in each case. The tragedy is that there are people like that already in leadership positions.

> No one will ever be a leader without a willingness to accept responsibility or accountability.

Whether we like the fact or not, there are aspiring leaders in the public eye who refuse to be held accountable. The term 'aspiring' is used because although they may be in positions of power that does not make them leaders, any more than being a 'public' success makes someone a leader. The fact that someone has power or influence or can buy power or influence, means that he or she is powerful. It does not mean that he or she can lead.

Remember, we said that leaders must have followers. Sycophants are not genuine followers, they are seekers after power or security for themselves. A leader has to be affirmed by the people being led.

Leaders must have followers.

This introduces a concept which suggests a leader as a sort of *first among equals* who has been given a certain amount of authority in order to achieve a task. This authority is affirmed by those who are being led as long as the leader accepts responsibility for what the organisation does or produces. A good leader can accept that responsibility whatever the endeavour the organisation is involved in. This means that a person can be appointed to a leadership position when they know nothing of the business. One could be forgiven for suggesting that most people would never affirm a person in those circumstances. However, the contrary is often the case and in fact sometimes it can be a distinct advantage.

TRANSFERRING LEADERSHIP SKILLS

If someone takes over a tomato soup company and doesn't know the difference between a tomato and a zucchini, he or she like any good leader, will be forced to defer to the real experts down the line. If the person has little idea of marketing, they are forced to defer to the marketing experts, and so on. If the person is a good leader who doesn't try to control everything, their subordinates will soon realise how much they are being relied on to produce the right answer. The leader will be obliged to consult regularly, listen to advice and take action according to that advice.

On the other hand, the leader must have the intelligence to discern when he or she is being poorly advised, and the character to do something about it. Previously we mentioned that corporate executives, military leaders and politicians are often able to take their leadership skills into a totally new environment and even transform that environment. The same thing happens from one business enterprise to another.

There is a trap. If I happen to be an expert in zucchinis I may unwittingly try to turn the company into a zucchini soup company, which is not why I was appointed. As an example of this, many ex-military people have come to grief trying to turn corporations into little militias and many politicians have stumbled when they have returned to the real world. Many successful corporate executives have also come asunder when they enter the government or not-for-profit enterprises. Notwithstanding that, the principle holds good. However, a good leader would be well advised to very quickly learn about tomatoes!

> History shows that a good leader can lead almost any type of organisation.

When a new leader joins an organisation a great deal of their effectiveness will depend on their *situational control*, a concept which was mentioned briefly in the Introduction. Situational control is very important when a new leader arrives in an organisation and starts learning the ropes.

Situational control is dependent upon three factors: *relationship with followers; task structure;* and *position power.* It may be that situational control will remain low to moderate until the new leader develops some task expertise. That may require some deliberate style adjustment, and it almost automatically means a greater reliance on the goodwill and expertise of followers in order to accentuate the leader–follower relationship. Alternatively, it may require some muscle flexing, that is, the exercise of *position power*, while the *leader–follower relationship* is developing.

In all this discussion we need to emphasise that leadership for its own sake is pointless. By definition, leadership exists for a reason, for the achievement of an aim or a goal. More often than not it is for the achievement of productivity and profit. After all, if an enterprise doesn't perform profitably it goes out of business and everyone loses. Most commercial businesses are created to make money for an owner(s). The service comes in recognising where a need exists that may be best served to create that profit.

Good leadership will ensure that an organisation operates optimally; therefore, the spin-off from an optimally performing workforce is an optimal bottom line. Improved leadership equals improved bottom line, whether the bottom line be service or cash. To achieve this needs a very clear aim and vision.

Key concepts

- Accountability starts at the top.
- Accountability for a particular outcome is indivisible.
- Accountability must be accompanied by authority.
- Acceptance of responsibility requires character.
- Responsibility means 'don't pass the buck'.
- Responsibility is not risk-free and implies a knowledge of what is going on.
- Risk taking means a flexible approach to a zero defects philosophy.
- To know what is going on a leader must shed trivial executive activity.
- Power and authority do not make leaders, followers do.
- A good leader can lead any sort of organisation.

CHAPTER 2
Second Precept

Provide a clear vision and direction

Any leader we read about in history had a *vision* and, for some, a belief in their own destiny. A vision has in many ways come to mean imparting a higher purpose to the things we do. In some enterprises this can be very difficult, if not downright impossible, yet what we are suggesting is that while not everything has to have a lofty purpose, it must have a reasonable and credible purpose. The purpose will be achieved more readily if everyone is motivated towards the achievement of their part in it.

The best leaders in history have been vision driven, as have the worst. In fact, some visions in the minds of some leaders have been so evil and preposterous that the world has treated them as the ravings of madmen and has ignored them, at a great cost. Hitler made his vision quite clear in *Mein Kampf* and was written off as mad.

Leadership is of the spirit, compounded of personality and vision.

Field Marshal Viscount Slim of Burma

On the other hand, who can fail to be moved even a generation later by the oft-repeated simple words of Martin Luther King: 'I have a dream'. It was a dream, a vision communicated by a master to a whole generation and beyond. While his dream has yet to be fully realised, it did indeed change the world and the ultimate vision is still shared by the vast majority of people. Most people would find that sentence very evocative even now and it is hard to hear it without having some sort of emotional response. However, it is given to very few people to have that sort of impact. Here we are also discussing matters somewhat more mundane than the freeing of a whole race of people from the bonds of formal and informal discrimination.

THE BIG PICTURE

What we are trying to convey is that any sort of enterprise needs to have a raison d'être to survive, let alone prosper. That should become the basis of the organisation's vision and it must become part of the goal of everyone in the organisation. Can you see problems already? What if an organisation is a cigarette company? How can any sort of vision be imparted there? Do we have a vision where every family proudly consumes ten cigars and two packets of cigarettes per day?

This is the first problem—the double bind. Some enterprises in which we are engaged may have no intrinsic worth. This is one of the negatives of entrepreneurial capitalism! Under those circumstances we might as well ask why on earth we are in the business? This is a fundamental issue for today's consumer society. How do you articulate a vision for a toilet tissue company without seeming to be somewhat frivolous? Alistair Mant, author of *Leaders we deserve*, says the first thing you should be able to ask is: What's it for?[1] If the answer doesn't make sense, then you or your followers—or both—need to do some thinking.

Let's look at a company that makes widgets, firkins and bodkins. The board enters into a series of takeovers, mergers and asset-stripping arrangements that make a good return for the shareholders but bring about rationalisation of staff in the companies taken over and a decision to get out of the bodkin market because of low returns. Lots of jobs are lost, lots of people are hurt, but the shareholders are delirious with joy at the returns shown by the company. What was the board's vision? What was the mission of the organisation? Clearly, it must have been to make the best return for the shareholder, in the short term.

To continue this example; bodkins now become impossible to get and somebody else sees the niche, starts a new bodkin company charging higher prices because of the demand and poaches some of the better staff in the first organisation who were being reskilled to make fish hooks, the latest venture of the first company. It is quite possible that the first company had an articulated vision to do with such noble ideals as making the world's most reliable widgets, providing the world's most serviceable bodkins or whatever. You can be sure its articulated vision didn't say 'to make the best possible return for the shareholder in the shortest possible time'. But that's the way the company behaved. It didn't behave in any way that would have provided its workers or customers with confidence about the company's vision.

None of this is to say that the company didn't have the right to do what it did or even that what it did was unethical. But it had confused the needs of the stakeholders. And as workers, external customers and shareholders are all stakeholders, clearly at least one if not two groups of stakeholders have been alienated for the sake of the remainder. There you have problem number two! There is a variety of stakeholders—the owners (shareholders), the managers, the customers and the staff. It would seem to be very hard for the owners to share a vision with customers or staff that was directed purely at making returns for the shareholders.

There is no reason for the vision to be mutually exclusive, although clearly in these days of multinationals a lot of visions are. Nevertheless, there are wonderful examples of visionary leaders with high quality organisations where the vision is related with staff participation and customer satisfaction which are, not coincidentally, showing great returns to the shareholders.

Any vision should be inclusive of the aspirations of all the stakeholders.

However, there are several ways of sharing a vision. An organisation could have a vision of becoming the best widget maker in the world and have no intention of ensuring customer satisfaction or staff participation. It could do this by eventually buying up all the other widget makers and then being the only widget maker. They may not be good widgets but they are the best in the world, because they are the only ones! It could articulate that vision to its staff with no intention of ever producing better widgets. And that's exactly what has happened in many cases. And that's problem number three!

PERSONAL VISION

In the Introduction we made mention of the legendary Brazilian company Semco. Semco's managing director and principal shareholder is Ricardo Semler, author of *Maverick!*, a refreshingly different book about the growth of this remarkable company.[2] Semler is very frank in his book about his absence of vision when he first took over the company. His only vision consisted of an urge for rapid change and a burning desire to acquire more companies.

As the story progresses, it virtually becomes an unfolding of his vision. This vision crystallises with time and becomes one of creating the most democratic and participatory company in the country, probably the world. However, he takes a long time to articulate it and there are remarkable sidetracks along the way. It is also clear that when he finally decided what it was he wanted to do he never lost sight of his vision and he did everything humanly possible to enrol his followers in that vision. More to the point, his followers played a large, if not overwhelming, part in the creation of his vision.

Theorists have waxed lyrical in recent years over the concept of shared vision. Peter Senge in his seminal work on the 'learning organisation', *The Fifth Discipline*, suggests that the only true way to share a vision is to ensure that it is part of the individual's personal vision so that the shared vision becomes one's own.[3] He could, of course, be making the ultimate cynical observation that people will only act in accordance with their own self-interest. But he clearly believes in imputing a higher purpose to human endeavours and he obviously believes that such a sharing of vision implies more than enrolment or compliance.

Those are fairly lofty ideals and, while admirable, may not be so easy to achieve in an organisation that makes toilet seats. Besides, what happens when staff change, as they regularly do? Does everyone stop and recreate the vision? Not likely! Clearly, there has to be a sensible compromise and that is that a vision becomes the philosophy of operation of an organisation. The leader must share the creation of that vision and all who join the organisation must be enrolled and imbued with that vision so that it becomes the essence of a staff member's loyalty. The vision becomes part of a person's life.

To do this it is necessary for a leader to not only examine vision but also values. No follower in any organisation is likely to share ownership of a vision if the leader's values and their own values do not conform, because we draw our values from our vision.

> *The vast majority of workers responding to an international survey*
> *claimed their values and the values of their organisation were in conflict.*[4]
>
> *International Survey*

AMBITION

Notwithstanding all that has been said, it is very hard to become involved in a vision on a higher or spiritual plane if one looks at the amorphous masses which many multinational or even national organisations have become. How often do we see leaders, and organisations, who have a vision that demands the loyalty of followers but for whatever pragmatic reason the leaders find they are unable to give loyalty in return? This is an occurrence all too familiar today. There is no loyalty in either direction because the vision is not mutual or binding.

One of the other hurdles we have to overcome in the realm of personal vision is to understand that there is a subtle difference between ambition and vision. Ambition is normally associated with an individual, but it can also be related to an organisation. Ambition is a driving force, vision is a leading force. Ambition is generally self-focused while vision is outwardly focused. There is nothing wrong with ambition; without it, there would have been no Churchills or Edisons or Einsteins.

It is valid for an aspiring leader to have the ambition to be the most successful CEO in the country or to make his or her company the most financially successful in the country. In this situation, not only is ambition valid, it is also necessary. It is not vision! It does not allow for mutuality. For example, a personal vision may involve a leader having a view of where the world should be, or what it should be doing in so many years time; ambition relates to where the leader wants to be in that world.

Unfortunately, a leader's ambition can sometimes distort a vision. Often, subordinate leaders may find themselves in a position of having to choose between a leader's ambition and the needs of their own followers. This is something which regularly happens at a political level, and the results of it are overall cynicism.

Ambition is self-focused. Vision is 'other' focused.

DYNAMIC VISION

When we earlier mentioned the prospect of regularly recreating vision we did so with some flippancy. However, a vision that is not dynamic and subject to regular updating is moribund. George Stephenson in the 1830s had a vision of building the best steam trains in the world. He also had a vision of a network of railroads throughout England. His company, which lasted well into the modern era, would have looked rather foolish if it had stuck only with steam trains by the 1960s. Its survival was due to its dynamic vision.

Other similar organisations have had to make similar shifts in the focus of their visions over time. Many organisations had to readjust to the fact that they were in the transport industry during the 1960s and 1970s rather than the railway industry. Those that didn't recognise that died. Tourism is another industry which has had to totally recreate itself in the last twenty or thirty years.

Therefore we should recognise that a vision needs to be dynamic and subject to change with the passage of time or the advent of new technologies or concepts. The trick is to *recognise* when and how much to change the vision or create a new vision—and that's where real leadership comes in. After all, leadership is very much about change and transformation.

Senge makes an observation that today's leader is rather more like a ship's designer than a ship's captain; the captain is the general manager as it were, but the vision comes from the design. It is also true that most of the great generals always created a design for battle and enlisted all their followers into that design, leaving subordinate generals (or ship's captains) to fight the battle or run the ship. In fact, the philosophy of PowerSharing is very much based on that concept. A good leader will have a grand design that is dynamic and all embracing enough to allow everyone to hook into it—rather like householders plugging into a power grid.

VISION FOR EVERYONE

There are numerous examples of individuals known to us all in recent times who have had visions into which everyone became enrolled.

Kennedy's stated determination to ensure that humans (i.e. the United States) reached the moon by the end of the 1960s was an idea that eventually became part of the vision of almost everyone in the Western world, despite the cost. Similarly, on a more mundane note, there is the example of Alan Bond's enrolling of most Australians (including the Prime Minister) in his vision of wresting the America's Cup from the New York Yacht Club in 1983.

Having discussed at length the overall concept, we should now point out that what we are really interested in is the vision that is necessary for the average organisation to survive. We are looking at the leader's part in that vision, how the leader uses the power he or she has plugged into.

The leader's part of the vision, or his or her own vision, doesn't have to be mystical or soul stirring. In fact, what we are saying is that it is more of a general direction based upon envisaging where the leader wants the organisation, or his or her part of the organisation, to be or what he or she wants it to be doing in say five (or ten) years time. It may even include what people will be doing with the organisation's product, how many will be doing it and why?

In an ethical organisation *that vision will be related to the customer or consumer and shared with and achieved through the employees.* Notice where the focus is—consumer and employee. A leader in such an organisation will be conscious that profit is an invariable byproduct of an organisation with a *sound* vision and all that flows from it.

A good vision is employee-based and consumer-based.

A vision should be creative and imaginative. It should come from dreams and not from thoughts. It should focus on what leaders of organisations and their followers want to achieve, not what they want to avoid. Some of the best visions have been the product of wild flights of fancy arising as a result of creative brainstorming in groups. Vision should be from the imagination, which is from where geniuses such as Edison drew their visions.

A vision should be a 'green field' or idealised vision of what is desired, unfettered by concerns for what is considered to be possible. The consideration of the possible comes later. In creating a vision, followers should even be encouraged to indulge themselves in fantasy. For instance, one consultant we know always prompts his young adult career-seeking clients to write their own job description before they write their CV or resumé. Then he has them write a job description for the job they hope to be holding down in ten years' time. Then they write their CV with those visions in mind. When they have done this, he urges them to create their own plan to achieve it. This approach is very motivating.

In the same manner a leader can dream about where he or she wants an organisation to be in x number of years—what it will look like, how many it will employ, what great achievements have been made, how much money it will be making!

However you arrive at your vision, that vision must be shared with your employees and consumers. Employees must share not only the vision, they must share in the achievement of the vision. What is more, they must be free to develop their own plans and ideas within that vision and be given the resources to get on with their part in it. That is why it is so important to mutually own a vision and why it is so much better if it can be part of a personal vision.

> A vision must be something everyone in an organisation can share and own.

One well-known commercial vision was Henry Ford's; it was reportedly 'to put the world on wheels' or words to that effect. Now it sounds trite and overstated. In the 1920s it would have been even more preposterous. The purists may say that he didn't achieve it, but few people would argue that more than any other man before him he made the car accessible to the working man. More than that, he revolutionised fabrication, engineering and marketing and caused the rest of the automobile world to follow.

Ford's vision began as a dream and it would have ended thus if he had not had the energy, sheer willpower and, some would say, ruthlessness to pursue his vision. As it turns out, it may have been a flawed vision because some would argue that he enslaved a generation of workers in drudgery. He also refused to countenance any change, giving customers what he wanted them to have, not what they wanted, and refusing to believe that the day of the 'T' model had passed.

Similarly, all the wonderful enlightening visions emanating from today's wide variety of sources will be worthless without leadership, strategies and procedures, and genuine espousal by all followers.

IBM reportedly had a very succinct vision in the early eighties: 'To change the world'. One could be forgiven for suggesting that such was the Ayatollah Khomeini's vision also, but for vastly different ends. A vision thus worded is not very inspiring unless there is some articulated end to it. Obviously we are suggesting that there needs to be some pragmatism! Of course, there always have to be the pragmatists even though, almost coincidentally, IBM has contributed in a significant way to changing the world. Pragmatism comes from having your feet on firm ground and being in touch with reality.

CURRENT REALITY

There is an old, well-known story about the typical Englishman who asked the typical Irishman for directions as to how to get to a certain place. The answer is the legendary: 'Well, if I were you I wouldn't be starting from here'. On the face of it, it's amusing—but it contains a great well of truth. Most visions come unstuck because of a distorted view of current reality. People start from the wrong place.

Peter Senge again postulates that that very thing happened to Lyndon Johnson. He was perhaps one of the most visionary US presidents of recent years, but that vision is forgotten in the welter of mistakes he made in trying to reach his goal. He introduced a record amount of enlightening legislation in his years as president.[5] In the end he lost sight of reality, played games with the truth and finally refused to run for further office. He died not too many years afterwards as a disillusioned man.

There are many parallels in contemporary politics and industry in all Western countries (and others)—many very close to home. We will look further at current reality in subsequent chapters. What this discussion immediately leads us to is a consideration of the realistic and practical side of having a vision.

One very clear example of the need for the practical, commercial side of a vision is the case of the Scandinavian architect, Joern Utzon, who designed the world-famous Sydney Opera House. There can be little doubt that the Opera House is one of the great architectural wonders of the modern world, but Utzon didn't complete the project. While there was probably political interference in the project, it is clear that Utzon's vision was not grounded in the reality of the day, either in terms of costs, industrial relations, or the pure technological capacity to complete it. A project of that size suffered from someone making day-to-day decisions on a dream rather than the possible.

We had this fantastic vision of how to make $10 million a year after tax in the first year but we couldn't get a bank loan to start up, so then we decided...

ARTICULATING A VISION

It is easier to understand that pragmatic side of the concept of vision if it is related to an aim or focus. What is my overall aim for this organisation over the next several years? Importantly, vision provides a focus or aiming mark and helps us to plan in reverse. That means we plan from where we want to be, not from where we are, and that is essential to progress.

Articulating a vision may take a long period of reflection and discussion, and often visions are never fully articulated. Companies and leaders regularly have great difficulty because they have never really defined what business they are in—and with the rapid pace of change today, opportunism is very tempting. Let us therefore articulate a typical vision for a mythical organisation that markets cut flowers and then see how we did it.

Giddy & Associates is an ethical and financially sound organisation producing significant returns to the shareholders by selling cut flowers of the highest quality and life to one in every three households in the country while employing only fully trained botanists who each have a financial interest in the organisation.

The vision is imaginative, a dream, green field, inclusive, an aiming mark, ethical and admirable. The vision says something about where we want to be, what the customers can expect, the quality of the product, what qualifications the staff will be expected to have, the benefits they will receive financially, the size of the business, the limitations to its expansion and its overall profitability. And it does all this in less than four lines. We also believe it is a vision that everyone can be enrolled in.

How did we get there? The first thing we determined was our *aim*. An aim is essential to the beginning of any planning process (which we will cover in more detail in a following chapter) and creating a vision is no less than a planning process in itself. Having determined our aim we look at the other factors involved, including where we are now, that is, our *current reality*. The difference between the two gives us our gap, or provides us with the *creative tension* that Senge speaks of.[6] Current reality is a *true picture* of where we are now, not where we would like to think we are. It *must be based upon truth*, not fancy.

Perhaps the best piece of advice we can give you at this point is to suggest that it is given to very few people to have the competence, foresight, wisdom and creativity to reach a vision on their own. A vision is not only better when it is shared, it is infinitely the best when it is jointly arrived at by as many people from as many levels as possible.

THE MISSION

Many organisations create a 'fluffy' vision statement or philosophy based on their view of who they are and what they do; they then stick it up on the wall in a prominent place and proceed to ignore it. If our *vision* tells us **what** we want to do and our *current reality* tells us **where we are now**, our *mission* should *begin* to tell us **how** we should do it to achieve the vision.

Once you have an idea of where you are going, then you can plan how to get there. That's the time when the mission is articulated. So, the mission is really the first part of the plan and the operational objectives will fall from it, whereas the vision suggests a general design. Clearly, a mission will often be similar to a vision but may have different emphases or parameters and may be subject to more regular review. At many levels, such as in departments, there will only be a mission statement relating to that department's share in the overall vision.

We don't want to dwell on the mechanics of relating vision to mission and objectives, because those processes are procedural and will be covered more fully later. There are also a number of schools of thought relating to missions, goals and objectives, and words mean different things to different people. In our context, while the mission may reflect and be similar to the vision, it is in fact the beginning of the plan; the important thing here is that good leaders don't confuse plan and vision. When you focus on a plan to the detriment of a vision, you become a practitioner rather than a leader.

We can liken a leader's vision to an architect's design. The builder is the practitioner and has to put the design into effect and for this he or she needs plans and procedures. Often the plans are straightforward, but most of them have a critical path involving set objectives, finishing times, and so on. Often plans need changing, snags are struck, obstacles arise and the builder generally uses his or her initiative to solve the problems. At other times, however, the architect—who is a regular attender and observer—is called upon to clear the way and clarify his or her intentions. However, if he or she is a good architect he or she never loses sight of the design, no matter what devious route the plan may have taken.

The vision comes before the plan. The mission and objectives are part of the plan.

Let's see what Giddy & Associates' mission might be.

'To produce cut flowers of the highest quality for the national market year round with a view to extending growth by 25 per cent each year and ensuring Giddy & Associates' cut flowers become known for their quality and long life, nationwide by 2000.'

The mission restates the business and gives a clear aim or statement of purpose, and then suggests how it is going to be achieved. It is obviously aligned to the vision, but it doesn't dwell on peripherals such as the qualification of the staff or their co-ownership. The mission is, after all, to sell cut flowers. The other components remain part of the vision and are acted upon *strategically*, but they are not necessarily part of the mission.

STRATEGIC DIRECTION

So now we come to strategic plans or, better still, our corporate strategy; because a plan tends to reflect something set in concrete while a strategy implies a general direction. Operational and business plans can be based on corporate strategy. What is more, the whole of the workforce must work with that direction and strategy in mind—always. If we go back to our original definition of leadership we recall that the operative phrase is *towards the achievement of a clear common goal*.

This presupposes a level of understanding of corporate goals not hitherto normally associated with 'down the line management'. It also presupposes a level of trust and flexibility that we have not necessarily been used to and an allocation of resources for independent operation.

All this needs a vigorous application by the leader of the PowerSharing concept. In fact, the practice is well tried and has been used by a number of enterprises as the basis of their management styles for many years. We have already mentioned Semco in Brazil but there are other examples; for instance, US executive Max De Pree's great little book *Leadership is an Art* provides some interesting insights into empowerment of workers.[7] In more recent times we have the example of Anita Roddick with The Body Shop chain of stores.

Interestingly, even in modern wars, organisations that have concentrated on individual devolution of leadership and initiative have invariably been successful. The German Army, up until 1942, was a case in point, and Israel has followed suit ever since. The concept was used in 'Desert Storm'. The early acceptance of management by objectives (MBO), so popular in the 1970s, was largely a result of a move towards PowerSharing. Under a leader invoking a PowerSharing philosophy, total quality management (TQM) and MBO dovetail perfectly on the basis that every objective is set with flexibility in mind and totally accords with the leader's—and ergo the organisation's—ultimate vision or aim.

If down-the-line managers then have the resources and authority, and are enrolled in their leader's vision and 'grand design', they are bound to take actions that further the aims or designs of the leader, *which includes ensuring that nothing they do conflicts with another person's ability to do the same*. This means that financial controllers won't cut expenditures in order to reach their own objectives without reference to marketers, who may need higher financial allocations to reach theirs—because the most important goal is the leader's (in which they have a stake anyway) not their own objectives within it. This doesn't mean divesting responsibility; it does mean a leader having the wisdom, confidence and ability to pass on authority.

Plans can then be adjusted as the need arises and such adjustments should be expected. Well-known US academic and author Warren Bennis postulated his second law of pseudodynamics along those lines: 'Make whatever grand plans you will, you may be sure the unexpected or the trivial will disturb and disrupt them.'[8]

> Strategic planning needs to provide for flexibility and opportunity.

Let's see what has been determined. The chief executive or chair of the board creates a vision for the future with broad input from everyone at *all* levels. This vision becomes the 'holy grail' of the organisation to which everyone aspires. Out of this comes the mission and the organisation's corporate strategy. The strategy is more in the form of a broad directive or strategic design, which must not only be divulged down the line but actively espoused by all levels so that all concerned can share not only the vision but its achievement.

Each level then makes its plans to accord with the ultimate strategy and is given the authority and resources to carry out their part of the strategy. This means that the individual departments or workers, depending on the size of the organisation, begin to make their plans. In the case of *Giddy & Associates* enough flexibility is given to ensure that departments and individuals plan in teams to ensure that all the various plans are mutually inclusive. Sufficient authority is given to each department to ensure that there is absolute freedom of action for their own outcomes. There must also be flexibility enough to allow for the carrying of opportunity targets and even for risks to be taken.

OPPORTUNITY TARGETS

From time to time in any enterprise a situation will arise that provides an immediate unforeseen opportunity that has been neither planned for nor budgeted for. It may be the opportunity for a takeover or merger at higher level, or it may be as mundane as getting extra fertiliser at the right price for *Giddy & Associates*. We have chosen to call these situations 'opportunity targets', which is just what they are—sudden unforeseen opportunities at which to aim.

There must be a limit to freedom of action, and that limit is defined by the boundary of a leader's vision. This means that opportunity targets can only be aimed for if they lie within the scope of the leader's vision. This concept allows free expression on the part of down-the-line managers, includes the concept of MBO and encourages the stretch and initiative required for continuous improvement. A good leader who is alert is quickly aware of any mutually exclusive objectives that can potentially arise, and foresees them.

> PowerSharing requires the allocation of resources and authority.

A word of warning. There is a school of thought that would suggest that only sufficient resources should be allocated for a team or department to reach an agreed objective. This *may* imply stopping if the objective has been reached. PowerSharing suggests that if the resources allocated can take you beyond your objective and it is still within and commensurate with the leader's and the company's vision, then go for it!

Nevertheless, it is important that the scope of the freedom has to be confined to the company's vision, so that procedures can be developed and people practised in them. If we go beyond the scope of the company's vision we are opening a Pandora's box. That's when organisations can get into real hot water, on the basis that it seemed like a good idea at the time.

That means that if opportunities arise that are likely to take an organisation beyond its strategy or vision, that decision can only be made at the highest level and desirably by all the levels that created the vision. Let's relate it back to our horticultural friends at *Giddy &*

Associates. Suppose an opportunity arises that, with the expenditure of an amount outside the budget, would allow growth into another state, territory or province a year earlier than planned. That opportunity should then be seized, because the vision is nationwide. However, if the opportunity arises for expansion into a market overseas, for example, then that needs to be referred back because it is beyond the scope of the vision. If the leaders and the company are true visionaries they will then amend their vision!

It goes without saying that there is an enormous amount of trust involved in all this and that organisational procedures and training are very important. The 1980s and 1990s have been so full of planning, as we intimated earlier on, that in the real world people have either stopped planning or become bogged down in their plans. But even within the flexible organisation of which we speak, there is still a need for planning procedures.

THE PLAN

We will cover training and standard planning procedures later in the book. Suffice it to say that it is often at this point that many organisations come unstuck. They make their plan based on the strategic direction and then scurry around trying to find objectives that will fit the plan they've just made. It used to be called 'situating the appreciation' instead of 'appreciating the situation'. The operational objectives often have not been clearly thought out based upon the strategy, or the strategy is too proscriptive.

John: A perfect example of that happened to me recently. I was planning some career management work for one of our local government councils and I was asked to put together a series of workshops, which were not inexpensive. On examining their situation I realised that what they needed could be achieved just as effectively, at no greater cost, and in greater depth by establishing a career transition centre and running teaching and counselling sessions over a period of months rather than stand-alone workshops over a few weeks. I was told in no uncertain terms that the decision was theirs and they had made up their minds—the workshops were how it was to be done.

One of two things had happened: they had either planned adequately but with inadequate information and their plans were too inflexible to change, or (and more likely) they had made their plans or decisions based on either the wrong mission or aim or no aim at all and I then had to situate the appreciation accordingly.

This anecdote illustrates the point of how important it is to get that vision—or in day-to-day operations, that aim—right in the first instance. If everyone is clear about the vision then there has to be flexibility of implementation, as we said earlier, because every day brings a new challenge. In business the fault is referred to as 'sticking to the solution rather than the aim'.

A good leader sticks to the aim rather than the solution.

This situation at local government level is regrettably repeated in many fields of endeavour. It comes about because there is either no leadership, or no adequate procedures, or inflexible guidelines from on high. Even if it is a combination of all three it tends to be reflective of poor leadership at some level, or at every level.

STICK TO THE AIM

If you are inclined to think we have introduced a further complication called *the aim*, you need to go back to our discussion on the vision where we mentioned that the process of determining a vision needed an aim in itself. An aim is simply a day-to-day definition of a particular purpose within a strategic direction. Every project you undertake within your mission, even every meeting you hold, needs to have a reason or purpose—and that purpose is the aim.

The use of the word *aim* is generic. A vision is an aim in itself, so is a mission, and every operational activity and every plan we make within that activity has its own aim, which is often easier to relate to in operational terms than is the corporate mission. Every action we take must be directed towards an end, even on a week-to-week basis. That end becomes our aim for that particular activity and it could be part of a given objective or even the objective itself. So also do all the little activities of the week have an aim. It is important to reiterate that we are using the word in a generic sense and we will use it later when we talk about problem solving.

You may well also be tempted to ask whether some level of super-vision is reached down the line where the supervisor just does what he or she is told without having to concern him or herself with company aims and objectives? No, the need to plan goes right through the organisation and every plan has an aim.

If planning is inclusive, then lower level leaders and supervisors will feel some ownership not only of the vision but of the whole plan-ning process. Indeed, many organisations take these things into account in the first instance and include unions in their planning so that issues relating to pay and conditions as well as training and devel-opment are built into project plans. Few organisations these days would make major strategic decisions without worker and union input. The trouble is that sometimes it is very difficult to motivate a comfort-able workforce to want to participate even when it involves their future. The only thing that will solve that is exposure to good leader-ship and active training in how to provide creative input.

> A good leader will seek input from all levels before planning begins.

However, it is no good seeking an opinion or input if all you really want is agreement. While sycophants may offer some comfort, they actually do an organisation a lot of harm. What is really needed is a leader who implements training and procedures, promoting indepen-dence of thought in both the planning and action phases.

Key concepts

- Every leader must have a vision.
- The workforce must share in the vision to the lowest level.
- The organisation's strategy and mission must be based on that vision.
- The strategy needs to be one of direction rather than too specific.
- Operational plans and objectives are based upon the corporate strategy.
- The concept of PowerSharing allows this flexibility.
- PowerSharing is based on openness and trust: it implies devolution of authority and responsibility but does not involve absolving leaders from responsibility.
- Objectives must be accompanied by resources and the authority to act.
- Plans will go wrong, initiative should be seized, independence of action is encouraged.
- Plans must comply with the objectives or aim, not with a desired solution.
- Planning should be participative and workers trained and encouraged to provide input.

Ensure that all followers have a sound understanding of goals and procedures

COMMUNICATING INTENTIONS

People in any working environment function more effectively when they have control over the outcome of their work. Total control may not always be possible because of the inputs of a large number of other people over whom an individual worker may have no authority, or even contact with. Nevertheless, the principle holds good: people should be responsible for everything within their sphere of control or influence, as outlined in Chapter 1, right down to the lowest level, including quality and safety issues, without interference.

This does not mean abrogation of responsibility at higher levels, nor does it imply anarchy in matters of supervision and control. On the contrary, the PowerSharing approach implies a greater acceptance of responsibility at higher levels because it is predicated on a very high degree of trust of one's subordinates. To do this with a degree of confidence, any leader must have confidence that subordinates understand the *mission* and their role and objectives contributing to it. The leader needs to also be confident in the fact that as well as subordinates being trained to use their initiative, there are certain procedures according to which subordinates are trained to act in routine matters. Finally, subordinates must have the resources and authority to act and leaders need to be committed to delegating the maximum amount of control that is feasible.

This means, first of all, that people must not only share the vision but understand the mission, understand the strategic direction, and have an appreciation of the leader's day-to-day aims. They must not just understand, but be connected to, committed to and imbued with these aims. This places a great responsibility on the leader to not only articulate these aims but to actively carry them to all levels of the organisation.

This presupposes a leader who can communicate and a follower who can listen and understand. After all, communication is a two-way process, which involves more listening than talking. If followers do not listen, it is often because they are so unused to being confided in that they automatically regard any direct communication from on high as irrelevant. Even if a leader has a very clear mission, or even message, there is every possibility of it being misconstrued by subordinates. Therefore, a leader shouldn't make assumptions regarding subordinates' understanding. It is a leader's responsibility to ensure that the mission is clear and understood. All operations must then be designed to support the mission. If it becomes obvious to a workforce that routine operational issues are allowed to interfere with a stated mission (which happens all too often in a bureaucratic environment) confidence in the leadership will soon be lost. Also, the mission should not be changed to suit the current operational situation or setbacks.

> A strategic mission should not be subject to the vicissitudes of operational needs.

MAKE THE MISSION MEANINGFUL

However, an organisation's mission *can* change. What certainly *will* change regularly is the strategy. Every organisation must have a mission. But—more than that—within an overall strategic direction there can be missions within departments, or missions for specific projects or specific periods. Remember the mission of *Giddy & Associates* in the last chapter. You will recall how it stated the purpose of the business, suggested how it was to be achieved, and the parameters under which it would be achieved.

The mission is the beginning of a plan. A mission can be long or short term and it can apply to a strategy; or there can be missions applying to contingency plans, annual plans, departmental plans or business plans. Departments could be told that 'so and so is the company's mission, our role in it is as follows and so on, and these are our objectives'. In all of this, the processes are as important as the final plans. Such subplans can be related to timing (annual plans), or level (departmental or sectional plans), or function (business or action plans).

A mission should be pro-active, and aggressive rather than defensive. It must also be continually presented to the workforce and not remain as some sterile and meaningless framed statement on a wall. It must permeate the organisation, be clearly understood at all levels and be aimed for consistently by all staff.

Whatever plan is involved, it must have at its source the organisation's vision and mission, which helps to give a holistic or systemic purpose. If plans are made in isolation then they will eventually become mutually exclusive and contradictory. Each year's plans need to contain a restatement of the leader's vision, intention, aim and strategy and then the organisation's or department's mission and goals for the year or for a given period.

Imagine that during any year a budget target is not being met for one reason or another and an executive finds it necessary to issue an interim directive about the impending deficit. If he or she simply says, 'I want such and such a department to come in with a balanced budget' it could mean that the financial controller sees it as his or her role to rein in expenditure in that department, whereas the department head may think it better to stretch the role of some staff to increase revenue. In fact, these staff may need an increase in resource allocation in order to reach their new targets. This would be quite contrary to the thinking of the financial controller!

In actual fact, that very situation happened with monotonous regularity during the recent recession. It became obvious that many organisations had very defensive and short-term missions and the only message getting through was to cut costs whatever the outcome; a sort of siege mentality seemed to exist. While the executive's intention is to balance the budget, as is clear from the statement above, it needs to be related to the overall mission and the longer-term vision. It may require a reduction in expenditure, it may even require some staff reductions, but these are steps that should represent a last resort in the scheme of achieving the mission. However, these often become the first resort. If a decision is made to take certain action then the appropriate person needs to be given the authority and resources to fully take the action.

THE PLANNING PROCESS

The planning process will produce a mission at whatever level. At every level the leader's vision is fed in and remains the guiding principle. The organisational mission for the finance and human resources departments will be the same, but the departmental missions will be quite different. In addition, the internal mission of one department may be different from one year to the next while at the same time the mission for the whole organisation remains unchanged. In fact the internal mission of a department may represent a segment of the organisational mission appropriate to that department.

If we go back to *Giddy & Associates'* organisational mission once more, each year will see a different *annual* mission with one thing in common—the growth of the business by 25 per cent until the year 2000. In the same way the marketing department's role will be quite different to the sales department, for example. One may focus on a strategy for expansion, one on a strategy for quality, another on a strategy for promotion and so on. Each will have its own mission to follow, and there should be a routine for the arrival at these missions.

Planning procedures or processes are probably more important than the plan itself, because, after all, that is where all the factors and options are considered and sometimes discarded. The first thing we start with is the already received or given mission from which we then determine what the aim of our planning process is. In the case quoted above, for instance, the aim of the marketing department may be *'to increase market share by 10 per cent in each capital city by the end of the financial year'*.

Any action we take is based on some form of reasoning. Even if we are only deciding to go to the football and we can't make up our minds whether to travel by car or train, we go through a logical decision making process. After determining what we want to do—our aim—we consider all the factors or issues, for example, the weather, likely crowd size, likely delays, car parking, train frequency, seating, number of guests, cost of train fare, next appointment and so on, in order to come up with various options. Having considered all this we make our decision on the best option. This, in fact, constitutes the basis of a *plan* of action, because out of the exercise will come all the considerations necessary for completing the task, such as departure time, taking or buying lunch, taking an umbrella and/or a coat and so on. The process is like this:

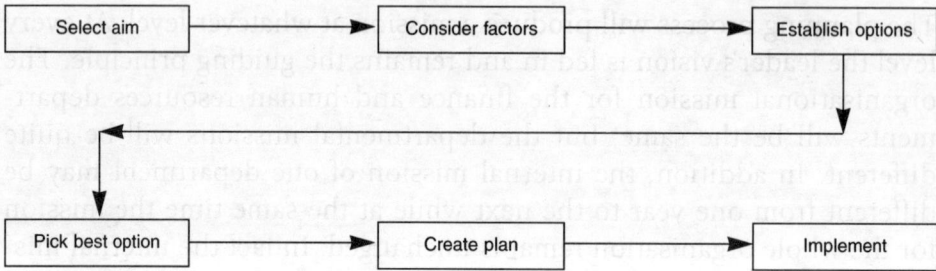

```
┌─────────────┐      ┌─────────────────┐      ┌───────────────────┐
│  Select aim │─────▶│ Consider factors│─────▶│ Establish options │
└─────────────┘      └─────────────────┘      └───────────────────┘
       ▲                                                 │
       │                                                 ▼
┌─────────────────┐      ┌─────────────┐      ┌───────────────────┐
│ Pick best option│◀─────│ Create plan │◀─────│    Implement      │
└─────────────────┘      └─────────────┘      └───────────────────┘
```

Fig. 3.1 *Rudimentary planning process*

If you make the wrong plan, it's generally because you had the wrong aim, failed to consider one or more factors or issues, or came to invalid conclusions. The principle remains the same: big tasks—long consideration; small tasks—short consideration.

ACTION PLANNING

Now we can quickly look at a more detailed process of planning. A plan is simply the embodiment of a course of action arising from a decision taken to fulfil an aim. What we are really interested in here, though, is the planning process or procedure, not the plan itself. Anyone can write a plan once a decision has been made—that's an administrative and mechanical process. The difficult part is in the planning or decision making *process*.

We can look later at what levels of plans there can be, but the ones most often referred to these days are *business plans* and *action plans*. Often business plans are confused with decision making processes. The reality is that a business plan as we generally know it is simply a set of administrative factors listed in a set order according to one of a dozen formulae that are available. Unfortunately, a lot of the material contained in many plans is guesswork or wishful thinking and the *decisions* arrived at have not received sufficient in-depth attention in the *process*.

It's how we arrive at the plan that is important. Let's look at some action planning processes. If you know exactly what your aim is, you can devise steps to get there. That process is more traditional. If you don't know exactly what your aim is, your process needs to be more circuitous.

The short process shown diagrammatically in Figure 3.1 is a traditional process. That process is ideal for a situation such as planning to go to the football, because we know exactly what our aim is and when we want to achieve it. Some parts of an organisation may have no such clear aim. In such circumstances they may initially have to describe their aim in very general terms and wait for the planning process itself to point out the specific direction. That's often called *gap planning*.

There are typically approximately six steps in any planning process. They are:

1. The statement of aim, either at source or inferred or drawn from above, either from the leader's vision or from a given mission or strategy. The aim should include the consideration of any operational limitations, such as time constraints.
2. The consideration of relevant factors or issues. This may mean evaluating the current situation, such as competitors, stakeholders, and other relevant plans, as well as current outcomes, opportunities, threats, strengths, weaknesses and so on.
3. The consideration of the options available.
4. Choosing the best option.
5. Selection of objectives or targets.
6. Implementation, which will include the formal writing of the mission and plan.

When you are not so sure of where you are going and you are using a *gap* method, then it may be necessary to review the plan to confirm its conformity with the intention of the higher authority. With a simpler planning process or in a PowerSharing environment, the plan probably only needs relating to the original aim we set, which of course already conforms to our leader's vision or strategy.

There are a great many action planning systems or procedures and one may well be as good as another. The important thing is to ensure that there is a process, and leaders at all levels need to ensure that their teams are trained in the processes and use them before any plans are set in concrete.

Look at Figure 3.2 to see the processes in this procedure. Planning for lower levels, for functional levels or for periodic purposes then becomes a further product of the corporate mission and strategy and would look a little more complicated. We have referred to the leader or corporate level as **strategic**, the annual period as **operational** and the departmental level as **tactical**. This process can be represented as shown in Figure 3.3.

```
┌─────────────────┐    ┌─────────────────┐    ┌─────────────────┐    ┌──────┬──────────────────┐
│ Leader's vision │ ─▶ │  Leader's aim   │ ─▶ │ Planning process│ ─▶ │      │ Corporate mission│
│                 │    │                 │    │                 │    │ Plan ├──────────────────┤
└─────────────────┘    └─────────────────┘    └─────────────────┘    │      │ Corporate strategy│
                                                                      └──────┴──────────────────┘
```

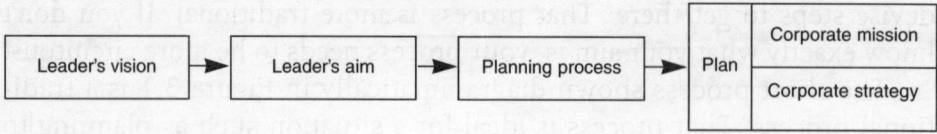

Fig. 3.2 *Strategic planning process*

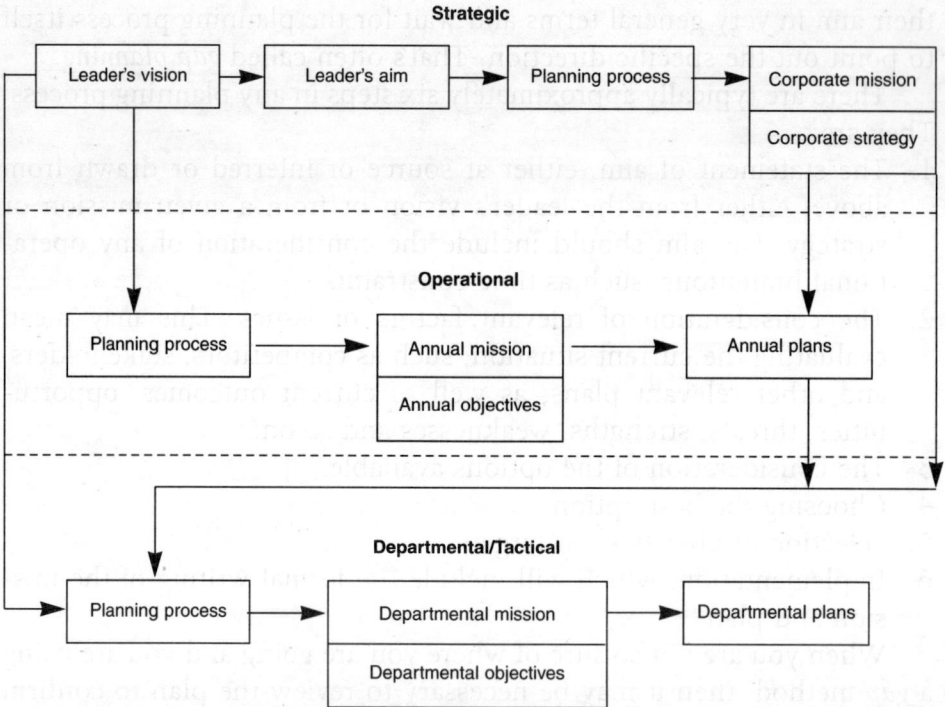

Strategic

```
┌─────────────────┐    ┌─────────────────┐    ┌─────────────────┐    ┌──────────────────┐
│ Leader's vision │ ─▶ │  Leader's aim   │ ─▶ │ Planning process│ ─▶ │ Corporate mission│
│                 │    │                 │    │                 │    ├──────────────────┤
└─────────────────┘    └─────────────────┘    └─────────────────┘    │ Corporate strategy│
                                                                      └──────────────────┘
```

- -

Operational

```
┌─────────────────┐    ┌─────────────────┐    ┌──────────────────┐
│ Planning process│ ─▶ │  Annual mission │ ─▶ │  Annual plans    │
│                 │    ├─────────────────┤    │                  │
└─────────────────┘    │ Annual objectives│    └──────────────────┘
                       └─────────────────┘
```

- -

Departmental/Tactical

```
┌─────────────────┐    ┌──────────────────────┐    ┌──────────────────┐
│ Planning process│ ─▶ │ Departmental mission │ ─▶ │ Departmental plans│
│                 │    ├──────────────────────┤    │                  │
└─────────────────┘    │Departmental objectives│   └──────────────────┘
                       └──────────────────────┘
```

Fig. 3.3 *Detailed action planning process*

OBJECTIVES

During the planning process certain key options or courses of action will suggest themselves and certain courses of action will become fairly evidently impractical. During the consideration of all the factors, including the traditional Strengths and Weaknesses of the organisation, department or work team, and the Opportunities and Threats in the environment—often called a **SWOT** analysis—obvious targets and objectives will begin to emerge. These will form the basis of the objectives in the forthcoming plan and the further planning process will begin to indicate a course of action to reach these objectives. These courses of action will form the basis of the plan. Departmental, operational or tactical objectives should not be imposed. This means they should either be self-selected or selected by agreement as a result of a planning process of some sort.

Under normal circumstances these objectives must be set by agreement. We have all seen situations where they have been imposed—and not always just in an emergency—with varying degrees of success in the ultimate outcome. Generally, an imposed objective, by its nature, is owned by somebody else and is seen by all concerned as impinging on responsibilities and even other objectives. Remember, one of the aspects of our definition was the engendering of willing co-operation and that generally means people setting their own objectives by agreement within the strategic direction. It also implies minimum interference in the processes.

Although we're not emphasising management by objectives, we do need to outline some ground rules for the setting of objectives, because that's where a lot of misunderstanding occurs—whether it be an annual objective, a training objective or what used to be called an enabling objective. The best way to define an objective is that it is a description of the exact situation that will exist at the completion of a given process. For example: 'by the end of the financial year the department will process 6000 cans of oxygen per week to a level of rejection not exceeding 5 per cent over a period of 46 out of 52 weeks'.

One theory used the acronym **SMART**. Every objective needed to be:

- **S**pecific—that means concise and unambiguous;
- **M**easurable—that means what it says; it must be able to be measured;
- **A**chievable—not unrealistic objectives prepared for PR purposes, but with some stretch or challenge;
- **R**ealistic—based on the mission and set at the right level;
- **T**ime bound—have a completion time/date.

It is also desirable for the statement to contain any exceptions, or the conditions under which the desired behaviour must be demonstrated. The measurement must also always contain the desired standard to be reached and for what period it is to be maintained. It can thus be seen that every mission is an objective and every objective becomes a mini mission. Following this sequence, the objectives emerge during the planning *process*. The final plan then includes a mission statement, objectives and a strategy for implementation.

There are numerous examples where theory and practice are separated by a huge credibility gulf.

Peter: Some years ago a colleague of mine worked at a senior level for a service organisation that had excellent planning procedures. They used to start their budget and planning early each year and excellent plans would come in from regional managers. These were then passed back up the line in anticipation of the final budget being approved on high.

Invariably, income would fail to meet expectations and they would have to cut expenditure, which in turn resulted in an inability to provide targeted services. Therefore, revenue raisers would have their target raised arbitrarily to an unrealistic level, which was never met. This regularly brought about the demise of the marketing manager, never those who were setting the unrealistic targets.

Objectives should always be SMART—so should leaders!

Nothing is more soul destroying than entering into a planning period knowing that the whole process, no matter how theoretically correct (and in many cases it is), is also meaningless. With so much frustration people very quickly recognise the prevailing wind and stop trying.

In the case given above, the mission—and probably the vision—were clearly unrealistic, given the known limited capacity to harness financial resources. In fact, the vision was really more of an idealistic philosophy which led to the mission being skewed. *The planners were driven by great ideals without great ideas.* They could have maintained their vision but made their mission much more achievable by being pragmatic. Basically, it appears the board adopted a vision, the implications of which a large number of members of the corporation had no idea. From then on things got worse.

- They didn't push decision making downwards.
- They allowed managers to make their own plans and set their own objectives within the framework of the annual corporate plan, then changed them or didn't give them the resources they needed to get on with things.
- They created unrealistic revenue objectives and set people up for failure.

- They had good planning procedures but took no notice of their outcomes.
- They had no procedures to support PowerSharing.
- They regulated everything for fear of budgetary problems.
- They didn't trust their managers because the managers regularly didn't meet their objectives, through no fault of their own.

A vision can be idealistic—a mission must be pragmatic.

That organisation, incidentally, was no worse than many others. Indeed, it may have been somewhat better; they had a vision of sorts and they did at least follow some planning and objective setting procedures. Some organisations have no procedures at all and freewheel through their planning and operating processes.

ACTION PROCEDURES

One of the difficulties people may have with the idea of PowerSharing as described in this book is that it gives the impression of freewheeling operations based on trust and initiative with a minimum of planning or procedures. That's not exactly true. The first step in PowerSharing is to ensure that there are adequate procedures to *enable* subordinate leaders to act independently. This means both planning procedures and action procedures. We've talked about planning procedures; now let's look at action procedures.

Use of action procedures means that when plans are made, under given circumstances an individual knows that he or she is expected to act in a certain way. It is essential for a leader to know that wherever he or she may be, the workers will be paid on Thursdays, or if there is a fire everyone knows where to go and what to do, or if there is a black-out everyone knows what to do and a minimum of information is lost—*because everyone has backed up according to procedures.* The list is endless. These are all procedures in which workers can be trained to respond automatically to minimise disruption or time waste. In addition, these procedures can help to clarify issues such as where the limits of authority lie.

The way to determine whether you have the right procedures is simply to ask: 'What if such and such happens—then what?' Once you can no longer answer, then you have to determine if the activity is routine or not. If it is—establish a procedure. If it isn't, that's when PowerSharing starts. The leader at the lowest level must then be empowered to take the next step on his or her own initiative—even if this means making a mistake from time to time or even disobeying a directive, if the step furthers the overall mission.

Procedures do not straitjacket people. Procedures do not mean over-regulation. There is a very real difference between a procedure and a regulation. Procedures are designed to streamline a process or to shorten a reaction time and are subject to continual change as new efficiencies are found. They normally represent the best way of doing something. Procedures are often used to give greater *structure* to a task and thus make situational control less reliant on position power (see Introduction).

On the other hand, regulations are created to enable checks and corrections to be made, and normally they are created to keep people behaving correctly or honestly. In addition, regulations often clarify laws and carry a weight of discipline—they tend to increase a leader's sanctioning power. Regulations establish the parameters of people's behaviour, procedures generally clarify people's activities.

Often there is confusion in the difference between regulations and procedures. Here is an example. Freda is a machine operator and her machine operates daily from 9 am to 5 pm. If Freda doesn't turn up at 9 am because she is ill or late, then Sam immediately starts the machine at 9 am; if Sam is absent Clara does it. That's a procedure. The machine has to be oiled and cleaned regularly. That's a regulation. It is therefore oiled every Friday at 5 pm. That's a procedure. Wouldn't it be better to just give Freda the responsibility and leave it to her?

Probably, but it's not always that easy, because there may even be overriding laws especially if safety or finances are concerned. Procedures are best when they are introduced by the workers themselves. Procedures can be continually refined to speed up a process, and often when certain operations are automatic some procedures can be skipped or even dropped. As a firm principle, once a better or more appropriate way is found, *the procedure must be dispensed with.* Procedures should not be allowed to become regulations unless there is agreement or there are overriding reasons.

If you want tea you fill in a green tea form T1, if you want coffee you fill in a blue coffee form C1, if you want sugar there is an appendix on each form, Appendix 1, headed Sugar. If you want biscuits there is a special form headed Morning and Afternoon Tea Solid Accompaniment – Form G. Morning tea is at 10.29½ and the award now allows 16½ minutes instead of 15. Now when it comes to lunch !!!

Regulations, on the other hand, are normally introduced by management as a means of increasing a leader's sanction, unfortunately are rarely scrapped, and are often enforced forever, so that eventually they can become very restrictive and burdensome. Procedures are task-oriented, regulations are authority or position power-oriented.

A procedure is a means of streamlining a routine process or giving a task more structure. A regulation gives a leader more sanctioning or position power. Both are outcome related.

Human nature is strange when it comes to regulations. When a regulation is broken the first thing we tend to do is tighten it up by making further regulations instead of determining whether it was followed in the first place.

Drink driving regulations are an interesting case in point that can be used to illustrate this previous point. It's agreed that 0.05 is a reasonable and safe limit. Nevertheless, when a drunk with a blood alcohol level of, for example, 0.25 is responsible for a serious accident, there is often a public clamour to reduce the limit to 0.0. Therefore, all the law-abiding citizens will eventually be punished because someone broke the first regulation. In many instances we forget that the problem was 0.25, not 0.05, and therefore we become inclined to impose a stricter rule for the wrong reason.

This situation occurs too often in the workplace when there is absolutely no need to continually tighten up regulations. They should be enforced in the first place. Often you will have regulations limiting all, because of the peccadilloes of the few. One organisation actually banned its workers from parking in a certain area of the company carpark because somebody once parked in the boss's space.

On the other hand, having sound procedures makes it easier to push the decision making down the line, particularly if the workers create their own procedures. Ideally, workers should also be allowed to create their own regulations. The only thing to watch is that a regulation has to be endorsed by the responsible authority, the one accountable for the point of impact. In most organisations that person would be at least a department head and often the chief executive. So even in those cases, once regulations are endorsed there is no reason why decision making cannot be decentralised. And decision making is one of the key issues in training for PowerSharing.

DECISIONS, DECISIONS

Getting people to make decisions is one of the hardest aspects of leadership. After many years of experience and observation, one is drawn to the conclusion that there are only three basic reasons why people won't make a decision:

- they are unsure of the limits or extent of their authority;
- they lack confidence in their reasoning ability; in other words, they don't trust their own judgment; or
- they are frightened of the consequences. This last reason is often a direct consequence of either of the first two.

Otherwise very fine leaders have been brought undone by an inability to make a decision.

Peter: I once worked for someone who took eight months to make a deci-
sion on an issue which affected my personal life. When I pressed
him he was very nice about it and said it was his policy to delay
decisions in the hope that the need for the decision would pass and
no one would be hurt!

His logic escaped me, but what was worse he had an opera-
tions manager who was just as bad. You can imagine the pace of
activity during their tenure.

> Decision makers need authority, confidence in their own
> judgment and an understanding of consequences.

As far as authority is concerned—insecurity about which is the first difficulty and reason for indecision—the concept of PowerSharing makes
the issue much clearer. If you have the job, you have the authority. If
the point of impact (see Chapter 1) is your responsibility, then you
have the authority. As we said in the first chapter, it's easier to get forgiveness than permission. This, in fact, means that if you are unsure if
you have the authority—assume you have! PowerSharing enshrines
that concept and gives it credibility.

> Forgiveness is easier to get than permission.

With the second difficulty, only training in the reasoning process will
help. Any aspiring leader must learn to make decisions in accordance
with a reasonable process. This is the case even if you are deciding
whether to have a hot or cold lunch. You consider all the factors,
observe the options and make a decision based on the most appropriate option. We have just covered that process in broad outline, but it is
the subject of many books in its own right and we can do no more than
scratch the surface. So making decisions becomes easier the more you
perfect your reasoning process. After a while much of this type of decision making becomes almost second nature; however, there seems to be
no substitute for training and experience.

The final difficulty to overcome is fear of the consequences. This fear is particularly strong in ambitious or insecure people, who often have a greater concern with not appearing to fail than in taking action. If you really think about it, many delayed decisions can be attributed to a concern over the consequences. Even delays that we attribute to laziness are often due to that same concern—fear of the consequences. We can only overcome this in the long run with a good dose of moral courage, which is a component of the character we spoke of in the first chapter.

Of course, there is the deliberately delayed decision that is awaiting further information. The reason for this kind of decision is related to the second reason. However, its delay is deliberate because of lack of information rather than a lack of confidence in the reasoning process. We will also see later that, by their nature, some types of people do tend to prevaricate and deliberately want to keep their options open. Such people often make tentative decisions but still keep their options open. Flexibility like that can be an advantage as long as it isn't seen to be carelessness.

When it comes to teaching people how to make decisions it is easier to do so by teaching them to follow a procedure, by considering all the relevant factors. That is probably adequate for making day-to-day routine decisions. However, the whole basis of PowerSharing is predicated on a fluid situation that implies that a leader can never be in possession of all the factors and that as matters develop new factors will emerge, which will create problems for the highly developed plan already in motion.

The use of the terminology 'gap analysis' is relevant when it comes to PowerSharing because it is predicated on the gap being flexible. It forces people to keep their eyes on the ultimate objective, because that is the only constant. The current situation is certainly changing almost daily and a lot of other factors will require the plan to also need regular review. The changing current situation will change 'the gap'. By keeping focused, leaders will regularly review their plans and won't be hidebound.

For instance, if *Giddy & Associates* set a target of selling ten thousand bunches of flowers per year in a certain city, one of the factors that they will consider in their planning is a certain level of staff. If suddenly they lose two staff, the gap between the current situation and the objective widens. They need to change their objective (not a good option considering the mission) or change their plan and recruit more staff, which will have an effect on the budget and require adjustment of costs and so on. A good and regularly used planning procedure takes the tedium out of planning and renders it almost automatic.

Experience shows us that so many people put so much effort into their plans that often they are the only things that remain unchanged. All the factors and the environment are changing constantly, particularly these days, so that a plan can be out of date as soon as it is written. PowerSharing overcomes this by incorporating an initial flexibility and by ensuring input and activity from all levels on a regular basis. This, in turn, satisfies the need for individuals to have some form of control over their working environment.

Sometimes a decision is going to be wrong because some of the factors will be unknown or the aim is poorly defined. In business it is often necessary to either reserve a decision or be able to respond flexibly in order to cope with newly emerging factors. This means that plans must also be flexible and subject to alteration in order to conform with the ultimate mission or aim. In order to achieve this there must be a lot of training and a maintenance of high standards throughout the organisation. The bigger the decision, the more detailed the consideration.

A decision to implement a course of action is a plan. The plan may be important, trivial, instantaneous or long term—the planning process is the same, the effort applied will differ.

MANAGING TIME

Proper use and application of procedures, especially planning procedures, will help to shorten process time, make planning easier, aid both leaders and others to appreciate what factors have gone into the consideration of a problem, and finally will lead to sound decisions. It also implies an acceptance of the need for training, a deal of open-mindedness and an ability to deal with priorities and opportunities. Dealing with opportunities is largely a matter of training and experience. However, learning to establish priorities is a matter of time management and this can be learned quite quickly by a motivated leader.

A good leader will have plenty of quality time. So the first thing to recognise is the difference between urgency and importance. While that definition can be found in any time management manual it would be well to cover the topic briefly here. We can grade matters with which we are required to deal, into four priorities:

1. important and urgent;
2. important and not urgent;
3. unimportant but urgent;
4. unimportant and not urgent.

It *should* follow that we tackle the important and urgent first and the unimportant and non-urgent last. The others fall in between. That sounds easy, doesn't it? However, let's look more closely.

We spoke in an earlier chapter about executive activity. Executive activity is the actual routine day-to-day work carried out by a leader or senior manager that could otherwise be carried out by a subordinate. Remember, we said that the more you indulge in executive activity the less you will be able to carry out overview activity. Most executive activity would seem to qualify as important, whether urgent or not. But experience shows us that if a leader continually deals with urgent matters he or she is getting involved in executive activity to the detriment of overview activity. If a leader is continually involved in *doing,* who is going to be *seeing*—in other words, who has the *vision*?

There should no intrinsic opposition to flattened structures, in fact they make good management sense. However, they may not always make good leadership sense if they involve a leader in *executive activity* to the detriment of *visionary activity*. A leader needs to act forward, out and up; a manager acts in, down and behind. But good leaders are always fully conscious of subordinate activity; they can *see* because they aren't *doing*.

What we are therefore saying is that the *important and non-urgent* things are those that the good leader will concentrate on. Important matters affect results, they have a bearing on our objectives, and we should treat them as though we are in control. Someone who concentrates on the *important and urgent* will end up having a nervous breakdown because of being continually in crisis. Anyone who concentrates on the *unimportant,* whether urgent or otherwise, is an escapist not a leader.

If we direct our attention towards only the important things, eventually we will no longer have to be bothered trying to work out priorities because we will only be handling things that matter. The problem lies in determining what types of issues are important, because in the scheme of things it could be construed that even a career itself is unimportant in relation to health or family, for instance. A leader must decide that issue for him or herself, and the decision could differ from person to person depending on value systems. Perhaps no one sums up the case for important but non-urgent activity to become a leader's focus better than Stephen Covey in his book *The Seven Habits of Highly Effective People.*[1]

Peter: A colleague recently recounted a story about his first performance appraisal interview with a man who had been his boss for about six months or more. It appears this boss used to get monthly written reports from his managers as well as holding monthly team meetings and individual face-to-face meetings. He obviously liked to know what was going on.

My colleague, who is a very good leader, was somewhat tardy in attendance at meetings and with his reports and he was very nervous about the stern warnings he was going to get about his punctuality and so on when he went for his appraisal. In fact, he had made a resolution and plan to improve.

The matter wasn't even raised. Instead, he was praised for his commitment to his values and his vision and encouraged to keep going with his good work. When he himself raised the issue of punctuality his boss brushed it off as a minor annoyance which carried no weight in the real scheme of things, pointing out that getting in a report on time was no real indication that what was in the report reflected excellence in performance. Doing and achieving was more important than telling others about it.

He, the boss, still reserved the right to get annoyed but that would never affect his judgment of my colleague's real contribution.

We do need to remember that if a leader can't see the big picture he or she is behaving contrary to the PowerSharing philosophy. A good leader will be looking to matters that deal with the future—planning, change, building character—and executive activity will be delegated to followers. We will speak about delegation in this regard in the next chapter.

A good leader will direct attention to *important* matters and let the rest follow in due course.

Key concepts

- People respond best when they have control over their outcomes.
- To do this, outcomes must relate to the mission.
- The mission must be unambiguous and imparted to all, even to the lowest level.
- People have a stake in the mission when the objectives are agreed, not imposed.
- When objectives are agreed, people must choose their own route or plan.
- People must learn to plan carefully.
- Plans must be subject to change and flexibility.
- Formulating a plan is essential to making even the simplest decisions.
- Procedures are essential to making decisions easier.
- Decision making is crucial and must be pushed down.
- Procedures can be many but must be simple.
- Regulations must be kept to the minimum.
- PowerSharing allows flexibility in planning.
- Establishing priorities is important in creating flexibility.
- A good leader sheds executive activity in favour of visionary activity; this means directing himself or herself to important matters.

Don't interfere with tasks or goals delegated to followers

Leaders and followers at all levels need to be given the freedom to find their own way, to do their own work, while at the same time being stretched within the limits of their knowledge and skill.

Leaders should always be under challenge—and one of the challenges is to keep followers challenged. This doesn't mean keeping people under stress or strain, far from it. It means keeping people excited, enthusiastic, and eager to come to a task each day with a light heart and a clear head. It also means allowing people to create their own challenges and to go beyond the limits of their training and skills, provided, however, they are not held accountable for tasks for which they have not been trained or prepared.

The keys to this freedom are delegation, training, encouragement and trust. The application of these keys, together with adequate supervision, will invariably ensure that objectives are fully achieved and that there are quality outcomes.

Delegation is one of the most misunderstood concepts in both leadership and management. It's almost as though there is some guilt associated with it. Certainly, encouraging people not to interfere with their subordinates can be very frustrating. This is related to concepts we explored in the second chapter. People seem to think that if they are accountable then they either have to do all the work or interfere with those who are doing it.

Following either of these paths can make subordinates very edgy, because they may see this behaviour as lack of trust—and trust is of the essence in all independent action. The trouble is that some people don't understand the nature of delegation, or comprehend the idea that when you give someone a task you should give them the whole task, including the outcome. And until you give someone the *whole* task you haven't really delegated.

TASK ASSIGNMENT

A lot can depend on the understanding and definition of delegation. Often what is referred to as delegation is simply initial task assignment. For instance, delegating means giving someone authority or power to do something. The dictionary definitions invariably use the word *entrust* '(authority, power) to a person acting as one's agent or representative etc'. There are two issues: first, you can't give people something that is theirs in the first place; and second, true delegation is empowering, it involves legitimising the power of a subordinate—PowerSharing.

If we say to someone 'Please sweep the floor', we are assigning a task. If we say to someone, 'The cleanliness of this room is your responsibility', we are assigning them an outcome, and that implies some empowerment and a level of trust—that's delegation. He or she may then decide to do other things in the room first and then *vacuum* the floor or whatever. The outcome is their responsibility and they have all the authority to act within that.

There are two types of delegation: routine delegation—normally to a role; and non-routine delegation—normally to a person. In the first instance, delegation is to a position and its degree varies with the incumbent's readiness. We will cover this in more detail shortly. Even so, it is not really true delegation until the whole role is assumed. The second type of delegation is to a person in order to achieve a specific result.

The word *entrust* is very important and needs to be related to Chapter 2. In delegating we give someone authority to act on our behalf. While that person is responsible to us for his or her share of our ultimate outcome and for his or her whole outcome, in no way is our responsibility for the ultimate outcome diminished. In the instance quoted above—relating to the room cleaning—we may still have responsibility for the satisfaction of the customers who use the room; however, our responsibility doesn't diminish because we are placing extra trust in someone to keep the room clean.

> Delegation involves trust, because a leader is prepared to take responsibility for someone else's outcomes.

Peter: *Years ago I worked for a man who thought he was a great delegator. He even had an office boy come in and sharpen his pencils every day. To him this was very important and he insisted that it was done perfectly. During the day he would call the young fellow to his office whenever his pencils were blunt and then sit at his desk and watch them being sharpened. Every now and again he would criticise the way they were being done.*

One evening I raised this issue with the man and he patiently told me that he was a busy man and didn't have time to sharpen his own pencils (he had time to watch while they were sharpened), it was good training for the office boy (only if he intended to make a career in pencil sharpening), and besides, he was showing us junior managers how to delegate.

I did learn about delegating. I learned what it wasn't. I learned the difference between empowering a subordinate and humiliating him with menial tasks. Tasking a subordinate to make a cup of coffee is not true delegation (it may not even be a good idea)! Making someone responsible for all office catering is delegation. I am not saying that the managing director should make coffee for the board, just that he or she recognises the tasks for what they are. Getting someone to do something for you is not illegal or even unwise—it's just not real delegation. That's what I understand people to mean when they talk about gofer delegation.[1]

In addition to what we have been saying, when we assign *tasks* we have to check on each task—that is, if we are doing our job properly. However, if we assign *responsibility* and *authority* we only have to validate the end product.

Imagine an activity that contains six tasks. The activity has a final outcome. In Method 1 we assign the tasks; in Method 2 we assign the outcome. What are the effects? Method 1 involves a leader in six checking activities; Method 2 involves only one checking activity.

```
┌─────────────────────────────────────────────────────────────────┐
│  Method 1                                                         │
│              A Assign Task 1      ───────────────►  Check         │
│              B Assign Task 2      ───────────────►  Check         │
│              C Assign Task 3      ───────────────►  Check         │
│              D Assign Task 4      ───────────────►  Check         │
│              E Assign Task 5      ───────────────►  Check         │
│              F Assign Task 6      ───────────────►  Check         │
│              G Validate outcome   ───────────────►  Check         │
│                                                                   │
│  Method 2                                                         │
│              A Delegate outcome   ───────────────►  Don't interfere │
│              B Validate outcome   ───────────────►  Check         │
└─────────────────────────────────────────────────────────────────┘
```

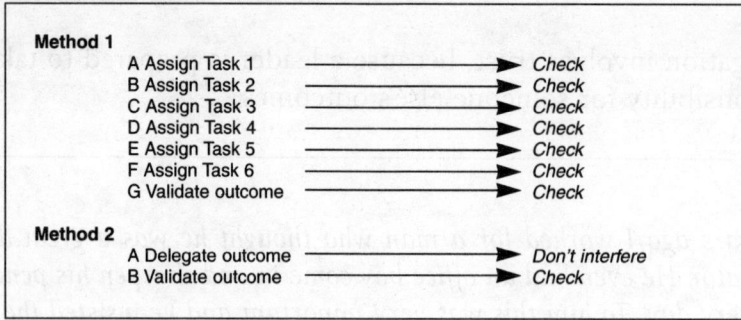

Fig. 4.1 *Comparison of delegation methods*

> Delegation of an outcome allows a leader to decrease executive activity and increase overview activity.

Delegation as a whole increases a leader's leverage and allows a leader to achieve a manifold output with a single input. In the case of the manager or leader, the ultimate output is the sum of the many outputs of the followers. To increase our own output we can either increase the input or get smart and increase our *leverage* by delegation. The follower has no leverage; in other words, the input equals the output.

> Delegation compounds output.

ROUTINE DELEGATION

We said earlier that there is routine and non-routine delegation. Routine delegation is normally to a role. For instance, a chief executive will delegate financial matters to the finance director, marketing matters to the marketing director, sales matters to the sales director and human resource matters to the human resources director. Some of these positions carry automatic authorities and approvals up to certain levels, especially when it comes to limits of expenditure.

In many cases the chief executive would perhaps not be as qualified as some of his or her directors and would therefore rarely step in to check on technical outcomes, although remaining responsible for the ultimate outcomes. Thus it is necessary to have regular external audits and so on. As a good leader, however, he or she will check regularly on general outcomes such as timeliness or general achievement of goals. These are *routine* delegations and they exist no matter who the incumbent director is. This type of delegation involves delegating to a role or position.

There can also be routine delegation to a person. This means that particular issues are always delegated to a particular person and they continue to carry that delegation no matter what their role or position. Possibly the person has a particular skill, or it may simply be a matter of tradition. It can normally be expected that someone filling a specialist role will have responsibility for technical matters immediately and will receive role delegation accordingly. For example, an organisation may import a specialist with certain skills. Any outcome associated with those skills is delegated to that person. If that person leaves, then activities associated with those outcomes cease until another person with similar skills can be found.

There may also be other generalist skills needed for certain aspects of a position for which the incumbent is not prepared. In this case it involves routine delegation to a person whose skills may still be developing. A good leader will therefore gradually ration responsibility and authority to the incumbent, perhaps task by task, until the person can be given full responsibility and authority.

> *As an illustration of that, just recently an old friend was waxing lyrical about his early years in Malaya. He was telling us how he was given standard responsibilities like all the others. He told us how he had been given very basic directed routine tasks on his arrival. If he succeeded he would be given a more responsible task the next time. If he did particularly well, the next task would be very difficult.*
>
> *Task by task he learned by experience. If he succeeded—more responsibility; if he did exceptionally well—a greater piece of the action at a higher level; if he failed then he was either coached or berated depending on the circumstances.*
>
> *After nearly a year he was asked to write a detailed plan at a higher level than his position would dictate. What's more, he was now being called by his first name and his boss was prepared to go on leave and even listen to his advice. Evolving delegation in action in 1958! Many years later it was formalised as* situational leadership.

> Routine delegation is giving a person the responsibility that
> goes with the job.

TRAINING

A good leader, in delegating to a person or role, will recognise the mentoring nature of their own responsibility. As someone once said, don't
delegate a *watermelon* outcome to someone with *grape* training or
experience.

It's not our aim to talk about situational leadership here other than
to encourage readers to understand that it is a leader's responsibility to
prepare his or her followers to accept responsibility—and that means
handing out responsibility in bite-sized pieces. That's how anyone is
trained really, so it is debatable whether it should be referred to as leadership or whether it is only a training or personnel development technique that is one of the elements of leadership.

Training is certainly one of the elements of leadership and it is so
important that it is the subject of a chapter on its own (Chapter 9).
That's why it's so important to recognise experience in a concrete way.
It gives us a guide to the expectations we can have of a performance.
After all, we can still entrust someone with a task but because of our
expectations we may need to observe the outcome–performance more
closely to ensure quality control. However, we look at the outcome
and we don't interfere. It also means that we may have to treat subordinates differently because of their different development levels.
Inconsistency is not an issue with a person if that person understands
the reason why, and is fully aware of his or her own developmental
level.

We have to be conscious, of course, of inconsistency of ability or
learning from one person to the next. For instance, if a person is learning too slowly or consistently makes mistakes, the delegator may be
inclined to give up on them. We hear it all the time: 'Well, I tried to
delegate it but it was never done properly so it's easier to do it myself'.

If one has taken all the steps and reverted, as we have all done at
some stage, to assigning tasks and regularly checking progress and still
a person doesn't seem to achieve the desired result, there comes a time
when something must be done. If, after examination, a leader finds that

all the appropriate steps have been taken but a person's motivation or capacity has not progressed, then for the sake of the rest of the team the incumbent may have to be told that he or she may be better elsewhere or doing a lower level or different job.

After all, if we return to the definition of leadership outlined in the Introduction, we need to remember our words '*respect and willing co-operation*'. Often, perseverance in such a case will diminish the respect and willingness of the rest of the team to co-operate, particularly if a leader is perceived to be wasting time inordinately on one member, or the team is required to make up for the shortcomings of another.

NON-ROUTINE DELEGATION

Non-routine delegation is normally delegation to a person. There is often an element of training and development in non-routine delegation also. Non-routine delegation often provides stretch and challenge to the *delegatee* but it also eases a leader's executive activity burden.

Experience has told us over the years that there are normally four non-routine times when tasks are delegated:
- when the task is rogue, that is, the task was beyond the scope or job specification of everyone;
- when either the manager or a more junior manager to whom a task would usually fall is absent;
- when a subordinate would benefit from the experience; or
- when the task most nearly fits the skills or job role of the *delegatee*.

Some of these reasons contained further reasons, and after reflection we believe that non-routine delegation can best be broken up as follows: *role* delegation, *skill* delegation, *stretch* delegation, and *team* delegation.

Role delegation means that any non-routine task that arises is delegated automatically to the role that has the skill to provide the solution. Take a bus company for instance. Suppose there is to be a new piece of road safety legislation introduced by the government, and users are being given the opportunity to comment on the draft. It is most unlikely that the general manager would handle it himself or herself, although he or she may if he or she didn't know about delegation. More than likely he or she would give it to the operations manager, who may well seek assistance from the maintenance department. It is unlikely that it would be delegated to the finance or marketing department, although there could be a role for, say, the public relations department in its public affairs role.

Skill delegation simply means giving something to the best person for the job, no matter what role a person has. This sort of delegation is more likely to occur at a higher level and in a bureaucratic environment where a lot of reactive management is necessary. There is an old adage which says: 'If you want something done give it to a busy person'. This saying is certainly unfair and may not even always be true. Give it to the individual with the most obvious skills *provided it is commensurate with their workload.* Or, if it is appropriate, give it to the person who would most benefit from having to perform the task. This leads to the next type of delegation.

Stretch delegation is giving someone a task for their own development. We have to be careful here to make sure the recipient can see the reason and the benefit in giving him or her the task. A colleague once remembered a parent at one stage saying to him that she hadn't bought a dishwasher because the children needed to learn how to wash dishes and the delegation was good for their development. He tried hard to think of all the benefits that had accrued to him over the years from having had to do the dishes three times a week as a child. He came to the conclusion that she would have difficulty convincing him.

Team delegation is fairly self-explanatory. It just means the sharing out of jobs to team members as a result of a decision that may have been collegiate or individual in the first place. It's akin to 'That's a good idea—would you like to try it?'. This sort of delegation needs to be treated with care because if someone gets good ideas and always ends up having to implement them it's remarkable how quickly ideas will dry up! On the other hand, someone may be a continual volunteer for non-routine tasks. The delegation needs to be shared around, because willing horses can be flogged to death and sometimes people's motives for volunteering can be suspect.

Warren Bennis, whom we have previously mentioned, recounts a salutary tale in his book *The Unconscious Conspiracy*.[2] Bennis is an expert on leadership in the USA and he is highly regarded. He described early in the book how he was consistently working until 4 am when President of the University of Cincinnati. He was overwhelmed by the mail he had been receiving about the behaviour of one of his deans in bringing his baby to the college in a bassinet twice a week and leaving the baby on his desk while he did his work. As a leader Bennis had to publicly defend the dean and deal with all these condemnatory letters. Bennis's position was correct, admirable and far-sighted.

He could have dealt with the situation differently. He should have publicly supported the dean and privately encouraged him, but he should also have given him all the correspondence, and maybe all the authority thenceforth, to deal with the issue himself. Leaders often make a rod for their own backs in taking up the causes of subordinates, and meanwhile subordinates may not have to deal with any of the consequences. The leader absolutely *cannot be absolved of responsibility* but he or she can definitely be absolved of a lot of the work. And if subordinates are not made responsible for the consequences of their own actions they may never learn to be responsible. This could be described as 'You broke it—you fix it' delegation, but it is really only a further instance of 'that's a good idea' delegation.

Non-routine delegation involves a leader shedding non-routine tasks to the most appropriate follower on the basis of *role, skill, stretch* or *team*.

In any of this, of course, there must be no motive of 'getting even', and no thought of the leader trying to shed responsibility. You also have to be careful not to destroy initiative or condemn people for making mistakes.

Peter: *Something happened to me years ago that may illustrate what we are saying. It also provides a good lesson in the need to address the consequences of delegation.*

    During one of our team meetings we heard that a well-known department store was conducting a program that, while with the best of intentions and certainly in the best interests of the client group we purported to represent, was nevertheless discriminatory and segregationist. I had no strong feelings about the subject but the team did, and it was decided that the store should be asked to reconsider its decision. I delegated the task of writing to the store to my regional manager in whose region the store was located. He wrote a very reasonable letter asking the store to consider doing things, in this case, another way.

    The manager of the store was not amused and threatened to withdraw sponsorships and so on. I went with a senior colleague from another department, which was most affected by the incident, to see the store manager and he was understandably angry. I told him that the regional manager was acting under my delegation on behalf of the whole team and could not be held responsible. The store manager protested that as he had written the letter, the regional manager should be called to task. Eventually he accepted my apology.

A lot of lessons emerged from this, not all to do with delegation. The team felt strongly about an issue, I agreed. I had delegated the task on behalf of the team to the most appropriate person; he accepted responsibility for it. The team was responsible for the outcome, but I was the team leader so the ultimate responsibility was mine. The sequence we followed was correct.

However, none of us had thought the consequences through. I had delegated a task not an outcome and therefore the regional manager had no flexibility in dealing with the issue. If it had been a sacking matter I would have had to resign. What was unclear was, if I had had to do so what would have happened to the regional manager who was acting on my authority? He too may have been fired from on high to mollify the store manager. What about the role of the team? We had a great vision but we hadn't matched our objectives to that vision.

Clearly, I had exceeded my authority, and probably because I had no strong view on the subject, did not apply my mind to it sufficiently. However, I wasn't a slow learner and after that I can assure you that the team could have all the philosophically sound ideas in the world but unless they could be tempered with pragmatism they remained just that—ideas! Fortunately my mistake was accepted in good faith by my superiors.

THE CONSEQUENCES

There were a number of other holes in that little exercise. After all, there is no reason why delegation shouldn't follow the other rules we have been establishing. Was the *objective* of the delegation perfectly clear to the regional manager? Were the *procedures* clear-cut? Did he have all the *resources* and *authority* he needed? While the objectives may have been clear to the team, it seems that they *certainly* were not clear outside the team. The same with the *procedures*. The team procedures may have been followed but were the company's? Did the company have any procedures?

The regional manager may have had his immediate superior's *authority* but unfortunately that authority was not his immediate superior's to give, because the consequences had ramifications for another department in the organisation. There was certainly some confusion about accountability. Finally, there seems to have been no clear indication as to how the success or failure of the exercise was to be measured.

This involves PowerSharing again: clear mission, sound procedures, resources and authority where they are needed, acceptance of mistakes in good faith (consequences of the action), and the new issue we have unearthed—how we judge those consequences.

Delegation requires a clear objective, sound procedures, resources and authority, an appreciation of the consequences and an agreement on how results will be assessed.

Judging the consequences, or evaluating any action, is today rightly regarded as part and parcel of any procedure or activity. So far we haven't talked much about consequences or judgment of results other than in the context of accepting that people will make mistakes and, provided the mistakes are a result of reasoned judgment and not incompetence, must not be penalised. But what about results themselves? How are they recorded and evaluated, and isn't there some accountability on the part of the delegatee?

By this we mean 'When is the task complete? When is the outcome complete?' We are suggesting that once you have delegated a task or an activity let the delegatee finish it. When you give someone a job, give them the whole job. That's what is known as the philosophy of *completed staff work*. The task must be completed down to the dotting of i's, crossing of t's and cleaning up. We've all heard it said that a leader should never accept an uncompleted task. But it all means the same thing. The person to whom something is delegated must be absolutely clear what is to be done, must know the procedures to follow, must be given the authority and resources, must know how the task will be evaluated and what the consequences of completion are. It makes things much easier if, as we said before, a leader delegates an outcome not a process. Then there is less likelihood of an incomplete task.

> When you give someone a job, give them the whole job.

This means being given the whole job but without being denied assistance where needed. It also means that the delegatee must be perfectly clear that no judgment or evaluation can be possible on a half-finished task. That way people look to take responsibility for a whole task fully completed. It encourages people to think for themselves and not to go running back to superiors with problems not properly thought through. It also encourages people to take responsibility for their own ideas in an environment where those ideas are welcomed.

When you go to a superior, go with solutions rather than problems. When it comes to paperwork, for instance, you should never accept a proposal that doesn't contain recommendations at the conclusion and, in fact, a recommended course of action or options. It's also a good idea to have people write in the first person, no matter what the document. It encourages ownership.

It also encourages people if you accept and implement their recommendations even if you do not totally agree. By this we mean that if there is very little difference between two recommendations it is a good idea to choose the one from the person who is less experienced or less qualified. *However, this doesn't mean lose the battle for the sake of not hurting somebody's feelings.* If people experience one or two wins or successes they will blossom, because their morale is affected. On the other hand, constant rejection leads to loss of morale and eventually loss of interest and effectiveness.

John: A friend of mine once worked for a very efficient man who was a compulsive proof reader and habitually corrected or changed the style of whatever was put in front of him. The inevitable happened. My friend was given a task to write something and he decided not to do it. After a number of reminders he was called in to his boss to explain where the document was. He replied that because everything he wrote was always appreciably changed he thought he may as well let the boss do it the way he wanted it in the first place.

I wouldn't recommend the above as a standard course of action, because not all bosses are as reasonable as in this case. This one accepted the situation, re-assigned the task to my friend with clear evaluation criteria and clear consequential criteria. My friend didn't try the same trick again, but by the same token his boss stopped compulsively correcting his written work. Morale and respect returned and initiative was no longer stifled and it has remained a great story for over twenty years! And they are still good friends.

It is important to remember in any delegated task, written or otherwise, that if you expect something done *exactly the way you would write it or do it yourself—then do it yourself!* Remember the old saying: 'Don't keep a dog and bark yourself'. Of course, the dog must know what to bark at. That means teaching him good barking habits in the first place. So you tell someone what to do, not how to do it. However, he or she must learn what it takes to do it to your satisfaction. That presupposes clear expectations. It also means that a leader must accept that there are a variety of ways of accomplishing something.

Eventually, delegation becomes a habit for both leader and led so that a person will recognise that something is in his or her sphere of influence and will undertake a task without reference to a higher authority as the need arises. All that is then required from a leader is affirmation that the action taken was correct and the next problem can be faced.

Three tenets of delegation
1. Don't come with problems, come with solutions.
2. Don't come with questions, come with answers.
3. Don't keep a dog and bark yourself.

RESOURCEFULNESS AND INITIATIVE

Resourcefulness and independence of thought and action are out-growths of proper delegation. The resourcefulness of followers makes a leader's task very much easier because the leader is not tied down by trivia and even necessary executive activity.

John: Some years ago when I was in the army I was about to take my unit on a major exercise.

I got to work at first light on the morning of departure and was casually told by my operations officer that a potentially serious problem had arisen overnight which may have led to the aborting of the exercise but that it had already been solved throughout the night by subordinates.

This involved 60 men working through the night, supplied with food and hot drinks by the sergeants' wives. The ops officer and the regimental sergeant major decided that as there was nothing I could personally do to solve the problem, and in line with our practised philosophy of individuals accepting responsibility, action and results, they had simply got on with ensuring that the battalion was operational by the morning.

There was obvious pride in their being able to inform me of a serious problem and its subsequent solution. Needless to say, I was somewhat proud too that the battalion could respond quickly to a serious problem, without having to get the commanding officer to approve an obvious, but demanding solution.

I see that as a good example of delegation in action. It was the ops officer's responsibility to get the unit to the exercise area, and he had solved a problem that could have stopped it. Naturally, as the person ultimately responsible for the unit I would have liked to have known of such a critical situation, but it was actually more important that my subordinates were prepared to assume the full weight of their responsibilities. It's also a perfect example of initiative, teamwork and resourcefulness.

Resourcefulness and initiative are two of the hidden benefits of delegation. We must not discourage ideas. It was written some time ago in a trade union journal that *no worker can justifiably be held accountable for work for which he or she is not specifically trained.* While we would agree with that, and advise that one has to think carefully just what the development level of the delegatee is before delegating, a lot will depend on the content, importance, urgency and other implications of the task.

After all, people are remarkably resourceful and it is amazing the number of developments that have taken place that have come about as a result of someone's initiative rather than specific research and development. It would be a shame to lose that. How do you stop stultification when people are discouraged from experimenting with things for which they have not specifically been trained? A statement which makes a lot of sense was contained in an article written in the last few years based on the Fort Hood Leadership Study. It said:

> If action is too expensive you get stagnation. If truth is too expensive you get lies.[3]

Initiative will not be stifled provided there is trust. Learning to trust and to accept accountability are some of the traits of character and integrity that this book is encouraging people to adapt to. Where there is trust and initiative, people tend to respond to challenges in remarkable ways.

Peter: I recently got an insight into the innovative Japanese character. I know that the Japanese are regarded as great imitators and improvers, but they are also great innovators.

We had a couple of very demanding clients who wanted something done a particular way. My advisers made it clear to me that it couldn't be done and I agreed. To be reassured I asked my advisers to get feedback from both the UK and the USA and anywhere else where the knowledge may have been held. The answers were clear and unequivocal in every case: we have been involved in this business for sixty or more years and it can't be done!

Under a lot of pressure we decided to give it a try. And it worked! Only partially, but enough to convince us that it could be possible to improve with more effort.

Some months later, one of my advisers was in Japan and found that they had been using this particular technique and other impossible methods for a number of years. They were very apologetic, but they explained that the business we were involved in was foreign and new to Japanese culture and they didn't realise that what they were doing was impossible! They asked if it was advisable that they stop doing it immediately!

In fact, our word *crisis* is roughly translated into Japanese and also some Chinese dialects as *danger-opportunity* or *dangerous opportunity*—which surely says something about taking initiative. In all leadership the calculated risk is often what wins the day.

Peter: When I was a boy my father used to separate people into experts and inperts. He used to say that an expert was someone who knew all the parameters of the task in which he was engaged. By contrast, he defined an inpert as someone who was too ignorant to know when something was impossible and just went ahead and did it!

An *inpert* is someone who doesn't know when something is impossible and just goes ahead and does it.

Years ago there was a famous US story used in army training circles called 'A Message to Garcia'. A general calls in a fresh-faced youngster and says: 'Take a message to Garcia'. No word of who Garcia was, or where he was—although presumably he was in the jungles of Central or South America because this story was during the Spanish-American or the Mexican war. The young man reached Garcia after some months of gargantuan effort. Presumably he remembered the message, because the story ended happily ever after.

The point of this story is that leadership, on the one hand, involves allowing subordinates room to take initiative; and on the other hand, it means the leader seizing initiative whenever possible. Both leaders and led need to deliberately develop a thirst for challenge. They need to actively seek out unusual and difficult tasks in order to build up their *inpertise* and to become more aware of the need for innovation in others.

THIRST FOR CHALLENGE

We have all had workers or followers who, when given a task, immediately make a problem out of it and ask a great series of irrelevant questions that make you wish you had done the job yourself in the first place. On the other hand, asking questions is the only way to learn, so it often depends on who is being questioned.

Mastery of challenge is often the key to leadership. That's why it's a good thing for some people to change their jobs regularly, either within an organisation or into other organisations. Some organisations do this well. They keep leaders challenged by either assigning them new tasks in the current role, changing their role, or perhaps sending them some different people to work with. Whatever way, the challenge is increased. This is going to become a more common practice in business and industry also, with leaner and flatter organisations. Leaders who find the challenge disappearing should think hard. Take up an external challenge or seek another job. A word of warning! It is not wise to artificially create a challenge just for the sake of a leader in an organisation if it involves followers being inconvenienced.

Challenge is something you have to continually train for and undertake in order to better answer challenges as they arise. You often find that you have risen to a challenge and done something which in the cold hard light of retrospect looks impossible. Even some adventure or initiative training is used by industry these days to give people a sense of challenge. However, we have to be careful to ensure that the people doing these things understand why they are doing them. You can't challenge others unless you yourself are kept challenged, either intellectually or practically. There is a flaw in the saying 'Why take the hard way when you can take the easy way?' The easy way may not necessarily be the best or right way and we should always take the best or right way.

Delegation is an essential element of PowerSharing. PowerSharing is not only the delegation of an outcome in total trust, it is also the sharing of the decision to place that trust. Thus, when we discuss with someone and agree on an objective we not only give the person the responsibility for, and resources to reach that objective; we give somebody their share in the ultimate objective.

We will cover the nature of power and authority later, but there is a great analogy in a statement that says that power has a habit of rising to the top—like oil on water.[4] It must be continually pushed down again. The minute you make a decision that should have been made below you, then you will find yourself making all sorts of trivial decisions. What's more, you'll tend to find yourself pushing, back up the line, decisions which *you* should have been making.

Key concepts

- Delegation implies trust and responsibility.
- Delegation allows a leader to lead instead of *doing*.
- Delegation of an outcome rather than a task reduces executive activity.
- Routine delegation is normally to a role.
- Non-routine delegation can be to a *role* or a *person* or *team* and can involve *skill* or *stretch*.
- When delegating a task, delegate the *whole* task including the outcome.
- Any delegation needs adherence to the principles of PowerSharing.
- These principles are: clarity of mission or purpose; clear procedures, allocation of resources and authority; clear evaluation criteria; and recognition of consequences.
- Challenge promotes innovation, initiative and risk taking.

CHAPTER 5
Fifth Precept

Maintain a genuine interest in your followers

The greatest asset or resource any *leader* has is the people who follow or have the potential to follow. The greatest resource any *manager* has is the workers who produce. It is a strange irony that these are often the resources least valued, least maintained and, tragically, most readily discarded or dispensed with. The highest in the land to the lowest supervisor too often treat people with indifference, as though the time, effort and money invested in them is of no consequence and as though they are only a means to an end.

In any leadership environment the needs of workers or followers must be paramount. This means that personnel must be trained, developed, empowered and supported. To do this successfully leaders must have a knowledge of personnel needs and aspirations. This is a *line* function, not a *staff* function. The *staff* can only ever be a resource. These issues are the responsibility of the leader, not a union supervisor or shop steward. It is necessary that leaders at all levels obtain and retain the trust of their subordinates and in turn demonstrate that they themselves return the trust. This requires openness and, in many cases, learning to listen.

OBLIGATION

An old school book from the 1940s and 1950s used to contain a short prose verse by Thomas Carlyle, the last sentence of which is still relevant:

> *If the poor and humble toil that we have bread, must not the high and glorious toil for him in return, that he have light, have guidance, freedom, immortality?*

There are two ways of looking at this concept. One suggests that it is jingoistic English noblesse oblige; the other is that it is noble and heartfelt, the essence of compassionate leadership. There is possibly an element of truth in both views. Today few people understand just what noblesse oblige meant and how seriously it was taken, at least in England, in years gone by. There really was an obligation on the ruling classes. Unfortunately, by the time of the agrarian revolution the concept began to smack of charity and paternalism. By the time the Industrial Revolution was at its height the concept had become a burden in the eyes of the nouveau riche and any thought of a mutually beneficial covenant disappeared.

The idea of mutual obligation goes back to feudal times when the liege lord was obligated to provide for the welfare of his retainers and their families in return for their responsibility to him of military and other service. In his turn the lord had privileges granted to him by the baron. The baron was in turn obligated to the king to a greater or lesser extent depending on the period. The whole was predicated on mutual dependence and support.

> The leader–follower nexus is a process of mutual obligation.

There is no thought here of making the situation sound idyllic, because it wasn't. The people of the so-called lower classes had barely emerged from serfdom at the time the agrarian revolution began, but at least they began to get dignity, if not almost freedom. By the early eighteenth century the greed of the growing merchant and industrial classes rather than the old aristocracy gave rise to poverty, squalor and associated crime on a scale hitherto unprecedented, certainly in England. These squalid conditions gave birth to agitation, which over the next century led to universal emancipation and the rise of the trade unions.

All this leads to the inevitable conclusion that the (hopefully defunct) union–management antagonisms of the past really had their genesis with the nouveau riche management of the nineteenth century turning its back on tradition and abrogating its responsibility for those for whom it should have cared. The unions were a natural outgrowth of an abrogation of leadership.

Too many of today's industrial problems also relate to management being incapable of performing in a leadership role. When management turned its back on its leadership responsibilities it created a vacuum that was filled by unions and later by specialist management sub-sets such as personnel departments. The consequence of passing the responsibility for people management to a specialist area is that more often than not it becomes just another resource; just one of the factors to be considered in the management equation, instead of the overriding consideration.

There is a tendency in many managers to want to stick to their level of expertise and leave the management of their human resources to the human resources specialists. The very terminology 'human resources' supports that contention. Karl Albrecht, the highly respected management consultant and author, has articulated the need to get back to calling people, *people*, instead of just human resources.[1]

People are an organisation's and a leader's most valuable asset.

After all, the 'human' resource is the only resource (perhaps apart from various jobs involving certain animals) that has psychological needs, can be trained to improve performance, can improve the performance of other resources and whose own performance can fluctuate wildly, even when inputs are the same from one day to the next. Robots are rarely subject to mood swings, computers don't suffer stress or need counselling and very few building assets get mid-life crises. Of course, non-human resources have needs as well, but they don't suffer from morale problems, except as an indirect result of a lack of morale among the people supposed to address the needs of those resources. And the needs of other resources are not the subject of *leadership* but rather of *management* efficiency.

FUNCTIONAL LEADERSHIP

If we look at any group engaged upon a task it has those three inter-related needs which we explained earlier in the book:

- *the needs or demands of the task;*
- *the need to be held together as a team;*
- *the needs of each individual in that team.*

It is a leader's task to balance the three interrelated needs. In previous chapters we concentrated on leadership functions relating to the task. The need to be held together as a team will be dealt with later. The needs of the individuals on that team is the subject of this chapter. The model in long use is the three-linked eccentric circles.

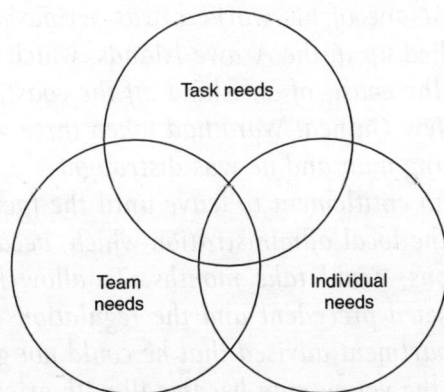

Fig. 5.1 *Functional leadership—interrelated needs*

If you remove, diminish or over-concentrate on any one of the three circles it will be to the detriment of the other two. Of course, in such cases as the military and some police operations, the needs of the task are of such overwhelming importance that the needs of the individual have to be sacrificed. Hence, people have lost their lives in the course of duty. A leader balances those demands and needs. It stands to reason, therefore, that whoever is responsible for addressing the needs of the task is also responsible for the needs of the team and the needs of the individual. That doesn't mean you do away with the HR department, it simply means that that department is a resource to the line manager. After all, it is the line manager who is ultimately responsible.

Some people with vested interests would express doubt that such a situation could be possible in a large organisation. This doubt springs from seeing people simply as another resource—which, while it might make organisational or management sense, more often than not is leadership nonsense.

> Line managers are responsible for the three functional leadership needs; a personnel or HR department exists to *assist* the line manager.

Peter: When I was in Papua New Guinea in the early 1960s, I became what would be regarded these days as the assistant personnel manager. We got a message from the manager of an isolated outstation that one of his workers was seriously distressed. His mother had died up in the Arawe Islands, which is rather like on an island off the coast, of an island off the coast, of an island off the coast of New Guinea! Word had taken three weeks or more to reach this young man and he was distraught.

He had no entitlement to leave until the facts could be verified through the local administration which, because of primitive communications, could take months. To allow him to go home would be to set a precedent and the regulations were clear. The personnel department advised that he could not go!

However, the young man became ill with grief, the whole outstation workforce suffered a serious morale problem and ceased performing well. The outstation leader's very ability to carry out his task was now in jeopardy. He was clearly in a cleft stick of either obeying regulations based on the advice or direction of a non-line personnel department or meeting his leadership obligations to his task, the group and the individual.

Working on the principle that forgiveness is easier to obtain than permission, he chose the latter and sent the worker home with consequent positive results. I am pleased to say he was supported by the general manager located on the other side of the country who also had a leadership focus.

I still remember the issue very clearly all these years later and continue to wonder what the outcome would have been with a less courageous leader–manager at the helm.

There are so many lessons in this story: loyalty, compassion, pointless regulations, *specialist staff* influencing a line decision, lack of independent authority, lack of on-the-spot knowledge of issues, and—the main lesson—the effect of the non-addressing of individual needs on the other two circles of *team needs* and *task needs*. This simple example should set in mind clearly the idea of specialist staff advice and line authority. It also gives a very clear example of how a simple, inappropriate, though technically correct decision, can affect morale.

MORALE

The importance of morale cannot be overstated. Despite Napoleon's statement that 'Morale is three to one' it is actually very difficult to measure and quite hard for non-leaders to comprehend. It's as though bricks are the skill level of a workforce and morale is the mortar. Good mortar will hold poor bricks up for a long time but with poor mortar even a wall of good bricks will soon collapse. The leader is the artisan, who chooses the bricks, mixes the mortar and lays the wall; and leadership competence equates to laying skill.

Personnel departments are a line manager's resource. They provide advice and assistance. The flatter the structure the more imperative this becomes.

> In a flattened structure leadership in management becomes critical.

As discussed in Chapter 1, you can delegate a task but you cannot avoid responsibility. The personnel department can advise, but whatever the process, the line manager carries the eventual responsibility.

A large span of control is not an excuse to avoid leadership responsibility. We know of leaders who were responsible for thousands of people but who still had time to get to know the names of hundreds of their workers, and even took time every week to visit those of the organisation's workers who were in hospital. Other successful leader–managers even send greetings to every person on their birthday or significant celebration day. Good leaders are attentive to all a worker's needs, whatever they may be, and this becomes a way of life.

John: There was a story from Darwin at the end of 1974, when the city was destroyed by Cyclone Tracy. John Holland Constructions had a significant presence in Darwin at the time. One of the junior engineers had his family with him and they had to be evacuated while the husband–father stayed behind to help with clean-up and damage assessment.

The wife and young family were flown to Brisbane where they were met by a senior representative of the company. They were driven to the Gold Coast and given Sir John's apartment as accommodation while matters were sorted out. They had nothing but the clothes on their backs. No sooner had they entered the apartment when the phone rang—it was Sir John Holland, the man who ran this very large organisation employing hundreds of people throughout Australia. He apologised for not *being in town, asked after their welfare and needs, explained that the company would meet the expense of refitting the family with clothes and other essentials and guaranteed the safety of their husband and father. He even explained where the drinks cabinet was, having assessed from his own experience what the most likely immediate need would be.*

Clearly, Sir John's actions were those of an employer who cared for his employees. What did it cost the big man in terms of time? An hour or two. What did it cost the company financially? In the scheme of things, only petty cash. What did the organisation gain? A lifetime of loyalty and certainly enough goodwill for the story to continue to be told over twenty years later. What did these actions really demonstrate? Sir John Holland truly cared.

This was a first-class example of an individual and his organisation who recognised that a good leader not only looks after the *career* needs of a worker but also cares for the *personal* needs. This implies a holistic view of the person and indicates recognition that the needs are inseparable, because they are on a continuum.

A leader recognises all the needs of his or her followers.

NEEDS

At this time maybe we should look at Maslow's hierarchy of needs (Fig. 5.2); after all, no work on leadership has any validity these days without discussing it!

Abraham Maslow was a psychologist in the 1940s and 1950s who was doing extensive research and study into human motivation. He found that a person's needs became more sophisticated as they were fulfilled. This meant that a person was not motivated by higher order needs until basic needs were filled. Maslow found that there were essentially five levels of need. These can be represented by a model similar to that in Figure 5.2.

To see the reality of Maslow's hierarchy one needs to look no further than the behaviour of people who lived at the edge of life daily in the concentration camps during World War II.

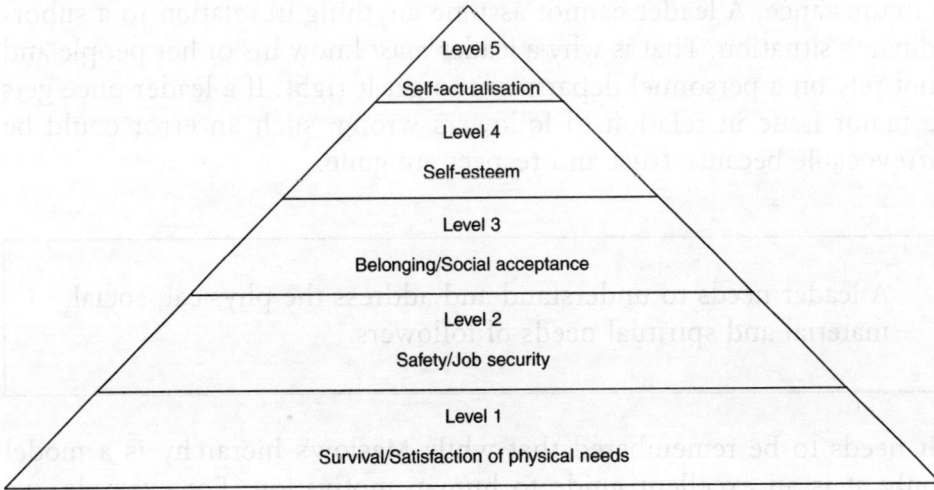

```
                    Level 5
                Self-actualisation

                    Level 4
                  Self-esteem

                    Level 3
            Belonging/Social acceptance

                    Level 2
                Safety/Job security

                    Level 1
        Survival/Satisfaction of physical needs
```

Fig. 5.2 *An adaptation of Maslow's hierarchy of needs*

The lowest level of need is the satisfaction of physical needs. This includes eating, sleeping and drinking. When the fulfilment of these needs is made difficult, needs of the next higher level become irrelevant. Not too many people whose life is seriously threatened would spend much time concentrating on job security. As Dr Samuel Johnson once said, 'Hanging wonderfully concentrates a man's mind'.

There even seems to be a hierarchy in the satisfaction of physical needs. Prisoners of war reported a very much reduced sexual desire during their period of captivity—and it couldn't always have been bromide in the tea! Maybe it is only in movies that a man's mind strays to romance in times of great peril.

After Level 1 comes Level 2, which is concerned with such issues as safety, security and job security. It is often at this level that people begin to co-operate more with each other for the achievement of a common good. The focus is still very much on self but there is a greater inclination to seek the help of others to achieve the security needed.

As each level is attained a person becomes motivated by higher order needs. It is important to remember that as far as the hierarchy goes, once a need is fulfilled it tends to become irrelevant (unless interrupted of course), as motivation then becomes focused on the next higher plane. It is important to remember that this is a *model* not a social scale.

A leader needs to understand that a follower's physical, social, material and spiritual needs will depend on each individual's circumstance. A leader cannot assume anything in relation to a subor-dinate's situation. That is why a leader *must* know his or her people and not rely on a personnel department to get it right. If a leader once gets a major issue in relation to followers wrong, such an error could be irrevocable because trust and respect are gone.

A leader needs to understand and address the physical, social, material and spiritual needs of followers.

It needs to be remembered that while Maslow's hierarchy is a model only, it is an excellent guide to human motivation. For example, we have been able to see the effects of the growth in unemployment in recent years on the self-esteem of those affected. Leaders could do worse than to recognise how they can help followers from one level to another through the hierarchy.

It has been suggested by any number of management–leadership philosophers, that it is the very fulfilment of the first two levels of needs that has created the crisis of emptiness in workers' lives. Learning organisations have to find out how to help fulfil the higher level needs of their workers. The whole is predicated upon a leader try-ing to be fully aware of each follower's needs at any time. It also fol-lows, of course, that if one can, by good leadership, help people from one level to the next, then by poor leadership one can destroy a per-son's confidence or self-esteem.

COMPASSION

The word that best describes a leader's responsibility to his or her fol-lowers is compassion. For some obscure reason the word compassion has been confused with weakness. Compassion means sympathy and concern. Sympathy is the sharing of a similar feeling or even an idea with someone else. A boss who is concerned for a worker's family or health is showing compassion. A leader will show the strength to do something about it, and there is nothing weak in that.

There seems to be a conventional wisdom that workers or employ-ees will resent any intrusion into their private needs. When someone from the Marriage Guidance Council interviewed on radio suggested that managers of the 1990s would do well to watch for signs of marriage breakdown among members of their staff, the radio journalist suggested that it would be an interference in a person's private affairs and that what happens in a person's home was his or her own business. 'Presumably so is domestic violence!' was the reply.

The truth is that a leader needs to understand the variety of personnel problem areas—both personal and of a business nature—that will continually arise in any workforce. All need to be recognised and addressed, although in different ways. Concern and assistance for Mr A may be appreciated, but if the same is shown to Mrs B it may be regarded as intrusion. Hence the need for a leader to know his or her people and understand how to deal with each of them. Those differences in personality will be treated further in a later chapter.

The belief, while not widespread, that compassion is weakness is nonetheless observable in many workplaces. This concept that real men don't eat quiche—or need compassion—comes from confusing the needs of the *task* or *team* with the needs of the *individual*. It is not correct to assume that if a team needs to demonstrate certain characteristics then all members of the team must show the identical characteristics (all out of the same mould).

The assumption is quite often wrongly made, for instance, that the physical image needs of the team are what each of the individuals also need. Too often you will find non-acceptance of an individual whose needs are different from the group 'image'. This will often be to the detriment of the task. We will explore this further when we discuss teamwork. The film 'A Few Good Men' was a clear exposition of this phenomenon. It depicted a situation where it was expected that every man had to think the same, act the same and have the same values and personality as everyone else or else the task would suffer.

There is, after all, something of value in the old Marxist philosophy: *From each according to his means, to each according to his needs.* The essential meaning of this is to treat everybody fairly having regard to their skills and capacities. This is something the communists failed to put into practice.

Treating everyone fairly doesn't mean treating everyone the same way.

John: I had a boss years ago who never had the courage to confront any-
one with a misdemeanour. If someone came late to a meeting he
would chastise all of us. If someone developed a bad practice we
would all get extra training. He found it easier to blame us all
than remonstrate with one.

Group punishment: All it does is confuse the disciplinary needs
of an individual with the disciplinary needs of the group. Sure, that
person's shortcomings will affect the task and the team, but it's the
need of the individual that must be addressed in order to complete
that circle.

There has long been discussion over where concern and compassion end and paternalism begins. There would be very few people who
don't believe in the obligation a leader has for the professional training
and development of followers. This is dealt with in a later chapter.
However, there continues to be a variety of opinions concerning
whether a leader has any obligation to an employee or follower for
other than work or career related needs. Today's leadership philosophers rightly point out the holistic nature of people: needs cannot be
separated into discrete packets. In this sense the leader of the learning
organisation and the enlightened leader of tomorrow would be advised
to recognise how wide the net of obligation now spreads.

This means that a leader will provide training or encourage an
individual to undergo training to better his or her career prospects both
in, and subsequently out, of the organisation. It means providing
encouragement, advice, time and maybe even financial assistance. It
means helping and teaching people to recognise their career goals and
to provide assistance in achieving them. Some organisations not only
run courses but also provide mentors for newly-joined employees.
These mentors provide the support that the newcomer needs. The years
to come could well see a significant development of the mentoring and
patronage system, especially in flattened structures with slower vertical
moves.

As well as the career needs there are developmental needs. These
involve helping people to set life goals, helping them to understand
more of their social responsibilities. They involve encouraging people
to learn to balance their lives, to match ambition with capability, to set
realistic objectives in relation to family and travel in the context of
work and career needs, and to encourage them to recognise the necessity to give in order to receive.

Key concepts

- Managers will treat people as a resource, leaders treat people as people.
- Control of all other resources emanates from people.
- Leaders have a responsibility to care for their workers–people.
- Leaders must know their people as individuals.
- People have a right to be trained, empowered, developed and supported.
- Leaders must deal with the employees directly, not through personnel departments.
- Groups engaged on a task have three interrelated needs: *task* needs, *team* needs and *individual* needs.
- Maslow's hierarchy of needs helps us to understand human motivation.
- Leaders should seek to help people to further themselves on the hierarchy.
- People need to be treated as individuals.
- Fairness does not mean treating everyone the same.

CHAPTER 6
Sixth Precept

Create organisational harmony and teamwork

TEAM-BASED ORGANISATIONS

No book on leadership would be complete without reference to teams, particularly in the 1990s. The team based organisation (TBO) is a concept whose time has arrived. Industry has begun to embrace TBO with the same alacrity reserved for MBO in the 1970s and TQM in the 1980s. Unfortunately, the concept of teams has taken on a narrow definition and it is assumed that when we talk of teams we naturally mean the self-directed work team. We want to examine a much broader idea of teamwork.

The value of teamwork has always been recognised in such organisations as the military, and it played no small part in the ethos of the nineteenth century, when colonialism was rampant and the playing fields of Eton produced the stuff of which empires were made. In that period and before, the concept of the common weal was very popular and young people were not only encouraged, but were expected to submerge their own needs to the common good. However, in the world of enterprise it seems to have been lost among other popular concepts as they have moved on and off the business stage, and a sort of dog-eat-dog mentality has grown up. Like many things, we find a new name and it assumes the mantle of the novel.

One of the crucial inhibitors of teamwork has been the acceptance of the idea that there are certain aspects of personnel management that are best left to specialists. This meant that until recent years an adversarial style of management not only existed, but was condoned.

Management in some cases was not only discouraged from negotiating with its own workforce but in many cases was actively prevented from doing so, by both the unions and the bargaining system. Imagine if the captain of a sports team was only allowed to communicate with his team through the players' association.

COMMITTEES

Oh give me your pity, I'm on a committee,
Which means that from morning to night
We devise and advise and contend and amend,
With ne'er a solution in sight!

Anon

Most teams these days act more like committees than teams, although fortunately this is changing. One of the reasons why teams act like committees is because so many people don't know the difference between them. Everyone has heard the old story about a camel being a horse designed by a committee. If you think about it seriously it does the camel an enormous injustice. After all, there are few animals more totally attuned to their environment than camels, and they perfectly fulfil all the requirements needed of a beast of burden. It depends largely on the terms of reference that the committee was given.

A committee is a group of people trying to arrive at a consensus that is the most acceptable for everyone. Each person comes with their own hidden agenda, a position of power they want to protect, and their own 'mental models', as Peter Senge calls them.[1] These are, at their simplest, preconceived ideas of what will and won't work. Generally, committees are happy if they reach a compromise.

A team consists of people whose individuality is sacrificed *for the role in question*. Each person exposes any hidden agenda, there is no power play and the mental models are taken out and examined by all and discarded if the team so decides. A committee may have designed a camel if they had been told that the end product was to be a horse. A team would have designed a camel if they had been told that what was wanted was: a tameable beast of burden; one that would operate in the presence of other animals; one that could accept loads in a prone position and still rise to its feet; one that was comfortable to sit upon for months on end; and one that could go without water for long periods. There is a subtle difference.

Creating a team is not easy when you consider the disparate backgrounds from which people come and the cultural and other baggage they bring with them. Blending people from disparate backgrounds into teams is something that the military fully understands. It is too easy and trite to suggest that the considerable position power which military leaders have is the reason they blend people so well. First, they do not necessarily hold that much power; and second, while the power theory may help explain early successes in team creation, it doesn't explain the continued loyalty over many years, long after any power has been withdrawn. Therefore there must be more rational explanations for this phenomenon.

SYNERGY

Teamwork will flourish in any soil that has management in a leadership role and where direct and constant communication on all matters to do with the workplace is freely available between management and worker. Only in such an environment of trust can proper synergy exist. Only with synergy is real teamwork going to be effective. Synergy is more than just co-operation or cohesion. It is the demonstration that in relationship terms, the whole is greater than the sum of its parts. The combined efforts of two people are greater than the sum of the efforts of the two individuals.

> Synergy means one plus one is greater than two.

Conversely, when there is discord between people or they are not working to a common goal then the combined efforts are often less than the sum of the individual efforts, in which case one plus one is less than two.

How often do people in organisations come to work on a Monday to be confronted (if they are fortunate enough not to be *downsized*) with the new buzzword—*self-directed work teams*. But teamwork cannot be mandated. A leader needs to have a deep understanding of how people socialise, what motivates them to co-operate with each other, and how profoundly an organisation's culture will affect the very ability of people to work within teams, and teams to work with each other.

Self-directed work teams are just one aspect of teamwork, which is in itself one aspect of organisational harmony. The organisational harmony will produce the synergy we are seeking. True synergy has almost a spiritual connotation because it implies taking that extra intangible step.

TEAM SPIRIT

The spiritual connotation we speak of is not that which leads people to more deeply practise their chosen religion, although they might do so. We mean the sort of spirituality which is referred to as team spirit.

One may well ask how an army manages to take somewhat unwilling, if not downright angry, young conscripts off the streets or out of industry and career and in three months have them working as part of a team. People tend to assume that it is done through fear and even brutality. But what is it that draws people, both leaders and led, together thirty years after the event to talk of the good old days and the good and bad times? Is it common goals, comradeship, challenge, loyalty, caring and leadership or is it a common memory of fear and brutality?

We use that example, because any army gathered together for any cause could, over history, repeat that experience and could do so today. The truth is that the armed forces change forever the perceptions people have of themselves and each other because of a deeper sharing of experience. It also makes everyone aware of their responsibility and importance in the scheme of things. In this age of cynicism it may sound jingoistic, but all credit to any industry or organisation that can retain the loyalty and concern of its members forty, fifty and sixty years on—year after year.

> True teamwork implies a sharing of experience.

There is a description of an infantry battalion in a book by a great Australian, Henry Gullett: *Not As A Duty Only*. It sums up what we are saying about real teamwork.

> But six hundred men do not make a battalion. The six hundred men have to learn the soldier's trades and disciplines. Even then they are not a battalion. An effective battalion in being ready to fight, implies a state of mind—I am not sure it is not a state of grace. It implies a giving and a taking, a sharing of almost everything—possessions, comfort, affection, trust, confidence, interest. It implies a certain restriction and at the same time a certain enriching and widening of the human spirit. It implies doing a hundred things together—marching to the band, marching all night long being hungry, thirsty, exhausted, filthy; being near but never quite mutinous. It involves not the weakening but the deferment of other bonds and interests; the acceptance that life and home are now with the battalion. In the end it is possible to say 'the battalion thinks' or 'the battalion feels'; and this is not an exaggeration.[2]

Within a battalion there are thirty-six ten-man self-directed work teams, each physically identical and each containing specialists within them and each of whose role is specific. There are also other identical teams whose supporting roles are different.

> Except for the weapons they carry and the sophistication of their equipment, similar teams to these have existed with the same basic role since the days of the Greek hoplites who fought for Leonidas and Alexander the Great. There were a variable number of these teams in a maniple, up to fifty in a cohort, and up to ten cohorts in each legion Julius Caesar used in the conquest of Gaul. This is a team that is designed to perform at its optimum under great stress and it lives, laughs, loves, cares and cries together.
>
> Each team has a clown and possibly a malingerer. Each has a smart talker and a whinger, some might have a drunk and a couple of ambitious hard workers. There may even be a couple of would-be bullies and a card sharp for good measure. But most of them are fairly straightforward, honest, and compassionate and they have a very remarkable hold on each other. Almost invariably they complain about the boss and they can always find a better way of doing things than he can.
>
> And so it continues to this day, called either a section or a squad depending upon what army you are in. Everyone knows their job, every person is just as important as the next, no one has any extra

privileges and they were, have been and are led by possibly the most underestimated leader in any organisation in history.

This knowledge helps to give us a further insight. In a successful organisation, lower level teams are the most fundamental. In each successful team everyone is responsible to everyone else in the team so that in a sense each person is *interdependent* which, as explained by Stephen Covey, is the next step on from *independence* and is indeed a higher form of independence.[3]

In a team no *person* is more important than another; individuals are interdependent.

It is easy to assume that one of the ways of socialising recruits was to put them in small groups where team spirit was fostered by competing with others and then getting together and competing in larger groups and so on. This thinking leads to the belief that it is the challenge and competition that fostered the team spirit. This is not so. Response to challenge is a natural outgrowth of team spirit, it doesn't make the team spirit. Nor is external competition necessary to challenge, although it can help.

Team spirit is not an outgrowth of challenge, response to challenge is an outcome of team spirit.

Team spirit is fostered by a common vision, a belief in a cause, implicit and total trust in your team-mates and a confidence in their behaviour and how they will react. Recently a colleague of ours, a marketing consultant of some experience, made an observation that business in general and marketing in particular was only beginning to realise that they needed to turn their triangle on its head and start their training and culture at the other end. Organisations that rely on true teamwork appeared to concentrate their efforts on the customer end of the scale, and seemingly had been doing that all along.

STARTING AT THE POINT OF IMPACT (POI)

The police force, and also the fire services as well as the armed services, start from the premise that the most important team is at the final *POI* and *all training and culture starts from that point and premise*. The most important function is at the POI, numbered 1. See Figure 6.1.

Business tends to, although not always, turn the triangle base over apex so that not only does the most important team become the managing board, but training and culture starts off with that premise. Whereas a firefighter and police tend to undertake several years of basic training and progress further away from the point of impact as they become more experienced, many business people these days have never even experienced any relevant POI. Therefore, in training and in practice there is a directional focus as in Figure 6.2.

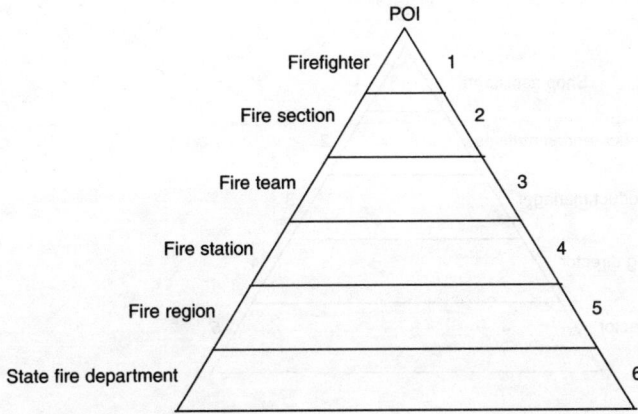

Fig. 6.1 *Point of impact—focus 1*

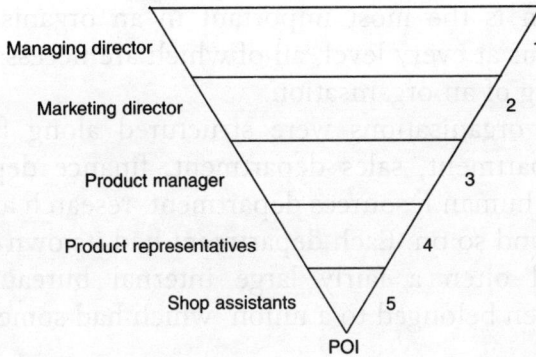

Fig. 6.2 *Point of impact—focus 2*

The tip of the triangle is at the bottom. This is the opposite to Figure 6.1. In the first figure, the focus runs from the POI back, whereas in the second, the focus runs the opposite way. Managers have now begun to turn the triangle around, as shown in Figure 6.3. You might ask what this has got to do with teamwork. Just this. The concept of the work team starts with the principle that the work done by the basic work team is the most important in an organisation. For centuries, the section was the eyes and ears of an army as well as its arms and legs. These days of sophisticated communications have lent armies other means of gathering information, but mostly it is still confirmed by the section. And ultimately the section still fights and wins the battle.

POI

Shop assistants   1

Product representatives   2

Product manager   3

Marketing director   4

Managing director   5

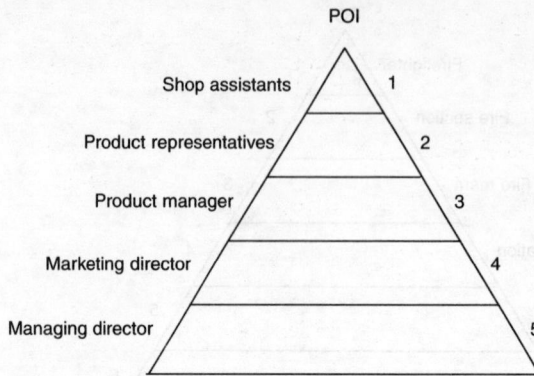

Fig. 6.3   *Point of impact—focus 3*

THE SELF-DIRECTED(?) WORK TEAM

The basic work team is the most important in an organisation. Of course, there are teams at every level, all of which are necessary to the successful functioning of an organisation.

For a long time organisations were structured along functional lines: marketing department, sales department, finance department, training department, human resources department, research and development department and so on. Each department had its own organisational structure and often a fairly large internal bureaucracy. In addition, workers often belonged to a union, which had some call on a worker's loyalty.

The inevitable happened in such organisations. Departments dealt with themselves, and people specialised over time to such a degree that someone could get to the top of the marketing ladder without any personnel experience or even interest in personnel or personnel matters. People had deep but not broad experience, and hence there was a lot of poor leadership seen. What was worse, it was considered normal for people not to have knowledge outside their field of expertise and so people at lower levels became used to not having enough information or knowledge to make other than the simplest decisions in the narrowest of fields.

Enter the *flat* organisation. While some considered that downsizing was created by market forces and that in turn created the flat organisation, it is our belief that it would have occurred anyway, because organisations had become *fat*. More importantly, barriers were being broken down as it became more evident that not only could greater

effectiveness, but more work satisfaction be guaranteed if people became multi-skilled at all levels. Demarcation disputes began to disappear and it became evident that decisions could be made at much lower levels if the functional groupings could be distributed.

So at lower levels, we began to see groups of people at the *coal-face* consisting of a marketer, a researcher, a salesperson, a personnel person and so on. Thus the inter-disciplinary team was born, and with it a recognition of the need to be trained in greater breadth for all levels.

The net effect of this is the disappearance of a number of levels of specialised middle management. However, unless the power or authority that used to accompany those levels is passed down, all that will happen is that senior managers will work longer and harder and become more stressed. And the team will also not survive unless it has authority to act in all disciplines at that appropriate level. The answer, of course, lies in PowerSharing.

The team that has been created is, in fact, a work team and the theory is that it can be self-directing. It may well be so. There are no doubt many instances of apparently leaderless teams succeeding. It is our contention that in any such work team someone has to take charge if for no other reason than for that of co-ordination. This co-ordinator can change according to the needs at the time. Remember the *contingency* theory discussed in the Introduction? This says that as the situation changes so then can the leader. There is little difference in this to the old theory that suggests that all leaders must know when to lead and when to follow. This is true for appointed leaders as well. So in self-directed work teams the most appropriate person becomes the leader for that occasion. Someone emerges for the situation.

> *Lead—follow—or get out of the way.*

However, a team must share something other than the work they are engaged in. You can't just train individuals in a team and bring them together and expect that they will function as a team, no matter how well trained they are. A group of individual champions can be beaten by a team of also-rans.

SHARED EXPERIENCE AND TEAM SPIRIT

There must be a thousand books and videos available today about building bigger and better teams—it's the flavour of the decade—and yet there seems to be only lip-service paid to the fact that a good team *shares* something of value. A group can be together for years and never become a team because they have never shared anything other than a mundane work task. They have never been called to go beyond what has come to be regarded as the minimum in outcome. Many people work hard and long but their outcome is either unspectacular or minimal. The same principle applies with a team—it must be challenged.

> A team must share more than a routine work task or objective.

Let's face it, most work, however hard we try to change it—at the process line or at any level for that matter—will often be repetitious and frankly boring, and if that's all a worker can share with his or her fellows then a team is going to be hard to build. But if an imaginative leader can give that team a 'raison d'être' then a team will blossom. The incentive may be more authority, it may be more autonomy, it may be encouraging teams to become more innovative, but at the source it means making a team self-contained and responsible for its POI with sufficient challenge that the team gets a special understanding and pride in its output.

Crucially, the only people who can normally change the parameters of a team's output are the members of the team itself. This means that within the bounds of agreed procedures and regulations, and a shared vision, a team sets its own agenda. To do this a team needs to receive special training so that members develop a deep trust and respect for each other. It also means that special steps must be taken to build a knowledge of, and confidence in, each other that will often go beyond the bounds of the work environment.

This may involve social get-togethers or it may mean special training sessions that involve some sharing. It may mean teaching people to loosen their hold on their prejudices and 'mental models'. It may be as mundane as starting a sporting competition. These activities all help build team spirit, but insofar as anyone feels left out, so will the team suffer.

> Every member of a team must share in the whole enterprise, whatever it may be.

Gullett is right when he talks about a 'state of grace'. The grace he talks about is the 'spirit' in team spirit and it's the same sort of sublime quality that makes the difference between an acquaintance and a friend. It's also the quality of an organisation or team that will not allow a change in culture no matter what the change in climate may be. Team spirit certainly implies an openness and trust on the part of the individuals in the team. That involves taking risks on an emotional level, and that means letting one's feelings be seen and felt. No doubt this is why combat strengthens the bonds of reliance and trust.

There is a wonderful description in Stephen Covey's book *The Seven Habits of Highly Effective People* of a sudden moment of revelation he had with his class. This arose as a result of one of his students making himself vulnerable by sharing some profound experience. This prompted others to do the same—*to synergise*—and Covey goes on to tell how they threw the rule book away and the class still reconnects every year and relives the great experiences they had. Does it sound familiar?[4]

Team spirit means just what it says. There is something other-dimensional about a good team, be it a family or a business. It is almost tangible and must come from the deep sense of sharing. There are wonderful examples from both history and folklore, such as the twelve Apostles at Pentecost or the Knights of the Round Table. Something happened in both cases that was profound and changed the way they worked together.

CREATING THE MYTH

There is something folklorical about a group of people who have shared an experience. Look at how on reunion days, the stories of the experience become more preposterous each year. What is happening is that the myth is growing, and mythology is an important ingredient of any culture, including organisational culture.

Many corporations are now sending their executives on camps and courses in order for them to share an experience, even if it is physically or emotionally gruelling. While the experience itself is valuable, one of the hidden values understood by the armed forces is the effect that recalling the experience has on organisational mythology. Many purveyors of such courses don't understand that factor themselves. Corporations often don't understand it either, so they send their executives on separate experiences and they end up bonding with people from other organisations. There is a difference between *knowing* what constitutes a team and *becoming* a team. Worse still, some aspiring leaders send their followers on such courses and don't go themselves, so they end up not being part of the growing myth and become alien to the culture.

THE CULTURE AND CHANGE

Culture is the sum of the values and principles that have been gathered together in an organisation over a period, sometimes years. It is a collection of traditions, history and customs—it is 'the way we do things around here'. These principles dictate the way the workforce will respond in given situations. It provides that 'state of grace'. Climate is simply the way things are at the moment. It represents the current collective feelings, expectations and working relationships of the workforce.

Peter: A friend of mine many years ago used to talk about this MD coming into a company. Apparently he was incompetent and a very poor leader. He said that this MD, as a result of his ineptitude, did his best to destroy the organisation but the old hands wouldn't let him! I always remembered it. It is a clear example that no matter what the climate in the organisation at the time, the culture can remain solid. There can even be high morale in a bad climate.

Organisational culture represents the values and principles of an organisation; it is built up over time as a result of shared experiences. Climate tends to be momentary.

A culture is built on shared experience and the climate is only something that exists at the time and will pass. A shared experience can be in a marriage, a family, a business or a football team. They are all teams, they all develop a culture, and loyalty to that culture depends on the intensity of the experience. What is more, that loyalty can't be obliterated except by a change in the culture. And changing a culture is very difficult.

Not all cultures are positive. If an organisation has a culture of confrontation, that culture cannot be changed simply by a new boss coming in and saying, 'We are now going to be non-confrontational'. The climate may change but underneath the culture doesn't change unless the new boss is a real leader and a culture of trust is planted and nurtured. That in itself could take a long time and requires a transformation in the workplace.

How can a culture be changed once it is entrenched in an organisation? Only with a change in attitude. Earlier in the book we spoke of leaders with vision recognising when change or transformation was necessary. A good leader, having recognised the need, sets about changing followers' attitudes in a non-threatening way. And this can be best achieved through PowerSharing and allowing workers to determine what changes are necessary to create the new paradigm. This may involve a sort of death of the 'old' and a phased transformation, and that sometimes involves a lengthy process involving disorganisation, recovery and recommitment.

In other words, you can affect an organisational climate just by directing a change in behaviour, but that will not be permanent or

meaningful unless you change the culture by bringing about an alteration in attitude which will rearrange behaviour permanently. That only
happens with a change in perception or a paradigm shift. Once again,
such a process is described well by Ricardo Semler.[5] Some of the greatest opposition to liberalisation of his workforce came from the workers
themselves. We have all witnessed this on a grander scale in Eastern
Europe with the return of the communists in Poland and Hungary;
admittedly it is a far more politically liberal communism, but it is
nonetheless a reaction born out of a people not being properly prepared for a cultural change, and more importantly it is a reaction to the
pain and discomfort of change.

> Cultural change requires a change of attitude; a change of
> attitude involves a change in perception. This cannot be
> momentary.

This also explains why some organisations are having such trouble
adapting themselves today to such things as the growing number of
women in the workplace and other sensitive issues. It also explains the
height of the glass ceiling in some organisations and why women are
voting with their feet.

People are often expected to behave overnight in a manner that is
contrary to their culture. You can prepare all the 'force field analyses'
you like and convince every living chairperson and MD. You may
change the climate but not the culture, *until the paradigm is changed,*
and the problem is that the paradigm in some organisations is
cemented by tradition, history, union and 'tribal' loyalties. For
instance, a unionist worker and a white-collar employer can both look
at the same reality and come to a totally different conclusion—one sees
justification for going on strike, the other sees irresponsible behaviour
leading to loss of productivity. Each group will have its faithful followers who often nearly come to blows over the way they perceive the
same issue. They are living in different paradigms.

Positive discrimination such as 'affirmative action' is a case in point.
Often it only changes the climate. The underlying attitudes don't
change, hence there is often a conflict between climate and culture, and
ergo morale can be seriously affected until the attitudes have changed.

Sometimes external assistance may be needed but turning to 'the law' should be a last resort.

LOYALTY

Often workers will develop a loyalty to a particular culture or even a sub-culture within an organisation despite the best efforts of the leadership of the organisation. There are many startling examples; for instance, where workers in an organisation with a good climate will follow their less satisfied workmates on a particular route for reasons of solidarity, even though they themselves are not unhappy. This is why it is so important to enlist the support of workers and followers at all levels, and why excluding workplace leaders such as shop stewards from planning change is so counter-productive.

> *In the drive to cut expenditure in recent years there has been consistent 'downsizing' at many levels in both public and private sectors. The downsizing has been of personnel, not of work levels or expectations of outcomes.*
>
> *Indeed, the advent of technology has increased workloads because information is so freely available and therefore more and more information is constantly sought.*
>
> *With the drive to trim costs it is often lower and mid-level staff who are let go. Now, fewer people are being asked to do more work—a sixty-hour week is not unusual. But is there a better way? Enlightened organisations first modify their procedures in order to reduce the need for employees; and then staff accordingly to meet the new requirement. The solution seems simple but is something bureaucracies (who seem loathe to reduce at the top) find difficult. In circumstances where the changes are made with no effort to change work practices or transform the culture, only resentment can follow.*
>
> *After some years, alienation becomes the culture of such organisations. And no amount of work will put the trust back in a hurry. So a climate of confrontation has in many cases been replaced, unfortunately, by a climate of distrust.*
>
> *Where once there was an expectation, indeed a culture of loyalty even in organisations with a degree of confrontation, the last few years have seen an opting out of loyalty at both ends of the spectrum. It will take many good leaders to replace that culture of loyalty because culture, like teamwork, cannot be mandated.*

The interesting point is that the teams and loyalties within an organisation may be contrary to the prevailing culture but of course their vision, values and goals may not coincide with those of the organisation. The result is dysfunctional organisations with workers' efforts and loyalties being misdirected. Sometimes there is even a situation where pockets or departments with a positive culture occur within bigger organisations with a negative culture. This is the height of dysfunctionality.

By the same token—and we'll cover this in more detail in the next chapter—even if a culture is positive, it may be inappropriate for the time, particularly if an organisation is heading for financial disaster. In this case a good leader may need to rapidly change the culture, but will do so by involving the whole workforce in determining the new appropriate culture, in other words through PowerSharing. This way the workforce loyalty can be maintained in the most difficult of circumstances.

THE TEAM AS AN ORGANISATION

Teamwork at any level is based on harmony and unity of purpose. Harmony is based on a positive and appropriate culture. Harmony does not necessarily mean that everyone agrees or has the same idea; after all, a piano and a violin sound entirely different and to play them requires different skills. Each has its strength in different types of music, but with the right music and in the right hands they harmonise beautifully.

Earlier on we learned that a team wasn't a committee and that its members, by definition, gave up something of themselves for the sake of the task in hand. A dictionary definition suggests that a team is simply a number of persons associated in some joint action, but that falls far short of today's common usage. A team has also been described as a group of people of any size who share a common goal and who are jointly responsible for the achievement of that goal. A business can be a team. It can also consist of a number of smaller teams. And as we have seen, sharing adds value to that team. Just being engaged in a common purpose is not enough in itself. Unless there is a sense of giving, and even sacrificing, for the common good then the team could cave in under pressure. So it presupposes that a good team *will share the same values* in relation to the work they are doing, and as individuals will be prepared to give at more than a surface level.

> True sharing invariably means giving as well as receiving; giving implies sacrifice.

In a good team everyone has a role but normally no one role is more important than any other. For instance, who is the most important player in a football team? In some codes captains are chosen on whether the team is attacking or defending and the captaincy is often a moveable feast among the more senior players. In most teams there are specialists, although even in cricket these days all-rounders are better for certain types of cricket.

The crucial issue in team work is to have the right mix of skills to ensure full all-round input. This doesn't just mean different professional skills, it also means different personalities. Some people are creative, others are practical; some are objective, some are idealistic; some are drivers, others are shrinking violets. A good mix of different skills, personalities and views is essential to creative teamwork.

The team may have a shared vision of being the most successful club of all time. It has a shared mission to win this year's premiership. Each week there is a shared objective and a plan to achieve it and every player knows his or her part in that plan. But he (or she) also knows that he or she is just one of eighteen or thirteen or eleven. He or she doesn't only play for him or herself, he or she tries to ensure that everyone else is helped to play their best as well: because he or she knows that even if he or she is best on the ground, if the team loses no one is exempt from responsibility, and if they win—everyone is responsible. How often does a *bunch* of champions go down to a *team* with a better spirit and cohesion?

> A team shares a vision, mission, objectives and plan.

A well-led team is committed to its vision and mission and therefore has a shared sense of destiny or purpose. Each member is prepared to forgo a certain amount of individuality and will not let the team down. In other words, each becomes accountable to the rest of the team—the other stakeholders. And in this sense each team member shares the same values as another.

We suggested that small self-directed teams may function without a specific leader although they still need a spokesperson or co-ordinator. As the team becomes larger, so there develops a need for an on-the-spot leader. For instance, a work group supervisor (maybe even chosen by the workers), is perfectly adequate as a team leader where there may be eight to twelve workers. He or she would still identify with the workforce and be identified by them, but at the same time has a defined supervisory role, and is trained by management in the skills of team building and leading.

In any workforce junior leaders are generally chosen by management (often by the HR department) because they are malleable or loyal or have specific work skills. It would be better to choose people who are leaders in the first instance, even if they may initially be somewhat troublesome. Follower selection of leaders is currently becoming fashionable again after two thousand years. After all, the Romans did it.

TRAINING

It is a leader's job to ensure that the teams that he or she is responsible for are properly trained, kept informed, understand the expectations of them, understand how responsibility will be allocated and who the co-ordinator or facilitator is to be. Above all the team must understand that as a team they have authority and responsibility for every outcome under their control. If they do not have authority, training, skills, and resources they cannot be responsible. The team must be empowered, because the success of the organisation depends on the success of that team. PowerSharing provides that empowerment.

Whatever the task may be, and however well matched a team is, there will be no positive outcome unless the team is prepared by training; training in team skills and needs, and training in problem-solving skills. The team also needs the right *mix* of skills among its members, implying training in individual skills. How often has a whole project failed because of the failure of one element? 'For want of a nail'! Does this mean the individual is responsible? No! The individual is responsible for one POI, as we said in Chapter 1. If the project fails, the team and ultimately the leader, is responsible. The team therefore needs the authority and resources to train and prepare together.

> The team needs training, skills, authority and resources.

Having seen what the operational requirements of a good team will be, it will be useful to apply the earlier characteristics of organisational harmony to the team itself, regardless of size. We spoke of loyalty, culture, transformation and synergy among other things, all in relation to organisations in general. Let's have a look at some of the characteristics.

CHARACTERISTICS OF TEAMS

Loyalty. Loyalty is a fairly easy issue to grasp. The basis of loyalty is trust. Loyalty is the outward demonstration of that trust expressed by the degree of co-operation. If I give my loyalty, I am unconditionally trusting you to act in a particular way and I agree to co-operate with you whether or not I have any influence over the outcome. Real loyalty is a covenant as opposed to a contract. A contract says: 'If you do this then I will do that'. A covenant says: 'I will do this whatever you may do'. A team must have internal, lateral and vertical loyalty, both up and down.

In leadership, loyalty downwards is paramount. If every leader gave unconditional loyalty downwards they wouldn't need to worry about looking over their shoulders, because their backs would be covered from above. In a team internal loyalty is also of the utmost importance, for obvious reasons. One of the reasons for the success of teams in most heroic endeavours is their fierce loyalty to each other.

Loyalty is covenantal, not contractual.

Fierce loyalty tends to be tribal—an 'us or them' mentality. It can be destructive if not harnessed properly. However, it is the sort of loyalty that should be encouraged in business. This doesn't mean the 'spilling of blood' type loyalty, but no leader should ever put a member of a team in a position that will compromise the person's internal team loyalty. In other words, they should never be encouraged to 'dob in' their colleagues.

One organisation of recent times had an unwritten operating policy that encouraged middle managers to report secretly to the board of directors on the performance of their seniors or their peers. While it may have given the board some interesting insights, it did nothing for teamwork, trust, cohesion, loyalty, productivity or pride.

Pride. Pride in a group is often referred to as ésprit de corps. Pride essentially comes from achievement. If a group gets an accolade, as it should when it achieves a goal, it can take pride in itself. The group is becoming a team and should be encouraged to celebrate its achievements in an appropriate way. Eventually the pride will lead to greater efforts and higher achievements such that even newly-joined members of the team will feel that pride and want to conform with the team. Achievements can be anything from solving a major distribution problem to reducing the accident rate in a particular part of the workplace. Pride comes from and leads to better performance. It therefore enhances continuous improvement.

An organisation that only awards individuals will have great difficulty instilling group pride and therefore group performance.

Performance. To perform competently, a team needs to be composed of competent people; not just competent in working as a team but also competent individually. Even the best teams have good players and better players. However, no team can afford to have any *bad* players. It's up to a leader to ensure that any member of the team has the skills he or she needs to competently carry his or her share of the task and so ensure team cohesion.

Cohesion. Earlier we mentioned synergy, which is probably a better term than cohesion. It represents the concept that the total output is greater than the sum of the parts. It is like a multiplier effect, or gearing up.

Apocryphal or not, there are stories of mothers and fathers performing prodigious feats of strength to save their children in emergencies. But synergy is more than just two plus two is greater than four. Synergy is a *feeling* of strength and cohesion in a group. It's the strength that you draw from another as a result of a bonding, so you have the other person's strength as well as your own—and, conversely, he or she has both your strength and their own. People need to be quite open and vulnerable for that to take place; that's why it is often evident among people who have seen each other at their most vulnerable. Cohesion is probably all that can be expected in the average team in the beginning and a good leader acts as a catalyst in this regard.

There are ways of developing this cohesion—and, eventually, synergy—by encouraging team activities that are not specifically related to work. As mentioned earlier, some organisations run lunchtime and after work sporting events. But other organisations take their teams out of the production line or off the shopfloor or out of the office for two or three hours once a week to conduct exercises in brainstorming, or planning processes, without having any specific work-related content. In some cases they just do team-building or sharing exercises—and it's working. It certainly motivates them.

Motivation. Motivation, as someone once said, is: 'Getting people to want to do what they don't want to do'. That's probably putting it as succinctly as one can. Motivation is the stimulation of someone by another person, or by some external influence such as a reward, towards the achievement of a goal. Motivation tends to be a continuing process, therefore implying a determination to continue until the task is complete. Maslow's hierarchy is a scale of motivation. It stands to reason that if a leader wants to motivate someone to a task involving belonging and social acceptance, then he or she had better make sure that he or she contributes to their job security, otherwise that person will not be motivated. This is definitely a lesson for these days of work-force reductions.

> Motivation—getting people to consistently want to do what they don't want to do.

In the team situation, motivation can have strange effects that quite candidly defy the conventional logic and wisdom of Maslow's hierarchy. People can and have been motivated to perform great deeds even though they're starving, because other factors come into the equation. That's where Maslow's hierarchy has to be treated with reservations.

Lord Wavell of World War II Western Desert fame speaks of the mystery of motivation:

> *To learn that Napoleon in 1796 with 20 000 men beat combined forces of 30 000 by something called 'Economy of Force' or 'operating on interior lines' is a mere waste of time. If you can understand how a young, unknown man inspired a half-starved, ragged, rather Bolshie crowd; how he filled their bellies; how he out-marched, out-witted, outbluffed and defeated men who had studied war all their*

lives and waged it according to the textbooks of the time, you will have learned something worth knowing. But you won't get it from crammers' books.[6]

The implication and the truth is that he *motivated* them before he filled their bellies.

You often hear the expression that at work people are only motivated by three things: their jobs, their jobs and their jobs! Yet actual studies carried out in the 1970s indicate that what people are looking for at work (in other words their *motivations*) are: the respect of peers and superiors, interesting work, recognition for effort, skill development, being listened to, autonomy, an efficient work environment, complexity of job (i.e. not too easy or monotonous), and up-to-date information. Down the bottom of the list are job security, good benefits and good pay!

No doubt the above was predicated on job security in the first place. Recent unsearched, anecdotal evidence suggests a lot of ill-will and backstabbing going on as people fight to hold their jobs. It could suggest that the chronic unemployment of recent years has undermined confidence to the extent that job retention is now assuming major importance. Certainly there seem to be serious morale problems in some areas.

Morale. Morale is the great unexplained and sometimes unexplainable factor. If a person is unmotivated it's possibly because morale is bad and if morale is bad it's because the team needs motivation. That's how closely connected the two concepts are. Morale is a state of mind or spirit that is related to belief in the task (motivation), confidence in the outcome (and in the leader), willingness to endure hardship or to sacrifice something, and the courage to face the consequences of all that with something approaching enthusiasm. To that must be added the effect of the organisational culture. Morale can nevertheless be high even when the climate is poor.

Morale is very dependent on success and in a team situation is related to pride in achievement. Unfortunately, because morale cannot be quantified, managers with a singular bottom line focus tend to ignore it and then wonder why results don't meet expectations. Napoleon, a great leader, saw morale as 'three is to one'. Maybe bottom-liners should start factoring this in.

In creating a winning team always build from the bottom up so that the team gets wins under its belt early in the piece. Winning then becomes a habit, the more complex tasks are treated as a challenge, and with every success failure is less likely to follow. When failures occur minimise your criticism but don't ignore the reality. Morale, *or lack thereof*, is infectious and like the 'flu can pass from one department or team to another. So it is important at all times to monitor contact between teams, but whatever you do don't try to diminish it. Co-operation between teams is like the mortar that holds the bricks together.

Morale is infectious and can pass rapidly from department to department.

Co-operation. This is not the same as the co-operation we spoke of earlier when discussing *synergy*. Even competing companies co-operate to achieve goals. Co-operation is more for the convenience of all concerned and may be regarded as contractual. Teams need to be in a position to seek help, to offer help, to drop what they are doing to achieve a common goal with a neighbouring team and (going back to Chapter 2) to ensure that any team that is on the receiving end of their outcomes continues to get good, and increasingly better, service. Co-operation is like loyalty, both lateral and vertical, and it presupposes first-class communication between teams and departments.

Good teams are characterised by loyalty, pride, performance, cohesion, motivation, morale and co-operation.

It now is becoming evident that teamwork is not something that can be decreed to begin on a certain day. It is also evident that much of the, no doubt valuable, rhetoric that we hear about work-based teams sometimes pays little regard to the realities of human relationships. On the other hand, concentrating on only the psychological needs and characteristics of team members often leads to unreal expectations on an organisation, team or company in the hope that teams can solve what may be intractable problems of another kind. Teams don't provide all the answers to leadership.

We saw in the last chapter how a leader addressed the needs of individuals; this chapter has dealt with the needs of the team. We have not yet completed the loop. We need to examine what the team needs from each individual. What sort of special attributes do they need?

CHARACTERISTICS OF TEAM MEMBERS

There is an element of the heroic in being a real team member. In outline the following characteristics would seem to be at least desirable. Insofar as they are not present in separate individuals then the team will suffer. It is then not surprising that really good teams are hard to find.

Openness. This means an openness to the ideas of others and more especially an openness in giving. A team member needs to be prepared to be vulnerable enough to put his or her ideas and emotions on the line. This requires some doing and not a little courage. It means having the courage of one's convictions and the courage to admit fallibility.

Acceptance of others. This means accepting another as a person—black, yellow, white, male, female. Not just acceptance of another person, but a toleration of their culture and value systems. It means changing that paradigm again and learning to see something through another's eyes; it means changing your perception of another and his or her ideas.

Selflessness. This means simply what it says. Putting others and their ideas before yourself and your own; treating others as you would want to be treated.

Communication. We'll be talking about this characteristic in the leader in greater detail later. Communication means not only transmitting but receiving—something which many people forget. (Or else they can't find their *receive* button.) Team members need to be able to convey their own message clearly and assertively. Assertiveness is part of the communication process. But so is listening—active listening. Some 70 per cent of communication is listening.

Give and take. This is really the concept of seeking win/win solutions. It does not mean 'you give and I take'.

Surrender to team ethos. This, put crudely, is: 'Play the game or get off the team'. It doesn't mean surrendering personality, initiative, or independence, but moving to the next step—interdependence. It may mean accepting the majority view or the views of others. A tree doesn't grow as well in another's shadow, but a plantation of trees can protect each other from destruction in a storm. There is an old Japanese saying: 'The outstanding nail is the first to be hammered'. We are not saying that individuals should be hammered, but the floorboard is more secure when all the nails are hammered home. This is interdependence.

Willingness to solve problems. This point will also be raised later. It means that differences of opinion or values should be solved within the team and not taken to a higher authority for arbitration or adjudication. When that happens the higher authority normally has to take one side or another and the best that can be hoped for is win/lose. Normally what happens in those circumstances is lose/lose.

John: *Recently I had two people working for me who had great difficulty getting on with each other and who came to me independently with their woes. After I spoke to each of them separately about each other's strengths, and focused them on the tasks rather than the problem, they managed to reconcile their differences and become an effective team. Although I acted as a catalyst I refused to arbitrate or take sides. It quickly became a win/win/win situation. This would not have been possible without mutual respect between all of us.*

Respect. We should understand that without respect all of the above is meaningless. Respect, like loyalty, must be earned; it cannot be demanded.

Team members need: openness, acceptance of others, selflessness, communication, give and take, surrender to team ethos, willingness to solve problems, mutual respect.

STYLES AND TYPES

Recent years have seen the emergence of quite a lot of work in relation to personality, type preference and temperament, and the very ability of people with different styles and values not only to accept each other but to make the best of the strengths of other people's often very different styles and preferences. Relating this to the anecdote of the two people who couldn't get on, we can learn a lot from these studies and use that knowledge to help us get the best mix out of a team of differing personalities. We can help people to click rather than clash.

There are a number of issues involved. First, when we say that teamwork cannot be mandated, it nevertheless sometimes must be demanded and it's still a leader's responsibility to make it happen. A leader can't go around indiscriminately firing people because they don't get on, so some facilitation may be necessary. This means that a leader needs to understand followers and they must understand each other.

A whole industry has grown up around personality type and temperament testing which enables HR gurus to predict fairly accurately the skills, values and personality attitudes of leaders and workers. Such methods as the Myers Briggs Type Indicator (MBTI)™ and others similar to it, can be of great assistance in understanding how teams can interact and what you can expect from them, especially in the creative rather than routine and reactive environment. For instance, a team gathered to solve a complex design or engineering problem or even a complex financial or marketing problem may well benefit from input relating to individual's types and skills, whereas a team in a routine assembly line job may need less input of this kind.

We can look at types and temperaments in a bit more detail later. One of the advantages of the systems that have become available in recent times is that they are no longer the sole province of psychologists. 'Lay' people can use the systems with ease, although there is a tendency for them to now become the province of the HR specialist or the corporate trainer. Even these more recent personality indicators can only be a tool and should not be considered either infallible or a panacea. A person's personality type is only one of many things that influence their behaviour. And as we said above, no amount of knowledge about another's 'type' will have any effect if there is no mutual respect and acceptance between parties.

In all this discussion we must never lose sight of the leader's role in creating the teams. Though we say that the leader is a part of the team and needs all the understanding of the issues as well as all the characteristics of team members, he or she needs, in addition, other skills and characteristics. That, of course, is the essence of this book.

A leader of a team, or teams, needs to impart and share the vision and mission; accept but share responsibility; understand and practise

PowerSharing; encourage, coach and provide feedback. In common with the team, the leader needs to be open, share decision making and facilitate conflict resolution. Above all, a leader needs to trust the team. All these issues are part of PowerSharing, and those not covered already are subjects of subsequent chapters.

Clearly, leadership today appears to be a much more collaborative process than in the past, and accordingly is going to be considerably more difficult. Nevertheless, the principles—like people—haven't really changed. A good leader has always been part of the team, not the director of the team from afar, and the misunderstanding of that fact in itself may be one of the danger signals we can see at this time. In the heroic past leaders suffered as much, if not more so, than the led, and in any event shared the hardships to some degree. The privileges some senior people are giving themselves carry warnings. They imply that status warrants extreme reward.

Teams and teamwork don't just happen; they have to be worked at. Team members need to be carefully chosen; they need to be nurtured and matched. They need to be given meaningful outcomes; they need to be trained and practised. And finally they need to be given time to develop and improve. Only then will teamwork bear fruit.

We trained hard—but it seemed that every time we were beginning to form into teams we would be reorganised. I was to learn later in life that we tend to meet any new situation by reorganising; and a wonderful method it can be for creating the illusion of progress while producing confusion, inefficiency and demoralisation.

Petronius Arbiter 210 BC

Key concepts

- Teamwork encourages synergy. Synergy means one plus one is greater than two.
- Synergy comes from sharing and a willingness to be vulnerable in that sharing.
- A good team shares experiences at more than superficial levels.
- A team must be built and trained around the proper understanding of the ultimate point of impact.
- When people have a proper understanding of their own importance in the team they are prepared to be accountable to others in the team.
- Organisational culture is really the sum of team spirit and a result of history and tradition.
- Culture can only be changed by a change in attitude and perception.
- Climate is only a temporary marker of organisational health, and should not be confused with culture.
- A good leader can transform a team's culture.
- A team leader is first and foremost a team player.
- A team shares a vision, a mission, and objectives.
- A team needs loyalty, pride, cohesion, motivation, high morale, co-operation and trust.
- Team members should be open, accepting of others, unselfish, communicative, able to give and take, prepared to surrender to team ethos, willing to solve problems, and have a win/win focus.
- Team members need to understand each other's skills, personality types and values.
- A team leader is a coach, should practise PowerSharing and, above all, trust the team.

CHAPTER 7
Seventh Precept

Understand and influence the environment

The underlying message here is keeping in touch. However, more than keeping in touch, the leader must know what is going on at any time and know when to influence (not interfere) if objectives are not being met or if processes seem to be getting off track. Influence is the power to produce effects without the use of physical force or authority, whereas interference is simply meddling or hindering. Any influencing needs to be exercised with great care and discretion to ensure that principles aren't broken and confidence lost.

CONTROL

One of the functions of the leader that we covered in the Introduction was *to control*. In this age of self-expression, the word 'control' seems to have taken on a somewhat pejorative meaning. This is unfortunate, because we should be looking for a workforce that can exercise self-control under the guidance of an enlightened leader. It has been suggested that we should perhaps use the term 'guide' rather than 'control', but, as we shall see, guidance sometimes means taking control anyway. Even in an age of the 'learning organisation' and the self-directed team, some form of control is necessary.

We often refer to a function or object, say a car, as being out of control. This means that the person in charge can no longer influence the direction the function or object is taking. To take control of a car a driver needs to do more than steer; he or she needs to control engine revs, transmission performance, braking power and so on. In order to guide an organisation adequately you need to be in possession of all the relevant factors or issues. It means keeping your finger on the pulse. It means being in possession of, or having immediate access to, information to enable you to make an urgent, informed decision, confident that you have considered all the factors.

Above all, the essence of being aware and in touch lies in communication.

A good leader not only keeps in touch with the workforce or internal environment but also with the external environment. That means with competitors, colleagues, trends, the market, the economy and so on. All of this is necessary to enable a leader to make the appropriate decisions affecting his or her workforce. Both *benchmarking* and seeking *best practice* are examples of keeping in touch with the external environment.

The external environment more often affects leaders in very senior executive positions, and, in the case of smaller businesses, what may be regarded as senior middle management. However, we don't intend to discuss this issue in this book because the external environment is the subject of many books. It is clearly a fundamental leadership issue and it is very much connected to a leader's vision, which we have already dealt with.

ORGANISATIONAL CONTROL

Sometimes in a good organisation a team will deliberately keep irrelevant information from a leader out of respect and in order not to confuse a leader's judgment or waste time. Often you will hear 'Let's not worry the boss with that'.

As we said earlier, it is often better for team members to solve their own differences before referring to the leader. This is because once a leader is called upon to arbitrate, the best that the individuals can normally expect is a *win/lose* but more likely a *lose/lose* situation. A *win/win* situation comes from individuals responding to each other and reaching a mutually agreeable task- or goal-focused consensus. In such a case the organisation is tending towards internal self-control.

The idea of guidance and control can be likened to horse-riding. Anyone who has ridden knows that horses have either soft mouths or hard mouths. The ideal is a soft mouth, where just the slightest pressure induces the horse to respond: either to turn, or stop, or slow down, or back up. Riding a horse with a soft mouth is a sheer pleasure and it takes a minimum of strength. You can ride for hours. Often the reins can be largely unnecessary because you can use leg or flank aids even in difficult manoeuvres like jumping.

On the other hand, riding a horse with a hard mouth can be a trial. These horses can be very headstrong and frequently you have to fight them every inch of the way. It can be fun, but after a few hours it is exhausting. Every trailrider knows what it's like to feel elbows out of sockets and fingers red raw.

Good instructors won't put beginners on a really soft-mouthed horse because they don't want it spoiled. A soft-mouthed horse will become hard-mouthed if it is consistently pulled, or held too tight, or over-controlled. Nor will they put beginners on to a hard-mouthed horse because that would obviously be a recipe for disaster. They opt for something in between. A good rider can soften a horse's mouth if it has been spoiled, but some horses are so tough that even a good rider can't soften them up. They have been spoiled too badly and they end up in the knacker's yard. Of course, experienced riders can still ride them but why would they bother?

Organisations are the same as horses. They are soft-mouthed or hard-mouthed by culture. A good leader produces a soft-mouthed organisation that is easy to lead with the minimum of control. If it gets into the hands of a poor or inexperienced leader who pulls, jerks and over-controls, the organisation will eventually develop a hard mouth and will only respond to excessive control. A good leader can still control it, but why would he or she bother? It is better to consign the beast to the knacker's yard.

A 'soft-mouthed' organisation needs guidance but a minimum of control.

Leaders need to learn that control means keeping in touch with an organisation—exerting only gentle pressure on the reins and flanks. No pressure or tension means no guidance or control. Guidance and control means that an organisation is constantly aware of its challenges. This is the leader's responsibility.

> Over-control of a self-regulating organisation is self-defeating.

When a leader first joins an organisation or a team what is it he or she must do? Take control?

SITUATIONAL CONTROL

We spoke of *situational control* in the Introduction. You will recall that there were three factors that determined the level of situational control a leader has:

- the structure of the task;
- the relationship of the leader to the team (and between team members); and
- the amount of position or sanctioning power a leader has.

    It is time now to examine the concept of situational control in more detail.

Task structure. Some tasks are inherently structured, such as assembly line, distribution and so on. Unstructured tasks would be exemplified by face-to-face selling, emergency operations like fire fighting or any other work where there is no set process to reach an outcome. The more structured the task, the more easily it can be monitored and controlled.

Leader/team relationship. This can be seen as the most important element of *situational control*. It has been dealt with in some detail in Chapter 6. It is important to stress that the relationship at issue is not just leader to team, but team member to team member.

Position power. To understand the place of position (or sanctioning) power we need to understand a little more of what constitutes power and the types of power that are found in any organisation.

POWER

Power, in its fundamental sense, is the ability to control other people or events. It is not a friendly word and used by itself is not helpful in a leadership environment. However, power is an essential ingredient of leadership that needs to be qualified. Leadership power comes in two varieties: position power and personal power, both of which can be further sub-classified. The former is *given* or allocated, the latter is *earned*. It has been suggested by some that managers use position power and leaders, personal power.

Position power. This means that the power is the leader's by virtue of appointment. It can be limited by virtue of contract period or other constraints imposed by the appointing authority. It can be power by mandate—where a person is elected; or by appointment—where a person is selected. In some cases it is absolute, or lifelong as in the case of the Pope. Or it can be power by right of constitution as in, for example, a constitutional monarchy. In all of these cases the power goes with the job. It is often referred to as *legitimate* power.

> Position power comes with the appointment.

Position power often carries with it the power to reward or punish; this is often referred to as *reward power* and *coercive power* respectively. These powers are generally relational, meaning their strength is largely in the eyes of the beholder. If someone is subject to someone else, the subject will see the position of power as being legitimate and influential as well as being able to reward or punish; in other words, being coercive.

To maintain credibility when you are only in possession of position power, you as leader may have legitimate power but there may be times when you have to demonstrate or in some way convince a follower that you will use the coercive or reward power that goes with it.

It is similar to the situation where a country with a nuclear bomb tells the world that it has no intention of using it. The bomb then ceases to be a deterrent. Earlier in the book we referred to it as sanctioning power, because there is an element of coercion in it even if, as in the case of the monarchy, convention suggests that the power may never be used.

Personal power. This is a much more effective power in the hands of a good leader. It diminishes the need to exert any sort of position power and it is the stuff of which mutual respect is made. Personal power can come from the leader having superior knowledge or skills in a particular area. For instance, in a situation that required someone with a knowledge of engines to take charge, a mechanic would have a certain amount of *skill power*; sometimes called *expert power*.

> Personal power comes from superior skills or knowledge.

During the 1960s there was produced a whimsical film called 'The Flight of the Phoenix'. It had been a successful novel. In it, an aeroplane builder who was an absolute misanthrope emerged with a lot of power over his colleagues because of his skills. He didn't end up as leader but he had the power of life and death over everyone else in the film and accordingly he was deferred to while he had that power. Clearly, in different circumstances each one of the others would gladly have murdered him.

Personal power can also come from a follower's *perception* of a leader's access to information, sometimes called *referent power*. Referent power can also come from simply being liked and respected for your values or your connections.

Power can also come from being feared for the call the leader has on other resources; an example of which is the fear exerted by people running protection rackets and similar operations. This is a form of *coercive* power that is not legitimate. Bullies have it in abundance.

All other things being equal, a leader who is also popular is better than a leader who is unpopular. Once again our definition is relevant: *respect and willing co-operation*. It is the characteristics of personal power that—if held together in sufficient measure—can often lead to a leader being regarded as charismatic.

ASSERTING CONTROL THROUGH POWER

A newly-arrived leader in an organisation will have position power to sustain him or her as he or she settles in. A good leader will then build up a bank of personal power, either by becoming an expert or, as is more likely in such a specialised world, developing a reputation for having the answers, that is, access to information and personal appeal.

What is in fact happening is that situational control is being enhanced by the leader improving the leader–follower relationship.

> A leader should try to convert position power into personal power over time.

The correct use of authority or power is essential. There is bound to be an element of power in any guiding or controlling that a leader does in an organisation. The outcome depends on the legitimacy of the power and how it is exercised. A leader can abuse position power when newly joining an organisation. If a leader continues to use position power inappropriately in a soft-mouthed organisation then eventually the organisation will become hard-mouthed.

A new leader in an organisation where situational control is loose, has to work overtime to establish control by either asserting position power, by structuring the tasks more, or—most important—by improving the team relationship. Accordingly, at lower levels where a leader's position power is curtailed per se, and tasks are fairly structured anyway, then team relationships are paramount if there is to be any control at all.

Some organisations that are successful with unstructured tasks and with little position power being exercised, may appear to be somewhat uncontrolled but it is a safe bet that the organisation has great self-control by virtue of a very high team relationship factor. Once more, an example is that of Semco in Brazil mentioned in Chapter 2. So we should be clear that control is still necessary, but it is best when it is internal self-control, and that's what makes a soft-mouthed organisation.

Control is good and essential, but it should come from the team relationship rather than by imposition. A leader must take control, not in the classical or pejorative sense, but he or she must establish clearly that he or she is the leader. However, to do so insensitively can be very counter-productive. To go in 'boots and all' may destroy people's confidence in themselves, in the previous regime, and therefore in the organisation itself.

The first thing to do is to observe and get a feel for the culture. If there are things that are glaringly wrong, such as safety or financial issues, and maybe some quality issues, then they must be put right immediately. This may mean issuing interim directives. Staff should be told that they are interim and given reasons why. In an organisation where morale has been poor, sometimes the reasons are fairly self-evident. In other instances some things need to be obviously corrected but to do so immediately may not be prudent. In these instances a smart leader will take note and allocate a priority to change. There used to be a piece of very sage advice given to aspiring leaders: 'Take note of everything that is wrong, because after a while it will start to look all right'. Notwithstanding this, 'newbroomism' (to coin a phrase) for the sake of it, will eventually cause resentment, particularly in an organisation with a positive culture.

Newbroomism for its own sake can be counter-productive.

Peter: I remember that an organisation I was in had a pig as a mascot. Not a big aggressive angry wild boar, but a little roley poley pink pig. A new boss arrived after I had left and took some drastic action to sharpen up the organisation because the climate had become slack. I had been in a fairly senior management position but I was amused to hear that the new boss had also vowed that the pig would go. It was frivolous and not a suitable mascot, culture notwithstanding!

The more he determined to get rid of the pig, the more often little painted porkies appeared around the area. This apparently went on for months. The new boss was no fool and knew when he was beaten—the pig idea stayed and I believe is still there, getting on for thirty years later.

Personal power is the power a good leader will seek to develop as quickly as possible by improving the leader–team relationship. It is important to do so quickly and then to maintain it. This relationship is very tenuous and delicate and it can be damaged, often irrevocably, by one or two silly or thoughtless actions.

John: In another organisation I know of, the incoming CEO fired a whole level of senior middle management and support staff within a week of the retirement of the previous CEO. Nobody knew quite why, because most were replaced within a few weeks. I am told they were called forward one at a time in what was described as a 'hairy-chested' solution. One member of staff said it was like the 'Reign of Terror' with people being called forward from the tumbrels one by one. The organisation is apparently still full of mistrust and resentment.

The anecdotes above represent a good way and a poor way! The best way, of course, is for a leader not to have to assert any position power at all. The former example illustrates wisdom and the latter the naked exercise of position power. In the latter, the leader(?) clearly asserted his position power and gained control but it is almost certain that as soon as the foot comes off the position power pedal, the organisation will tend to get out of control, because the other two factors have not been addressed. There are all too many examples of the latter situation. Both situations involve the arrival of a new leader as a harbinger of change.

GUIDELINES FOR ORGANISATIONAL GUIDANCE

It is beyond the scope of this book to talk about managing complex change, although it is clearly a leadership issue. Even the concept of PowerSharing espoused herein may require a major change in culture in some organisations, because it will change radically, 'the way things get done around here'.

Often, complex change is best facilitated by bringing in external expertise. This is also the subject of many books in its own right. What we want to cover is how a leader will routinely develop personal power, which will enable him or her to guide and maintain influence in the average organisation. Here we are talking about organisational guidance, not individual guidance, which will be covered in a later chapter.

A leader can guide both *formally* and *informally*. Both styles have their place and are equally valid. Formal guidance tends to establish procedures and will help to make tasks more structured, though not invariably. Informal guidance, on the other hand, will tend to improve team relationships if used properly.

Formal guidance

Procedures. These are mentioned here only in their role as parameters and are not to be confused with regulations—although some regulations may have procedures. Procedures form the outer barriers or fences along a route and they keep people from losing direction. But there should be gaps along the way to enable people to take short cuts if that is appropriate. Procedures will lay down a leader's expectations of routine performance and minimum standards. Normally they will include such things as safety standards, accounting standards, leave, correspondence and so on; in fact, most of the *transactional* management issues. A leader needs to be a good manager and will have such things established by the administrative staff.

Reporting systems. It is normal to have a system of verbal and written reporting in most organisations. Again, how it is done is really a *procedure* (management issue) and will depend on the industry. Some reports are verbal, brief and daily; some may be written, lengthy and monthly or even quarterly depending on need. With recent emphasis on total quality management (TQM) and continuous improvement issues, a lot of statistical analysis may be necessary—normally in the form of routine computer printouts.

The important point is that in addition to knowing what is going on up the chain, a good leader will have an expert knowledge at his or her own level, a full working knowledge of what is going on at one level down and a broad general knowledge of what is happening two or more levels down (where those levels exist). *With the proviso that he or she has a* clear knowledge *of what is happening at the ultimate customer interface or 'point of impact.' This is not a licence to interfere.*

Keeping in touch doesn't mean touching everything or meddling.

Scheduled meetings. Again, these are *procedural.* They can be one-to-one or group or team meetings to a set routine. It's really just another way of communicating. Meetings can be an annoyance and should be kept to a minimum. While people are *meeting* they are often not *doing.* A leader must not rely on meetings to find out what is going on; however, they are a way of imparting the same message to a number of people in a short time, both in a lateral and vertical sense.

Keep in touch by having procedures, reporting systems and with regular face-to-face contact.

Notwithstanding all of the above, often the most effective way of keeping a finger on the pulse is by use of the more informal systems.

Informal guidance

Information sharing. A lot of organisations use the float file system or its technological successors. This system simply involves circulating open files of all correspondence to keep everyone more in the picture. It is used to great effect, especially in more bureaucratic environments. This way a senior executive can become aware of every piece of correspondence that goes in or out of his or her department. It helps a busy person to know what is going on and it has the added advantage of keeping all subordinate staff informed as well. Subordinates also have an expectation of knowing what's going on at a higher level, if not a right to know.

There are traps in this system. Some people sit on float files for days or even weeks. Float files have been known to suddenly reach the light of day from out of nowhere, over a year old. Also, some immobile executives use the float file as an excuse not to move around among their people. There also has to be care exercised in the level down to which the file should go, and in some organisations there may be sensitive material that needs to be kept confidential. Even in the average organisation most personnel and financial matters need to be vetted. Such a system must not become a vehicle for mutual criticism.

Information systems. There are management information systems packages available now that will keep all levels informed in a slightly different and often more efficient way. As with all technology it is a two-edged sword. Management information (or at least data) is now available by the trailer load at just the flick of a switch or the push of a button. A manager can be tempted to think that there is nothing more to gathering information and keeping abreast than the mastering of the latest piece of computer software or the absorption of the latest print-out. A good leader will not be so fooled. The advances in technology have serious implications for the way people interact and a computer screen *is no substitute* for human interaction.

What is also of concern in all of these admirable open communication systems, is the temptation for leaders to step in and interfere on the basis of knowledge transmitted through informal communication channels. All too often what passes for knowledge is only information and what passes for information is only data.

Personal contact. By far the best informal system is personal contact and this can be achieved by the use of the old 'open door' policy by which a leader encourages people to communicate by being accessible. We will cover accessibility in a later chapter, but one of the advantages of having an open door is that not only can people come in, the incumbent can get out. This enables the leader to indulge in some 'management by walking around' (MBWA). This used to be called 'visiting the troops' long before anyone ever heard the phrase MBWA.

Management by walking around. Whether we are talking about 'management by walking about' or 'management by walking around' one needs to be aware that it can also be a trap. While a good leader uses MBWA to help determine a climate and can take action accordingly, workers can resent what they perceive as spying and subordinate leaders can resent bypassing. It can lead to terrible confusion in the wrong hands. Seeking subordinate's views on intermediate leaders is cowardly, seeking subordinate's views on your own performance is foolish, asking for complaints is asking for trouble, and yet so-called leaders have been observed doing all of these things.

It is a great idea to get input during MBWA, and provided intermediate leaders are not bypassed, getting to know the workers is admirable. But here a list of do's and don'ts for MBWA is important, because it is an area where so many aspiring leaders make mistakes.

Use it to get to know people. Learn their names, their interests, their family. Talk with them, not at them. Don't intrude; respect a person's right to privacy even in his or her work.

Use it to familiarise yourself with systems. Ask people to show you how things work, express admiration for their skills. Listen if they suggest better ways. Don't get them to show you the obvious or things you should already know.

Use it to let the worker see you. Let them ask about you and your interests, family and so on. Don't boast about matters in which you have an interest. Let them hear your vision. Remember, your interests may not be theirs.

Use it to freshen your mind. Get out of the office to stop becoming jaded. Keep an open door except when there is a meeting or a private telephone conversation going on. A closed door not only keeps casual visitors out, it also keeps the occupants in.

Use it to get a sense of progress. See first-hand what the difficulties may be. Don't attempt to *fix* things that are somebody else's responsibility.

Don't use it to check on people without their knowledge.

Don't ask for complaints. As workers become more at ease with you, they will soon let you know if they have any complaints—often in no uncertain terms.

Don't use it to get workers' opinions, either about yourself or about those in intermediate positions who may be placed over them. If such information is offered use it in a very guarded fashion and refer it to a formal system as soon as possible.

Never use it as a means of 'one-upmanship' over a subordinate.

Never use it as a means of discipline.

Never do it surreptitiously. Don't snoop.

Never use it to ingratiate yourself. Being the workers' mate sometimes leads to unrealistic expectations on their part.

Always vary your calling pattern. Don't have favourite calling spots as this may give rise to accusations of favouritism.

Don't just talk to people you like.

Use it to get to know external customers. About the only time a leader is justified in breaking the chain of management communication is to handle a complaint or a difficulty with an external customer. But in that case . . .

Think before you talk.

Informal systems help a leader understand his or her followers and the organisation or team.

A final word of warning on informal systems. They are just what the word says—*informal*. Do not assume that any communication you have while walking around has the imprimatur of an established decision and never presume to ask a subordinate to pass on a decision or communication upward to an intermediate leader or laterally to others in a team. That's your responsibility. A decision has no force until the decider has passed it *downwards* directly to the next level—*formally*.

Use informal, as well as formal, systems to keep in touch.
Informal communications have no status until confirmed formally.

Peter: I worked in an organisation once where I had a boss who had great difficulty understanding the principles of MBWA. We had a system that my staff would ring me as soon as the boss had left them and let me know what sort of latest nonsense he was perpetrating. I would have to put them straight and ambush my boss when he came back and reiterate that it wasn't good policy to bypass me. He'd then get flustered and have to admit that he'd already told my people to implement whatever it was. Then we would sort it out until the next time.

John: I know of another organisation where one of the senior managers used to spy on the CEO and then inform the chairman. Needless to say, the CEO and the chairman didn't see eye to eye. That's reprehensible, but a lot more common than you would suppose. It is what we might call executive espionage. Good leaders will not allow spying and telling; obviously the chairman concerned showed poor leadership.

In relation to the above anecdote another political game people play is the deliberate withholding of information. There is an old belief that 'knowledge is power', and keeping someone in the dark means they are always one step behind. This is, of course, a serious distortion of the expert power we mentioned earlier in the chapter. Obviously, decisions made on the basis of ignorance will be poor decisions and withholding information will invariably be counter-productive.

DISCIPLINE

Followers in a well-led organisation will always respect the legitimate use of authority. A good rider may carry a crop but may never use it. If used it will only be so for the amount of time necessary and no more. And a good rider will not try to fight a horse while using the crop. In most cases even a bad-mannered horse will behave as soon as the crop is sighted!

In the same way, position power that provides for sanctions is best when it is not used. In business and industry today there are not many sanctions that a leader can invoke anyway, short of dismissal, which is a last resort. Of course, there is always the slowing down of promotion or promotional prospects, but that won't work in some cases anyway. All that is left is verbal chastisement, which is often ineffective, or colleague and team disapproval—both of which can be fairly significant.

It is often this peer pressure and team spirit that will give individuals pride in themselves. That in turn will create self-discipline—and that is what is ultimately being sought.

> Self-discipline and self-regulation are superior to any other form of control.

Whatever disciplinary sanctions are used they must apply to the transgressor only. That can't be stressed enough. And when regulations are broken there must be redoubled efforts to enforce them, not simply the creation of new regulations.

COMMUNICATION

A leader's major effort towards discipline must go into positive motivation, which means constant communication with workers.

It is quite surprising the number of people, aspiring leaders included, who deliberately tell their workers as little as possible because 'they always get things twisted and that's a sure way to create rumours'. The reality is that rumours invariably start as a result of insufficient information, not too much information. If workers always get things twisted, it is more than likely due to the way they are told rather than *what* they are told.

> Rumours abound where there is poor or insufficient communication and information.

All of the formal and informal systems we have talked about are simply one means or another of communication. Ease of communication is one of the sure signs that a leader is confident of his or her position. But communication must be two way and all leaders need feedback, both on their performance and on the communication process itself.

Two-way communication is necessary but there will be occasions when there is simply not time. And sometimes the circumstances lend a sense of urgency to a communication. Sometimes it is simply a case of 'just do it!' A leader who has built up a bank of valid personal power will not be questioned on such occasions. When circumstances change, followers know that two-way communication can resume.

There are many interactions in the communication process and one should be aware of how many things can go wrong. Look at the communication interactions outlined in Figures 7.1 and 7.2.

In a two-person group there is only one interaction (Fig. 7.1), whereas in a three-person group there are seven possible interactions (Fig. 7.2).

Fig. 7.1 *Possible interactions—two people*

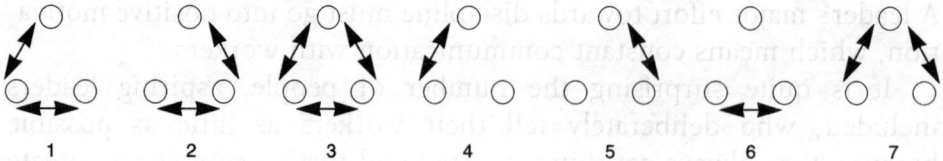

Fig. 7.2 *Possible interactions—three people*

In a group of four there are twenty-five possible interactions and in a group of five, ninety! That's ninety opportunities for things to be misinterpreted, going one way! The same number exists in reverse.

Then there are the psychological barriers caused by perceptual problems between both communicator and receiver and there can be variations in perception caused by such things as differences in cultural background.

John: I remember a classic difference in perception. One of my colleagues was a very difficult person. Apart from having a reputation for irritability he wasn't very efficient or effective. The people who worked for him disliked him intensely and he ended up with a none too complimentary nickname.

He eventually got wind of what he thought was his nickname and over a few drinks one night he was preening himself and made a statement along the lines of, 'I know I'm not popular, that's not my job, but I have people's respect. I know I'm called WAR DOG behind my back but I don't mind!'

You should have seen his face when he was told that he was actually called WART HOG!

The foregoing is an illustration that sometimes we only hear what we want to hear. This is a major barrier, considering that approximately 70 per cent of communication time is spent in listening, and only about 20 per cent in talking. We read and write the other 10 per cent, with writing coming a bad last. Doesn't it seem odd that we are taught these skills in reverse order—reading, writing, formal speaking and finally, for those fortunate enough, we are actually taught to listen.

Listening is a major form of communication.

Next time you go to a boring stand-up social function notice how people who don't know each other 'fish' for a discussion topic. Surprisingly enough, most people seem to do this by talking rather than listening. They are no doubt trying to establish a common ground or manoeuvre the conversation to something in which they can establish some expert personal power. You think you can tell who are the listeners—they are the ones who aren't talking—but more often than not they aren't listening either, they are simply waiting to talk.

John: I once worked for a boss who would have a one-to-one meeting each month and would spend the whole time on transmit. I don't think he ever found his receive button. When he talked, he always talked at someone rather than to them and it was always about matters as they affected him.

When he did listen he would listen with his engine running at high revs and then a week later demand to be told why he hadn't been informed that something was going on. Then he would proceed to tell the (supposed) culprit why he (the boss) hadn't been kept informed. It was like a run-away circus.

It is very easy for your mind to wander when you are listening, especially with some sorts of people. Often you will find yourself getting ahead of them. Or else you are predetermining the answer based on your perception, and it may be wrong.

Peter: I had a woman working for me once who was very gentle and highly competent, as well as being assertive and determined. We met regularly and I know we had a high mutual regard for each other. However, she once said to me, 'I get the feeling that sometimes you aren't listening'. I was perturbed and I asked for instances where I had not acted on her requests or discussed her advice. She admitted that I had been blessed with a retentive memory and that my questions and follow-up indicated a fairly clear understanding. 'But', she said, 'sometimes I don't feel listened to!'

On reflection she was right. I realised that my mind used to wander. Fortunately, because our communication was good she was prepared to tell me. I gave her my undivided attention from then on.

Communicating is more than just talking and hearing. One communicates with the whole person, not just mouth, ears and eyes. This comes back to what we were talking about in the last chapter about people understanding the underlying feelings of others. The messenger is often more important than the message.

Communication is a total process involving senses, emotions and intellect.

John: *That reminds me of a colleague I worked with who had the repu-tation of being a bad listener—it was not unusual for him to start reading in the middle of a conversation with anybody but the boss. The office joke was that if you wanted him to read something in a hurry you gave it to him and then started talking. On cue he would start reading.*

Here are some hints in the talking and listening area. They are listed because they are so important and so poorly understood.

TALKING

Leader

- Make your conversation unambiguous so that there can be no misunderstanding.
- Stick to the subject. Don't talk about people, talk about perfor-mances and expectations.
- Ensure that the content of the conversation is clear, correct, coher-ent, and concise to avoid the embarrassment of having to counter-mand because of an avoidable mistake.
- Question the recipient's understanding to confirm that the meaning of the conversation has been grasped.
- Observe and evaluate the subsequent performance to ensure that there is no slip between understanding and expectation.

Follower

- Stick to the subject. Don't waffle.
- Explain your own position in relation to the subject.
- Outline the problem if there is one.
- Suggest some alternative ways of looking at the issue.
- Suggest some options to be considered and recommend your preferred option.

- Be direct, respectful, personal, confident and not obsequious. Be assertive, not aggressive.

LISTENING

- Listen to the whole person in order to get the message behind the message.
- Concentrate on content, not on the speaker's mannerisms. However, be conscious of nervousness or difficulties.
- Listen to the whole message or argument before making a judgment.
- Don't dig for detail; relate any detail to the main point.
- Don't take unnecessary or detailed notes; it distracts from listening to the whole person. You can always ask the speaker to give you supporting documentation later if you need it.
- Don't let your mind wander.
- Question for clarification, participate in the feedback process and double-check your understanding.
- Help the speaker who is having difficulty with explanation, but don't pre-empt or presume a meaning.

A leader who is able to do all those things will certainly have a good idea of what's going on in the organisation, will have the confidence and respect of the team and need never feel alone. He or she will be able to keep the team on course with the minimum of pressure. The team will want to forge ahead of its own accord and may even need restraint. Sometimes it may even be necessary to gallop and leap obstacles. To do this the team will need continual training, but the whip will probably never be needed.

Key concepts

- A leader needs to have control of his or her organisation.
- Control in a PowerSharing organisation generally means keeping in touch.
- Keeping in touch means having access to all the relevant facts and factors.
- *Soft-mouthed* organisations are much easier to control.
- A leader must establish early control by determining an organisation's culture and adjusting the elements of *situational control*.
- Power allows leaders certain sanctions that they must be prepared to use.
- A good leader may start with position power but should seek to create personal power.
- 'Newbroomism', which seeks to change culture without attitudinal change, may cause widespread resentment in a workforce.
- Establishing procedural communications is an early management need.
- Informal procedures are valuable means of a leader keeping in touch.
- Informal systems need formal follow-up.
- Leaders must learn effective communication, which particularly means skilled talking and effective listening.
- Leaders must help people in their organisations to learn to listen.

CHAPTER 8

Eighth Precept

Do not isolate yourself from followers, their aspirations or their environment

> If you need to hire new staff the HR department will do it, if any of your staff need training, the training department will do it. Leave is approved by admin and pay matters by accounts, all expenditure is approved by finance, personal problems are handled by the HR psychologist, or the industrial chaplain. Casual staff bring their own lunch, permanent staff have their own canteen, management eats in the company dining room and we directors eat in the board room. With good management you should only need to talk to your staff once a week.

SELECTIVE INFORMATION

Isolation is the beginning of alienation. It is also endemic in the last decade of the twentieth century as the information revolution makes it continually easier to access and relate to data and information without having to relate to people. The message is becoming more important than the sender, the receiver or the messenger. This just adds to the day-to-day isolation from one's fellow man.

Added to this is the plethora of information that is available and growing daily at such a pace that leaders, at whatever level, are reliant on the filtering of information through experts and advisers. Many of these so-called advisers are sycophants rather than followers. These people have their own agenda, it is in their own interests to tell the leader what he or she wants to hear—a common failing at all levels. Keeping the truth filtered can often be the precursor to serious problems in an organisation because there is a tendency in everyone to seek their own advisers and counsellors from people of like mind. 'Yes' people are incredibly destructive.

This situation becomes exacerbated when isolation is deliberately, if unwittingly, sought. We hear of governments being isolated from the people, capital cities being isolated from reality, the cities being isolated from the country and so on and yet we continually have evidence of a growing urge to centralise and merge activities, both at governmental and business level, in order to gain *efficiencies*. It is forgotten that efficiency is about things, effectiveness is about people. Efficiency at the expense of people can only be followed by alienation.

How often do you hear things like, 'I think the government's doing a good job (or a bad job); everyone I talk to thinks they're great (or awful)'. What people seem to forget is that they are most likely to meet or mix with people of their own political or industrial persuasion. From the point of view of the blue collar worker mixing only with fellow workers, it would be very easy for that person to convince himself or herself that there is no such thing as a good industrial boss. Likewise it would be rather nonsensical to seek objective views about compulsory unionism from, for example, an 'establishment club' and assume therefore that it is the prevailing view in the country. Oddly enough, this is something which people tend to do all too often. They are indeed isolating themselves by only communicating with like-minded and similarly levelled people.

> People don't only tend to hear what they want to hear, they only listen to people who will tell them what they want to believe.

John: In my work with large organisations I often deal with many levels and stratas. I am continually interested by how the opinions on the same issues vary at different levels. It is almost as though each level has received its own injection of group-think. While the various levels seem to acknowledge the differing views of other levels, it is almost as if it is forbidden to ascertain why the other views are held.

Somehow there is a feeling that the way to overcome these things is to do more polling, to gather yet more information, so that senior management or government or whatever is replete with information. All the while they forget that their constituents are not so replete, and they will make *their* decisions on the basis of what *they* know, not what their bosses or leaders know or tell them. This can lead to selective information manipulation.

THE COMMON TOUCH

Historically, truly great leaders never lost the common touch, even looking as far back as the example of Hannibal, who lay on the ground in the Alps in the company of his soldiers covered only with his cloak. And in more modern times, the British royal family shared the lot and the danger of Mr and Mrs Average during the Blitz on London. While in the latter case it may only have been a gesture, the effect was profound.

Even so, people are not small-minded. They understand responsibility is accompanied by access to information and even privilege, within reason. It's when you have authority without responsibility, and when access to certain information or privilege is assumed to be a right of only certain people, that resentment sets in. What this means is that if a follower shares the gain he or she will gladly share the pain. People are invariably sensible if they know the reasons for a certain course of action, preferably beforehand!

> Don't expect followers to make reasoned choices if they are only in possession of half the facts.

Unfortunately, there are any number of examples where this doesn't happen. In the climate of economic rationalism many organisations have restructured and resized. It would be interesting to look at the percentage of those people who have lost their jobs at the top, at the middle and at the bottom. It would also be interesting to know how many senior executives actually took reduced pay packets before the downsizing started. Statistics indicate that a good percentage of organisations fail to achieve their financial targets as a result of downsizing.

Studies of downsizing or right-sizing in the United States have revealed that too many downsizings have been a failure. Studies also reveal that there is no link between an organisation's performance and the pay packet of its chief executive. Companies seemed to forget that it *costs* to retrain and replace, and that experience is not something that can be regained overnight. Many organisations downsized on the advice of financial advisers or consultants, who took their retainer and walked away from the resultant shambles completely oblivious to the sometimes mortal damage done to an organisation's culture, because they saw things only as short-term, bottom-line solutions. There were and are vigorous attempts to handle the out-placement of departing executives, managers and so on, and almost no programs designed to cater for those left behind, who are of course in a grieving mode with all trust gone and cynicism entrenched.

However, you can't blame the consultant. Consultants are not necessarily in touch with an organisation's culture. It is a leadership failure. A consultant can only do as good or as bad a job as the client's brief will allow. While they are admittedly inured against the real world in some ways and certainly often seem to be stuck in an ivory tower, consultants to a *client* who *is* in touch with reality and the workforce would not be allowed to make unwise personnel recommendations. The fault clearly lies with the organisation's leadership. Line managers must learn to treat people as their most important resource, to be interfered with as a last resort, and the HR or personnel departments must resource line management in this regard.

> People are the leader's ultimate resource.

PERSONAL AMBITION AND PERSONAL GAIN

Many of the problems that occur at the workplace are as a result of the isolation, deliberate or otherwise, of line managers from their followers. The isolation begins at the lower levels of leadership and gets steadily worse further up the line.

Alistair Mant, who was mentioned previously, makes the observation that when he goes into an organisation he asks two questions of the management team: 'How does one get on around here?' and then later: 'What does one do to get the job done around here?' If the two answers are different, as they often are, then there is a real leadership problem.[1] Any leader who puts his or her own ambitions ahead of the team, the task and the needs of other individuals, is already isolated.

Unfortunately, as indicated already, such occurrences are endemic in many organisations and organisational cultures. Personal ambition above all else, is not only applauded, it is actively encouraged by the set-up of the organisations themselves. Tragically, people are encouraged to better themselves at the expense of others or encouraged to leave many of the issues of leadership as represented by the needs of the team or the needs of individuals to HR specialists, while they themselves simply concentrate on the needs of the task.

As we said in Chapter 2, many people confuse personal ambition with vision, such that the only vision they have is of themselves getting ahead. Success comes in their own terms with better cars, bigger offices and more perks. The actual results they have achieved with their team may even be irrelevant to their personal success. Or at the very most they are only judged on their achievements and not on the broken bodies they have left on the way. We should be encouraging young leaders to *stand out not on.*

> Ambition is essentially individually focused, while vision has a corporate focus.

We have already said that ambition is not a bad thing. Most genuine leaders have personal ambition but it doesn't totally subsume all other characteristics, because they have learned to balance their life's priorities. They concentrate on the really important matters without worrying too much about the urgent. And the really important things are people. Good leaders seem to have good leadership as their main ambition—and it's amazing how successful they seem to be at their job as a result. The foregoing may seem to indicate a certain belief in the school of hard knocks—people should serve an apprenticeship 'before the mast' as it were, so that they don't lose touch. This is not strictly so. Although someone who has come up the hard way often has a better appreciation of followers, there are also glaring examples of the opposite being the case.

In previous times serving an apprenticeship may have been appropriate, but it doesn't necessarily follow today, especially with the advent of technological data gathering. These days the opportunities are fewer but there are a number of organisations that require aspiring employees to have had some years of experience in the *real world*. That's probably today's equivalent of the school of hard knocks. Some organisations even send young executives on physical adventure training courses to build their character and give them a taste of the hard knocks. Unfortunately, those courses probably do neither. They can be very good for team building and seeing how a person works momentarily under some physical stress, but there is no evidence to support the theory that having a cold shower every day in winter or standing terrified at the top of a cliff necessarily helps to build character for the work environment!

The solution lies in making sure that leaders at every level have responsibility for all the elements that go to make up those three functional leadership circles we first saw in the Introduction. Leaders must be able to see and feel things through the eyes of followers. They can't do that through a third party.

What is important is that the leader must recognise where the ultimate client interface (point of impact) lies and have a fully empathetic appreciation of the pressures on the worker at that point. Above all, we must begin to ensure that 'getting ahead' means 'getting the job done' and 'getting the job done' means attending to and being responsible for all the elements of those three circles.

One of the great examples of leadership in recent times in Australia is that of the late Sir John Williams who became the first chairman of a revamped Australian National Line (ANL) in the 1950s. Williams was in turn a ship's master, wharf manager, ran a steve-doring business, then freight, salvage and engineering businesses and had interests in gold mining, cool-stores, paint manufacturing and farming. He was chairman of ANL for sixteen years until 1971.

He worked until well into his eighties and as late as 1971 at the age of 75 he was still getting his hands dirty in the salvage business. He had all the characteristics of a leader, especially when it came to risk taking and innovation, but he never asked of others more than he would do himself. His greatest characteristic, which is clearly evi-dent in his life, was that he never lost the common touch. He main-tained touch with all that was going on in his businesses—but more than that, he was as happy at the coal-face as he was in a boardroom and seemed to be as much at home in a diving suit as he was in a din-ner suit.

Sir John's story is recounted in detail in his autobiography So Ends This Day.[2]

STAND OUT, NOT ON

Having once again established the importance of attention to the three circles it is time to create a set of guidelines that may help to keep that concept in its proper perspective. The reader will notice that at no stage have we suggested a leader shouldn't stand out from followers or peers. On the contrary, a leader will stand out by not trying to be out-standing. The paradox is that simply by being one of them, the people will more readily acclaim him or her. That acclaim will come from a leader's determination to serve followers rather than have followers serve him or her.

We have listed a set of guidelines that we think are important. The list is not exhaustive but it is drawn entirely from experience and we think it will help aspiring leaders to stand out.

1. *Beware the trappings of office.*
2. *Share the pain and the gain.*
3. *Empathise with followers.*
4. *Use specialist staff as resources.*
5. *No reward without achievement.*
6. *No advancement without responsibility.*
7. *Do not over-regulate.*
8. *Match actions to words.*

9. *Lead by example.*
10. *Be consistent.*

1. *Beware the trappings of office*

What are the trappings of office? Huge offices, corporate suites, corporate dining rooms, large ostentatious cars, long lunches, obvious fringe benefits. Note that we said beware! We don't say they are wrong in themselves, even as rewards in the corporate world. They aren't, and we all aspire to one or more of them in some form or another. The problem lies in the context in which they are used. If workers see them being flaunted by bosses who they think don't deserve them, then there is going to be resentment and envy.

A lot depends on perception. A large accountancy or legal firm in the city may well be able to get away with some things because the aspirations of followers do not preclude them eventually having such things themselves. The danger is in them becoming the important things of life or work. Some people make judgments of a person's success based on whether he or she drives a BMW or a Lada, or whether he or she dresses from the bargain basement or Gucci. It is not that workers down the line necessarily want to be in the same place, they just want the same consideration. To establish such privileges in a working-class area where the workforce sees the privilege daily and has no hope of aspiring beyond their current lot, rubs salt into the wounds of resentment.

On the other hand, there is the story of a very senior politician who insisted on travelling economy class on aircraft. People didn't see him as being egalitarian, they just thought he was nuts, because he had a lot of responsibility and should have used time on the aircraft to work, not to wrestle with a small seat and all its limitations. Thinking people aren't fooled by such hollow gestures.

Privileges *earned* by leaders are rarely resented by followers.

Peter: I was in a diplomatic post at one stage when a very senior departmental official came to the country on an official visit without either his wife or a personal assistant. Australia was on one of *those semi-perpetual austerity campaigns. Wives were forbidden to accompany husbands and we managed to save about $1500 by the exercise. All costs in the country were being borne by the host country anyway and I accompanied the official throughout his tour acting as his personal assistant. Apart from austerity we thought we were being very egalitarian.*

Wherever we went, I was drawn aside by senior officials and bureaucrats of the host country and asked what they had done to offend us that the official's visit should be considered so unimportant as to preclude his wife travelling at such a small expense. We put cost before value.

In both the above cases leaders were isolated from the real expectations of followers or colleagues and made incorrect assumptions regarding followers' reactions, on the one hand assuming resentment at privilege and on the other assuming unimportance of privilege.

> Privileges should be based on *value* rather than *cost*.

People do not have unrealistic expectations. Few workers at a working-class car plant would expect a visiting Japanese trade delegation to be fed on hamburgers down at the local 'Greasy Spoon'. (On the other hand, few auto executives would have come to work in the morning and helped to clean out the factory as the Japanese executives may well have done had they been at home.)

The issue of corporate privilege needs to be seen in context. All too often people are judged on the basis of how they look, what car they drive, and where they went to school and not on the basis of whether they have earned their privileges.

Peter: I used to have a lot to do with the Australian subsidiary of a privately owned US organisation. They are a very ethical group and committed to egalitarianism. Years ago an acquaintance of mine who ran the company operation in a country town used to say that he had the biggest office in Australia. The trouble was he had to share it with about a hundred other people! This massive office housed everyone and they claimed it made for excellent

*communication. Whenever you went to lunch you ate in the can-
teen and lined up with factory hands and the workers. If the MD
wanted to have a private conversation he booked the conference
room like anyone else.*

*Everybody was in the shop window. No privacy, no privilege, no
perks. But away from the factory the executives stayed and travelled
in luxury. I visited one of their plants in the UK—the same thing.*

*I remarked on this to the driver on the way back to London
and his view was that the workers resented the lack of privacy
more than management did because it precluded 'goofing off' and
indicated a lack of trust up and down. But in the manner of all
wise English chauffeurs he claimed that it was more than compensated for by the generosity of the company, which showed in so
many other ways that they did trust their workers. It worked for
them and the privileges (including remuneration) that leaders at
all levels received were generous and tangible but not obvious or
ostentatious at the coal-face.*

Do not flaunt privilege.

We should fully endorse efforts to ensure that privileges are not
flaunted. That doesn't mean they have to be secret, just that they are
kept circumspect. And there must be efforts to ensure that workers
have their own privileges as well. Even a social club or bar at a couple
of different levels helps to reinforce the concept of privilege as reward.
Also, often what are perceived to be privileges are exercises in pragmatism, such as the increasing provision of the ubiquitous (and to
some iniquitous) mobile phone. In some places the provision of a car
and driver allows the occupant to work while travelling, or often to
socialise at a necessary level without the threat of a drink driving
charge. They are both sensible uses of what are often regarded as
perks.

2. *Share the pain and the gain*

Immeasurable harm was done to the credibility of corporate and political leadership during the 1980s, the decade of greed.

Social researchers are making interesting observations when it comes to the nature and future of work. More people are losing their jobs and yet more people are working longer hours. Some people are working sixty and seventy hours a week and as many and more are on social security. Many are paid overtime rates for thirty or so hours a week and others can't even get ten hours work a week. Some executives are paid salaries in the vicinity of $50 000 a week and many people consider themselves lucky indeed if they can earn half that much in a year. The many are beginning to wonder how the few can justify those sorts of salaries and how work can be so unevenly distributed.

This is happening all around the world at macro and micro levels. Too often the workforce sees itself bearing the brunt but not sharing in the benefits of productivity gains. Organisations that downsized are staying flatter and often replacing people with fast-growing technology. Retrenched workers see their former colleagues too frightened to speak out because—to use some well-known, accurate but unjust words—'the reward you get for doing your job, is your job'. If any so-called leader can see justice in that remark then he or she is totally isolated from the fears, concerns and aspirations of the workforce.

It takes so little to move about among the workforce, to explain the hardships and difficulties and to seek ideas and suggestions; to keep in touch with those who have been let go. If, for any reason, people are too frightened to talk to you on their own initiative, you have failed as a leader. By the same token, the rewards must be shared with a work-force. It seems that some smaller owner-managed businesses may have a better grasp of this than bigger firms. It's surprising, for instance, the number of organisations that see a pay freeze as excluding certain levels of management. There can't be a rule for the rich and a rule for the poor. It has to be one in, all in.

3. *Empathise with followers*

It's surprising the number of people who confuse sympathy with empathy and how often both words are under-valued. Empathy simply means understanding someone else's feelings. In order to understand someone's feelings you have to get quite close to them, so asking a leader to empathise with followers is no short order. Covey says it best when he says 'seek first to understand then to be understood'.[3]

In order to achieve this it is often necessary to go through the previous principle to understand a follower's fears, concerns, frustrations and doubts. The late Sir John Williams, already mentioned, gives in his book a clear impression of someone who can see both sides of any issue.[4] He could project himself into the mind of the ordinary seaman and he never lost the common touch.

A leader should wear a follower's shoes for a day.

The corollary to this principle is often forgotten when industrial democracy is discussed. Leaders have a right to expect their followers to understand the necessity for certain sometimes unpalatable leadership decisions. This is the 'then to be understood' part of Covey's equation, which suggests that having sought to understand, a leader has a right to put his or her point of view, which includes sometimes making unpalatable decisions.

4. *Use specialist staff as resources*

Everyone recognises the need for experts and careerists in human resources or personnel, or training or industrial relations or finance. Every business needs these experts at every level, but they must never be allowed to intrude between a leader and his or her relationship with followers or workers.

It was the separation of staff from line that was responsible in such a great way for the many tragedies on the Western Front of World War I. Senior generals inured themselves from reality by relying too much on their staff. Politicians do it today and, as we have said, they get filtered information about their constituencies as a result. Specialist staff should never be allowed to set policy at whatever level. Only leaders can set policy, staff can advise. This means that a line manager or leader must have prior right of veto on *staff-initiated* policy matters that come from above. In any sound system a leader must have immediate and direct access to a leader at the next higher line level, no matter how senior the specialist advisers or staff in between.

The flattening of organisations is one of the outcomes of the expansion of specialist powers in business. Unfortunately, if an organisation is *fat*, people think the solution is to make it *flat*. In other words—do away with hierarchy and make managers at all levels do the hack work. The problem is not the existence of a hierarchy, but the enormous bloating of the specialist staff at each level of the hierarchy which inures leaders from the realities of the next several levels down.

> The solution to a 'fat' organisation is not necessarily a 'flat' organisation.

Some people are already advocating a return to such specialisation in the light of the information and technological revolutions. It would be a tragic mistake. Besides, with the flattening of organisations (a trend that may or may not last) there is a growing recognition that leaders must be their own personnel managers, HR managers or trainers and act accordingly.

Specialist staff should be used to help a leader look outward. If a leader is too busy minding the store, he or she won't see that another one has opened over the road. So a leader needs the resources to enable him or her to keep in touch with both the internal and external environment. Let there be a hierarchy if need be, but let it not get too fat; let there be specialists, but as advisers not as executives in the line management system.

5. *No reward without achievement*

Reward relates to both individuals and groups. Leaders must have a very clear understanding of who or what is reaching objectives and targets and why or why not! Workers and subordinates are clever enough to know who is performing and who is not, and if they see advancement or preferment on the basis of politics, sycophancy or nepotism all that will follow will be resentment and cynicism—certainly not confidence and trust. Worse will follow; the promotee will more than likely become a 'yes' person, begin to filter information, and truth and trust becomes a casualty in the workforce. The result? Isolation. Remember the twin statements: 'How does one get on?' and 'What does one do to get the job done?'.

> A good leader will match advancement with results.

6. *No advancement without responsibility*

This means no 'jobs for the boys'. This includes 'finding' special jobs for special friends and to follow it is a test of integrity. Not only do some illustrious bosses find jobs, they create them, and when they can't do that, they pretend. In the context of leadership, an increase in status and pay packet must be accompanied by an increase in responsibility. Nevertheless, it's neither unusual for a politician or executive to appoint a personal assistant or press secretary from the ranks of the party faithful, nor is it unethical. It tends towards being unethical if the position is used unduly to secure the next advancement against others in the field. Even then it's more unwise than unethical.

What we are suggesting is that if someone receives preferred advancement, which may be the best way to promote, then it must be based on skill, qualification and achievement with an eye to potential, and not on nepotism. In political or corporate terms the appointed person must be expected to further the aim or the vision of the leader, and that may mean appointing someone of a certain political persuasion provided the incumbent can perform up to the task, and be fully accountable for that task no matter what the prior experience may have been.

On the other hand, being someone's patron is no excuse for accepting their failure (as opposed to occasional mistakes) on the basis that the person is still learning the ropes. If that's the case maybe they shouldn't have been promoted in the first place. Patronage itself is neither unethical nor unwise provided all the qualifications are fulfilled and the patronage itself is impartial. And provided that there is no advancement without commensurate increase in responsibility.

7. *Do not over-regulate*

We can relate this concept to the principle regarding *staff* and *line*, because it seems that it is generally the staff who create regulations. We mentioned earlier that regulations and procedures were there to keep an operation running smoothly and consistently. Despite this there is an 'all too human' tendency to over-regulate and to use the regulations to make a misery of the lives of workers. There are two parts to this. One says that a leader should not allow unnecessary regulations, and should keep regulations and procedures constantly under review. The other aspect is that leaders should not be bound rigidly by administrative regulatory trivia that can be legitimately set aside when necessary.

No regulation should be allowed to interfere with a worker's basic rights to achievement, natural justice and a living wage.

Peter: I was once at the pay office of an organisation in which I worked late one Friday afternoon while ten or fifteen workers tried to argue their right to pay. Someone in their section had neglected to fill in their pay sheets properly. They had been out travelling for the week and the pay clerk wouldn't budge. There were procedures and they hadn't been followed. He realised it wasn't the workers' fault but rules were rules, they could come back on Monday. I ascertained that he had the money and the acquittance rolls so I directed him to pay the workers. He refused initially and stated that it was highly irregular, but eventually he was persuaded to do so.

On Monday I was called up to explain my actions to my boss who had been advised of my actions by the finance manager. I told him what I had done. The finance manager gave his side of the story and mentioned how his staff had to re-open the rolls and what a bother it was and so on. He suggested that the people responsible be disciplined. The boss did no such thing and calmly pointed out that the pay staff should understand what their POI was. And that was the finance manager's responsibility.

It can become too easy to let procedures and regulations become the be-all and end-all. It makes you realise where the saying 'rules were made to be broken' comes from. You will regularly find people saying it's too late for such and such an application because it's past the closing date, and after refusing what may be legitimate and valuable late applications, the original ones sit on a desk for a week waiting for someone to action them!

It is a good thing to always remind oneself of what is important to a leader. People are important. All else follows. It is so easy to substitute efficiencies for effectiveness. It is much easier to centralise to save space, time and maybe even money. It is much easier to recruit centrally and leave the details to the HR department. It is safer to live by regulations than by genuine PowerSharing. In the short term it may even be more cost-effective. But we come back to the confusion between value and cost. Any bureaucracy by very definition will tend to isolate a leader from his or her constituents.

8. *Match actions to words*

The experts would say, 'actual behaviour must equate to espoused behaviour'. This concept really doesn't need a lot of explanation. Suffice to say that any worker can see through a hypocrite or a poser (and we will say more on that later), but what this point is really about is keeping promises. Don't make promises you can't keep or have no intention of keeping, and don't make threats that you can't or won't carry out. More than that, no leader should paint scenarios that are patently absurd or make predictions that are unlikely to come to pass as a means to motivate workers. Leaders must not make fairy tales of current reality.

Under a good leader who is in touch with all stakeholders, an organisation will have a mission statement that will actually predict behaviour. How often do you see 'Our aim is to serve' and you stand in the foyer of an organisation that clearly doesn't serve any better than its competitors. The words and actions don't match. If a leader was not isolated from the customer such things wouldn't happen. So when we say don't isolate yourself, we mean from all stakeholders, not just the workers or staff.

> If your motto is: *'To serve'*, then serve!

Peter: I know of a managing director of a big retail chain who used to go shopping at any one of his own stores on a regular basis just to get the feel of being a customer and to see if the company standards were being maintained. As you can imagine—they were! There was no way his staff could fool him with 'the customer believes etc'. He retired some years ago but the standards he set have never been forgotten.

The converse is where a leader fails to verify the reality of what he or she is being told. While this doesn't mean that everything has to be checked continuously, it does mean that the leader must ensure that rhetoric and process match.

9. *Lead by example*

This is a difficult point. Whenever it is suggested that there may be an expectation of certain behaviour from a leader, there is often the accusation of making judgments or moralising. However, if people take time to think rationally they will recognise that all we are suggesting is that whatever expectations of behaviour or performance a leader has *of* a workforce, that leader must first demonstrate *to* the workforce. This doesn't mean the leader has to be able to perform any task asked of a follower. It means that if you expect punctuality, then be punctual; if you expect high dress standards, then dress well yourself. If you expect your staff and workers to be fair when it comes to matters of discrimination or sexual harassment, then be absolutely scrupulous in your own behaviour. If, on the other hand, you are, for example, aggressive, then don't be surprised if others become aggressive.

John: *I know of an organisation where the senior executive team introduced an austerity campaign and read the riot act to the workers regarding belt-tightening and then went off to a three-hour lunch to discuss austerity measures.*

   If people see senior staff or aspiring leaders helping themselves to the stamp tin, or the boardroom booze cabinet or the stationery cupboard, what are they to think? More to the point, what are they to do?

   Likewise, if workers observe aspiring leaders turning in second-rate performances or not achieving targets or objectives and getting away with it, where is the personal or organisational integrity or credibility? A leader must model the performance, the standards, the attainments and the behaviours of both a personal and organisational nature, that are expected of workers and anything less is unacceptable leadership behaviour.

Posers are quickly exposed.

Any worker who observes these last two principles regularly broken will quickly lose trust in any leader. If a leader can't meet his or her own objectives there must be a question mark over his or her competence or judgment at the very least. And if he or she can't live up to expectations in his or her behaviour or performance then there must be a question mark over his or her character or integrity. Either way, trust is lost.

10. *Be consistent*

This last guideline is somewhat removed from the others. Consistency is a strange concept, because a lot of people think it's harder than it is. They get the term confused with being *constant*.

Consistency doesn't mean you're not allowed to have bad days as well as good days, and doesn't mean that you are supposed to turn up at work every day with a spring in your step and full of enthusiasm for every little project. Life just isn't like that! Nor does it mean that you have to follow the same routines consistently each day or only have favourite issues that are always examined at particular times. Sometimes it's good to keep followers guessing a bit, because it tends to keep people interested and enthusiastic for challenge.

Consistency doesn't necessarily mean consistency of behaviour; it means consistency of expectation, consistency of standards, consistency in culture and consistency in attitude. No one can be expected to behave consistently in all weathers, in all circumstances; as the saying goes, 'It just ain't natural'. Followers need to understand that and learn to read a leader's moods as leaders must learn to judge their followers' moods. This is not carte blanche for aspiring leaders to indulge their moods.

Consistency doesn't necessarily mean consistency of behaviour or style so much as consistency of expectation and performance standards.

Peter: I worked for a man once who had a fairly difficult personality on occasions and I was listening to some juniors one lunchtime declaiming how they learned to watch the boss's moods and they only took things to him when he was in a good mood. There was hearty general agreement that he was inconsistent. I had never found him so; difficult yes, inconsistent no.

I explained this to the juniors but they wouldn't agree. Sometimes he would knock a proposal back out of hand; on others he would spend more time and explain things. His message was consistent but his method of delivery varied. Did he demand high standards? Yes! Sometimes they were so high he made them do the whole proposal again from scratch. That's where he was so inconsistent!

It took a while for it to dawn on them that they were the inconsistent ones. Their performance was very erratic, as is often the case with juniors. Sometimes it would be so bad he made them start over again and then he got angry. At other times they were nearly there and he was happier with their performance. He never wavered in his expectations and in my view he was a model of consistency.

Most workers recognise consistency and appreciate it, even if it seems a little hard at times. What people need to understand is that a leader would need to be super-human to pick up every issue every time and the overlooking of something one day, or even one week, is not a sign of inconsistency. It may be a sign of tiredness or preoccupation with other things.

John: *I can recall pointing out to an individual the difficulties his inconsistencies were causing—one day it would be cost cutting, the next day cost was no problem; at times there was not enough fun, at other times people were being too frivolous. His response to my attempt to draw to his attention the problems his lack of consistency was causing was his claim that his inconsistency was consistent!*

One of the difficulties relating to consistency is making sure that you are *seen* to be consistent. It would be unnatural for leaders not to be drawn to some followers more than others and vice versa. While having favourites is not advised and showing favouritism is to be avoided, there will always be a difference between one worker and another, both in performance and personality, and a leader's attitude or treatment of each worker will need to be very sensitively handled. Because you like somebody, that does not entitle them to special treatment; however it also doesn't mean that you should hide the fact.

Consistency takes a great deal of moral courage and a strong commitment to team and task. Leaders must be conscious of their own commitment all the time. That means being in constant contact with the task and team—and that can't be done from a position of isolation. In a later chapter we will briefly touch on personality issues and how it is incumbent on a leader to really know his or her own personality and the personality of followers.

The last aspect of consistency is keeping one's eye on the main game and not being sidetracked by irrelevancy or taking expedient short-term measures because that will momentarily increase popularity or whatever. The chickens will always come home to roost.

> A consistent leader never loses sight of the main game.

THE 'MAIN GAME'

One could go on ad infinitum about the dangers of isolation between leader and led. Unfortunately, there is a lot of lip-service paid to the issue, in both business and at the political level. At both levels there is repeated evidence of squeaky doors getting the most oil and attention, and minority groups at a political level and minority trouble makers at an industrial level hijacking the agenda. Leaders then tend to manage by crisis, because their eyes are off the 'main game'. They cease to concentrate on the long-term important things and they can lose touch with the vast majority of the constituency or the workforce.

Leaders may well be surprised at workers' or constituents' feelings on certain issues if they truly keep in touch. They may even feel more secure in the directions they take and not be put off by sycophantic advisers.

There is no doubt, though, that it is also incumbent upon workers to let their leaders know when they are feeling isolated and there needs to be a foolproof system for that. This is also where the self-discipline of PowerSharing comes in—self-regulation in accordance with established procedures and reliance on the knowledge that absolute honesty flows both ways. That requires a lot of training and development on both sides.

Key concepts

- Isolation is a prelude to alienation.
- Isolation goes hand in glove with centralisation, large staffs and galloping bureaucracy.
- Isolation is becoming endemic with moves towards centralisation of power and growing concentration on technology.
- Specialist staff and advisers can isolate a leader from followers.
- People can inure themselves from the views of others by virtue of their social contacts.
- Ambition should not be confused with vision.
- In some organisations *getting on* and *getting the job done* are mutually exclusive.
- Leaders must learn to see issues through the eyes of other stakeholders.
- Isolation can be best avoided by adherence to ten principles. They are:
  - *Beware the trappings of office.*
  - *Share the pain and the gain.*
  - *Empathise with followers.*
  - *Use specialist staff as resources, not as directors.*
  - *No reward without achievement.*
  - *No advancement without responsibility.*
  - *Do not over-regulate.*
  - *Match actions to words.*
  - *Lead by example.*
  - *Be consistent.*

Guide, develop and protect your followers

A leader's attention to the three functional circles demands as clear a concentration on the development needs of followers, both as individuals and as a group, as it requires a concentration on the task. Development is more than just keeping their interests at heart. That presupposes a static view of followers' needs; we covered that issue in Chapter 5. In this chapter we need to take a more dynamic view of followers' needs.

It has been mentioned time and again throughout the book that people are a leader's ultimate resource. So it stands to reason that it is people who must be maintained above all else. This also means keeping them from harm's way. That can be a tall order. Most younger leader aspirants at some time in their lives seem to regard it as necessary to get into trouble; it seems like a rite of passage of some sort. But we aren't just talking about risk taking. We are suggesting that people should be encouraged to take risks without the ever present possibility of incurring the wrath of someone much further up the corporate ladder. This often means that leaders have to interpose between their own superiors and their subordinates.

To perform any function or complete any job a follower or worker needs skills, confidence and motivation. The three are closely related. The skills require a commitment to training, the confidence requires skills and motivation, and motivation depends on a variety of factors including skills, environment, confidence, challenge and reward.

Clearly, what we are talking about is some form of *situational leadership* as outlined in the commercial package of that name.[1] We do not need to dwell on this concept, because there are obviously plenty of materials around that give far better detail than we can hope to give in a portion of one chapter. However, even prior to the developments needed for the foregoing, it is necessary that any follower has an understanding of what will be expected of him or her. We will therefore examine the needs under the headings *expectations*, *environment*, *motivation* and *training*.

EXPECTATIONS

Let us return to the beginning of the leadership story and assume that a new person has joined your team. What does that person bring to the team and what does that person need from the team; more to the point, whose responsibility is it to provide it? The person may well be highly qualified but it is most unlikely that the skills he or she has learned will allow him or her to complete his or her allotted task without assistance. Therefore, most professions provide some form of on the job training (OJT), such as internship for medical practitioners or clerkships for lawyers.

Who provides? As we learned in a previous chapter, it should be a process of mutual obligation. There should be a clear understanding that whatever qualifications a person has when they are chosen for a job, any special extra skills that the person needs are the responsibility of the leader to impart—not necessarily personally, but to ensure they are imparted. We will cover that in more detail later.

It may well be that a leader doesn't have the skills the follower requires. In fact, that will be the case as often as not. But a leader will and must have expectations of the job and it is up to the leader to see that the person doing the job is fully equipped to come up to expectations. If you are that aspiring leader that entails on your part:

1. enough knowledge of the job or task allocated to know the results wanted;
2. establishing the parameters of optimum performance, clarifying how you see the role in relation to other jobs, and making sure your subordinate understands and agrees with expectations.

1. *Enough knowledge of the task to know the results you want*

This often unnecessarily causes a lot of misunderstanding. It's that misunderstanding that causes so much angst when it comes to the acceptance of responsibility and the inability to delegate. No one can possibly know the intricacies of a subordinate's job unless they have been promoted from it themselves. This is actually unrealistic. However, the answer is really quite simple. Take our cars, for instance. We know what we expect from a car and we certainly know if it's not performing, even though we don't know how to tune today's complicated car engines. However, we know the results we want.

> A leader may not be able to carry out a task, but must know what results to expect.

The same is the case with a subordinate's role. That also leads to the second point, relating to optimum performance.

2. *Establish the parameters of optimum performance, clarifying the role in relation to others and ensuring subordinates are in agreement with expectations*

We can tell a mechanic how well we want the car to run or how badly it's going. We leave him or her to fix it and we don't interfere—after all, we can't. However, we'll find another mechanic if it doesn't work! The same goes for a work task.

The whole point is, you must know what you want and the difficulties of the task—*and so must your subordinate*. This involves both leader and subordinate being clear of the impact others' outcomes and POIs will have on the outcome of the particular subordinate in question. Additionally, any follower is entitled to have a full range of input into expectations surrounding the outcomes for which they are responsible. While this doesn't have to be in the form of a contract, there needs to be an agreed system for discussion.

While slavish adherence to appraisal systems can have a negative impact, there is no doubt that such things as expectations and agreed optimum performance levels, are best imparted during appraisal and review discussions. However, this must occur at the beginning of an appraisal period, not after the horse has bolted—as happens in many instances.

A *performance appraisal* or *performance review* system is also a good way to establish how you see the task or role in relation to other jobs, and to make sure your subordinate understands and is comfortable with that. A well-conducted review is one of the few activities where *the process is just as important as the outcome*.

It will be of assistance to examine the major characteristics of a good system.

PERFORMANCE APPRAISAL AND REVIEW SYSTEMS

A system should probably have room for, and should at least lead to discussions surrounding, the following points:

- the *agreed* objectives of the past period in review with room for sub-objectives and results and the relationship of the objectives to the mission;
- the previously *agreed* objectives not reached and the reasons;
- the previously *agreed* objectives to be carried forward to the next period;
- the *agreed* new objectives for the next period, the sub-objectives and the impact on others laterally;
- others' objectives as they bear on the reviewee's tasks;
- agreement on the extra skills needed and the training and development to reach objectives;
- agreement on the above for reviewee's subordinates;
- agreement on personal developmental objectives related to their career goals;
- agreement on the financial and other resources needed.

A good performance appraisal and review is primarily for development rather than for promotion and although the purists would frown on their use in salary review they are regularly used as such in many organisations with little observed ill effect. It is *not* a disciplinary document, and a development system is an excellent leadership tool.

While the above represents only one possibility, it gives an indication as to how we can formalise and record expectations, achievements and relationships to others' jobs. As we said, the *process* is as important as the *outcome*. However, it is important that it be maintained as a tool with outcomes, because often a process can capture an event and the outcome must further organisational as well as personal objectives. Slavish adherence to objectives only can be counter-productive. It is one of the criticisms the great Dr Deming of total quality management fame had of management by objectives.

> In any appraisal system the process of agreement is as important as the result. And the result must have the effect of making obvious all a leader's expectations.

Not every worker is at a level where a detailed individual appraisal is either necessary or feasible. In fact, there are situations where some form of team appraisal can be conducted whereby the leader uses the process to facilitate the setting of agreed team or group goals.

> A leader creates a strategic environment, knows the results wanted, conveys that to the subordinate(s) and makes clear the impact of one task on another. He or she ensures the subordinate(s) understands and shares the implications and conditions to enable the achievement of optimum results.

THE ENVIRONMENT

Subordinates not only have a right to know what is expected of them, they have a right to an environment in the workplace that will optimise their performance. We recognise that a coalminer should not expect to have access to a personal mobile phone (although for safety reasons it wouldn't be a bad idea) or a carpeted work room. That's not what we mean by environment. We mean the conditions and the working relationships.

This involves:

1. *An environment of trust.*
2. *Stable working conditions.*
3. *Clear procedures.*
4. *Freedom from interference.*
5. *Attention to personal needs that may distract from performance.*
6. *Understanding subordinate's temperament.*
7. *Recognition of developmental and career needs external to the task.*
8. *The technical skills and attributes needed for the job.*
9. *Ensuring workers accept their own personal limitations.*

The conditions include the environment, the standard of training, motivation and readiness of the subordinate(s); in fact, anything that affects the personal motivation of the subordinate or follower at a given time. It is a leader's job to ensure those conditions are right.

1. *Environment of trust*

This is the cornerstone of all group activity. At the risk of being repetitive, it is a two-way process that transcends differences in style, personality, background, skills, or even values. Trust is very simple, but paradoxically it is also the most difficult quality to obtain and retain. It cannot be mandated, it can only be earned. Conversely, a leader needs to assume a position of trust in others and that will often take a degree of moral courage.

2. *Stable working conditions*

Anything in the environment or in the conditions of work which may impact on a job's performance must be taken into account. And if they impact negatively, efforts must be made to reduce the effect.

3. *Clear procedures*

This issue has arisen in nearly every chapter so far. The main concern is that people know what is expected of their behaviour and routine (as opposed to their results, which we covered earlier). This also includes matters relating to what we used to call 'good order and discipline'. However, when one uses the word 'discipline' it can conjure up visions of threat and punishment. 'Good order' is a better term. Understanding of this term seems to happen when you mention things such as policies relating to standards of behaviour, sexual harassment, punctuality, safety or financial propriety, because no responsible person could object to them as part of good order (discipline).

It is incumbent on a leader to ensure that followers are not only aware of those expectations, but also of the consequences of particular behaviour.

4. *Freedom from interference*

We have already dealt in detail with freedom from interference in the context of delegation. But interference is a fairly wide issue and includes within it matters relating to loyalty. Our contention is that a leader must protect subordinates from external interference and owes a debt of loyalty downwards—not exclusively, but predominantly. It is as a follower that one returns a debt of loyalty upwards. An individual in a leadership role whose main focus of loyalty is upwards is either foolish or simply looking after their own interests; an individual whose main focus of loyalty is downwards, is a leader.

A leader's primary loyalty should be directed downwards.

It would be so easy if as a leader all you ever had to do was look downwards, because you were protected as a follower by your own leader protecting your rear. It is easier to make a statement in this regard than to practise it, human nature being what it is. This principle relies on 'character'; it simplifies leadership enormously if it is properly understood and followed. It's a very old principle that you can't expect loyalty if you don't give loyalty yourself. Similarly, it is difficult to expect to have followers if you personally never experienced following.

By implication, a leader gives loyalty to everyone in his or her team and the team members laterally to each other. But a leader may also be part of a larger team and, as a principle, a team member must be protected by a leader from the predations of a leader's peers and/or superiors. This means that a good leader needs to be conscious and sympathetic to the need of members of his or her team to have internal loyalty to each other. Team members must never be put in a position where they are asked to compromise their loyalty to each other.

5. *Attention to personal needs*

This was covered in Chapter 5, but here we are referring to something more than sympathy at a bereavement, or consciousness of personal difficulties. We mean attention to personal development needs. For example, someone is a marketing expert, but may be painfully shy or insufficiently assertive. Is that a leader's responsibility? Yes, if it impacts on a role. There are two issues here. The first is to ensure that people are given the necessary training and support to enable them to carry out their duties or tasks. The second is where the leader ensures that nobody is given a task or responsibility for which they may not ultimately be suited.

Even if it isn't immediately relevant it may be in the best interests of both parties for a leader to accept responsibility for some of these matters. An example is in the arranging of training for women who work late at night in the art of self-defence. That could be a valid responsibility and may have an effect on teamwork, cohesion, morale and trust, but have nothing explicit to do with the work task.

6. *Understanding subordinates' temperaments*

This primarily means to recognise and read the moods of individuals. People have mood swings and they may not be as capable of performing as well on the same task on one day as on the previous day. It may be tiredness, boredom, exhaustion (related or not to the task), difficulties at home, bad biorhythms or just plain personality clashes that bring about emotional changes.

One of the incorrect assumptions often made with theoretical leadership is that situation A requires leadership approach B. This is all very well in theory, but the reality can be quite different depending on the mood or temperament of the people in situation A. The reality is that performances will often vary from day to day. Additionally, each person is an individual and leadership approach B, while working with Fred, may not work with Frank. A good leader will be cognisant of the differences between and within individuals and will adjust his or her style accordingly.

All too often we see a boss with expectations that a subordinate will adjust to the boss's temperament totally. A good leader will see this from a different perspective—that's the difference between bosses and leaders.

> A leader needs to recognise nuances in followers and be alert
> to changes in performance.

---

7. *Recognition of developmental and career needs external to the task*

This means professional betterment. Those with certain potential, and even those without, are singled out to improve themselves professionally.

The improvement may not be necessary for successful completion of tasks or objectives in the current role, but it is necessary for the further promotion of the person either in or out of the organisation.

Presumably, someone may be encouraged to do postgraduate engineering work or medical work or be encouraged to go on to an MBA, or whatever is appropriate. This is identified during an appraisal or review session and the step is agreed. It may or may not be at the organisation's expense but an outcome is agreed, that is, what happens after the person has qualified. Any personal development that enhances an individual's character will eventually impact positively on the organisation—a sort of reap and sow mentality. But there have to be limits.

These days when an organisation cannot guarantee people employment, it does have an obligation to assist employees to remain *employable*. While this is not universally accepted, the more enlightened organisations and leaders see it as their responsibility. This all presupposes an openness that may lead to a recognition that the worker or follower may eventually seek work elsewhere. How do you convince leaders that that's a good idea? Does it make sense to employ unwilling workers? What sort of message does it send to the willing workers? What happened to openness and trust?

Limiting followers' career options can be counter-productive.

When one door closes another opens. A good leader in a good organisation could do worse than sending a lot of successes into the world outside and keeping a larger number of committed, focused employees.

It also gets back to something we have previously alluded to. If a leader does what we are saying here and actually links work objectives to personal ambition and career objectives, then there will be less of a gap between career success and achieving work goals. So 'getting ahead' in an organisation will require the same performance as 'getting the job done'.

You can't separate the issues as easily as some people think. They are not discrete in that a person can have a personal need that is entirely unrelated to a development or career need. A person must be treated holistically, because one issue bears on another. If a person is a liar or regularly cheats on his or her husband or wife, then you can be sure that he or she will be tempted in the same way in a professional sense. There is no intention to moralise, but if you were hiring a person in an area of executive responsibility then you would want to know a little about how he or she leads his or her private life. So if you are looking for somebody who is going to be handling money, then scrupulous honesty in all facets of life would be a prerequisite.

A person's social and recreational behaviour will reflect work behaviour.

---

8. *The technical skills needed for the job*

This is fairly self-evident. Some aspects of this concept are still handled very badly though, mainly because often a manager is not aware of the skills required in a job and therefore has unreal expectations of an employee. A lot of this occurs at the point of recruitment where a job description is published and an appointment made which turns out to be a failure because management did not know what it really wanted.

Often a requirement will also change. Computers have made an enormous difference to the way things are done and, clearly, as new programs are introduced new skills are needed. In both the foregoing instances it is incumbent on the employer to have the employee trained up to the appropriate level. Where it becomes evident that a skill is beyond someone, or retraining is impractical, redundancy may be called for.

Redundancy requires special compassion and its likelihood or possibility should be signalled well in advance. In order to be just, any sort of redundancy should not only be accompanied by a generous cash severance but also by a proper out-placement and retraining or re-settlement program. Anything less is a recipe for industrial trouble and a demoralised workforce.

9. *Recognition of personal limitations*

This implies a recognition by both leader and led.

Peter: I had a man working for me once who was very streetwise and quite articulate. Because he impressed everybody with his confidence, he developed an inflated opinion of his own ability.

It also took me a while to realise the situation and so I sent him on all sorts of professional and developmental courses, all to no avail. Some people can never learn—there are none so blind as those who will not see.

There are also intellectual limits, which we can't do anything about. However, most people are responsive to motivation and if they aren't, maybe you just have to 'let them go', to use a euphemism.

MOTIVATION—REWARD AND PUNISHMENT

There are two aspects of motivation that need some further detailed explanation in addition to what was said in Chapter 7, and they are the effects of reward or punishment. One is positive and the other is negative, but they are both consequential upon a behaviour. Of the two, positive motivation is far more effective.

Positive reinforcement—reward

Positive reinforcement or reward is always more effective. Reward can be monetary; it can be in terms of conditions or promotion; it can be in the form of more responsibility or challenge; or it can be praise or public acknowledgment or whatever motivates each individual. Some guidelines are:

Praise publicly. Don't just let the recipient of the praise know. Let his or her colleagues know and inform superiors if it seems appropriate. Make the acknowledgment publicly if you can.

Praise in writing. Acknowledge good work on paper. It only needs two or three lines in a note written to the person. Or it can be an acknowledgment in the newsletter if there is one, or even on a bulletin board.

Acknowledge the process, result and performer. It's not only important that the person receive acknowledgment but that colleagues know what was achieved and how it was achieved. Imagine recommending someone for an award simply by saying 'so and so is an altogether splendid person'. It is a ridiculous statement. You are required to dwell on what was done, how well it was done and how often it was done.

Don't single people out from a team. While in a football match best players may be able to be singled out, even that is not always a good practice. When a team performs well or beyond the optimum the whole team should share in the acknowledgment. If someone among them has been performing less than adequately, both the individual and the team know who it is. If someone has been outstanding, they should only be singled out in the context of the team.

Never make acknowledgment conditional. This is straightforward bribery. 'If you keep going like this you will get a pay rise.' A corollary to that is the next point.

Don't use acknowledgment as a benchmark. This is the old, 'Now that you know you can do it, let's see you do it all the time', or 'See how Fred does it, that's how I want you all to do it'.

Of course, it is appropriate to set benchmarks of optimum performance; that's expected. But you should never use an *outstanding* performance as a benchmark. You can use it as a model. People can give the optimum for long periods, but the maximum cannot be sustained indefinitely.

> Don't use *outstanding* performance as a benchmark for others, use it as a model.

Don't have favourites—people, processes or results. This is self-explanatory.

Don't overdo acknowledgment. This is a real trap. It has the effect of trivialising performance so that people expect praise for an ordinary performance. A very well-known organisation had come to a stage some years ago where unless one received an 'outstanding' report it meant one had failed.

> Don't trivialise performance with excessive praise.

Negative reinforcement—reprimand and remediation

When reprimanding, almost the direct opposite applies, but there are some significant differences:

Reprimand in private. When someone has turned in a less than satisfactory performance or hasn't met objectives, it is more than likely that most people close to the action will know. There is no need to advertise it further. In fact, the individual can often be so acutely sensitive and embarrassed that it's hardly necessary to issue a reprimand. Sometimes it might be necessary to let others know by simply making a statement to the effect that the matter has been dealt with and is now concluded. Don't inform superiors unless there is some procedural or legal remedial requirement.

Do not commit a reprimand to writing, unless it is part of a formal disciplinary process. If the organisation has a procedural system that requires consistent under-performers to be warned and monitored, then committing the reprimand to paper may be a requirement. If a person is consistently making the same mistake or is under-performing then it may be necessary to keep a record. For routine or casual misdemeanours keeping records is unnecessary, time-consuming and frankly unfair.

Concentrate on the behaviour or result, not on the person. Nothing is more conducive to resentment or self-image problems than calling someone an idiot or some other derogatory name. Never indulge in character assassination or name calling. Simply dwell on the behaviour, the results, or the inadequate processes, not on the person. It has been a saying in leadership circles for many years that sometimes it may be necessary to 'humble' someone—it is *never* acceptable to 'humiliate' them; it takes away their dignity. Calling someone an 'idiot' is humiliating; suggesting that their outcome performance is unsatisfactory is humbling.

> *Humbling* someone can be good for their soul, *humiliating* them is good for nothing.

Try to avoid group chastisement. If a group or a team has failed, let them know but determine at what point the failure occurred and address that issue separately. Certainly, group punishment is a 'no-no', as we said earlier. Accordingly, we have to be careful about group chastisement, even if it means taking aside known good performers and explaining things to them.

Chastise only when an agreed expectation has not been met. Do not hold people responsible for something that may not be their responsibility. It is unjust to reprimand someone for failing to meet an expectation that was not agreed to. This doesn't mean that every single little thing is to be the subject of an agreement or discussion. The behaviour of both leader and led has to be tempered with commonsense; it means that you shouldn't reprimand someone for something that they wouldn't reasonably be aware of.

Reprimand immediately. This is self-explanatory. Don't leave a reprimand until the end of the year or until appraisal time or when you feel braver or you feel the time is better. Make corrections as soon as the fault is detected.

Never, never chastise for initiative. PowerSharing requires an acceptance of mistakes made in good faith. You should point out the mistake as a means of training, but it should never be associated with any sort of sanction.

There are not a lot of legal sanctions you have if retraining, counselling or reprimanding don't work. Some organisations can remove privileges, reduce overtime, dock pay for lack of punctuality or absenteeism—even fines are legal in some cases—but they are all fraught with employee relations implications. Still, if there are proper contractual procedures there, they can be used. And if all that fails, dismissal is an option.

Dismissal

Dismissal should only be carried out if the right procedures are followed, expectations and consequences are clearly known beforehand, and the objectives set have all the characteristics as outlined in Chapter 4. Any sanction that is used leading to dismissal should be:

- *Dispassionate.* Without fear or favour.
- *Compassionate.* Made with the consequences in mind, working conditions and the effect on others taken into account, *and the transgressor's story heard*.
- *Swift.* As soon as possible after the misdemeanour or behaviour but not until the subordinate has been heard.
- *Generous.* All statutory payments made immediately available, together with pay in lieu of notice, always erring on the side of the subordinate.
- *According to guidelines.* This means that there must *be* guidelines. Anything less would be unfair.
- *Only as a result of a clear inadequacy.* Not as a result of personality or convenience or lack of adequate training or counselling.

Of course, there must be times and instances where dismissal should be immediate—for breaking the law, for proven behavioural shortcomings and so on. Such things as duty of fidelity are important. The important point is that everyone must be aware for both legal and moral reasons what constitutes a transgression, particularly a serious transgression.

> An organisation's procedures must cover those behaviours that would be regarded as transgressions.

TRAINING
Formal training

It will not hurt to reiterate here the responsibilities a leader has for training subordinates, though these responsibilities have already been covered to some degree under the headings of *expectations* and *environment*.

There are two inviolable principles:

- When a person is employed with particular skills and qualifications, or when new equipment, new materials, new products or new procedures are introduced to an existing role, then a large or small gap will occur between a worker or subordinate's skill and the expectations of the outcomes for the job. *The training of the person in the skills needed to fill that gap is the full responsibility of the employer or leader.*

- If a worker cannot be retrained or if the newly-arrived worker is found not to have the entry skills required through no fault of their own, then it is incumbent upon a leader to ensure that the worker remains employable and is helped upon a different career either within the organisation or elsewhere.

Any leader must have a clear picture of skills required and training within the organisation, for organisational work remains the leader's responsibility. That training can take the form of OJT, as we mentioned earlier, or it may mean formal training on- or off-site, although clearly on-site training is desirable.

As well as training for the role in the particular position, which is clearly a leader's responsibility, is there a responsibility for a leader to train people who may eventually take their expertise elsewhere? We would say yes. After all, any training will make an employee more marketable elsewhere and training in matters outside their role will make them a more complete person. But the person must also take some responsibility themselves.

In these days of the flatter structure, people will move sideways many times in a working life and multi-skilling at all levels is an idea whose time has come. However, there will come a time when sideways moves are no longer feasible for a person and the only way up the corporate ladder in a flat organisation is to change the corporation the person is working in.

Career paths used to be four-lane highways along which you could move at speed; in the future they could well be dirt tracks along which you have to crawl. Leaders will find that in the future they will need to offer all forms of formal training to subordinates, not only to keep them up-to-date but also to keep them motivated. This may well entail an acceptance that you are training people to move out!

Informal training

Mentoring

Earlier in the chapter we briefly mentioned the idea of mentoring as a means of development. Mentoring is another word for coaching. Coaching is part of the training and development process and is as much a leader's responsibility as any part of the management role. When a young or newly joined person arrives in an organisation there is an immediate expectation of induction to enable the newcomer to understand the procedures and culture of the organisation. But a formal induction process has a finite time frame and sooner or later the newcomer is expected to perform.

There are, however, any number of practical skills and measures which are peculiar to a job or a role or career that cannot be learned at a learning institution. Leadership is one such skill! A person needs a coach or patron over an extended period, sometimes years, to help them learn 'the trade'. A mentor is even appropriate at senior level and can come from outside an organisation. The purpose is the same—to learn 'the trade'.

This is also an idea whose time has come in industry, both from the point of view of leader mentoring as well as peer mentoring. The concept of leader as teacher may be novel in some industrial settings but it certainly isn't or shouldn't be novel to anyone who has been a parent or seen how successful parenting works.

Years ago when a young man joined one military college with which we are familiar, he entered into an incredibly steep learning curve in which he needed enormous support to survive. Eighteen hour days were not uncommon for months on end in the early stages of training.

But he was not left to survive alone. Apart from peer support, which became automatic, a 'lord and master' was allocated to him whose role in life was to teach him how to survive; how to short-cut, how to clean, polish, arrange, move quickly, study and cope with the hundred and one cultural traditions and other nonsense which accompany that sort of life. For the first month any minor infractions that brought a sanction or a drill or a demerit were allocated to the lord and master. As the cadet learned, so gradually the process of support was withdrawn but the 'lord and master' was nevertheless available for the whole of the first year if warranted.

The cadet also had a 'father' from a senior class who was more of an emotional support to whom the new cadet was allowed to relate on a more personal first-name basis. The father offered advice on relationships, support in the case of homesickness and general friendship from a position of some seasoned experience. Traditionally, the father took no part in, and even tried to protect the cadet from the worst excesses of the bullying or bastardisation system.

The cadet also had a 'grandfather' who was a much more senior cadet, normally in his graduation year, who became a sort of distant but benevolent patron. On top of that there was a commissioned officer who was the company commander, but who came to be called a guidance officer.

None of these people were trained counsellors, they were mentors in the truest sense of the word, and by contact with these people, the cadet learned informally about relationships, loyalty, duty, systems, customs and a host of other things during very trying adolescent years. Even things like regular contact with parents, siblings and ex-schoolfriends were dealt with and taken very seriously.

One could no doubt mount a very reasonable argument about the value of some of the things that were taught at such a college, but there could hardly be a valid argument about the way the systems and values were imparted. Many of the mentor and peer relationships created then have stood the test of time and have lasted over sixty years.

When, after graduation four years later, the young officer joined a unit he was offered the same sort of support, such as senior peer support and more formal induction support. Apart from the teaching role of the immediate superiors, there was the extremely important role taken by the more experienced subordinate who was expected to help the young officer. The idea of old hand as mentor has been well covered by Hollywood, at least conceptually if not accurately. The experienced subordinate as mentor is very necessary in many professions and invariably provides a more rounded and humane leader in the long run.

Leaders have two roles in the mentoring process: first, as mentors themselves; and second, to ensure that a system of mentoring is available through others to all levels. Mentoring doesn't finish at the completion of induction but, as with everything else, it needs to have an agreed finishing time initiated by the *mentee* (to coin a phrase).

As we said, no one who has ever been a parent will baulk at the idea of mentoring; after all, it is such a process we use as we introduce our children to the wading pool, to the bicycle or to the roller blades. As in all situations, some learn fast, some are slower and need more patience and guidance. We are not suggesting a system of paternalistic oversight, and mentoring has to be discreet and voluntarily entered into by both parties.

Mentoring can be sought internally and externally. A growing number of people seek external mentors from business associates and from their own networks of like business acquaintances. Associations and societies of various types actually can provide significant mentoring; many are formed with that aim in mind and do provide another formal and informal avenue of development. The mentoring to which we are alluding, though, is part of a leader's responsibility, is normally internal, and can come from peers, seniors and often from experienced subordinates. It shouldn't be open-ended, but it must complete what it sets out to do.

Mentors should be chosen carefully and where possible matched by personality to the person they are coaching. Sometimes a mentor gets as much out of the extra responsibility as does the *mentee*. Anyone who has read *Tom Brown's Schooldays* will remember the great value to Tom of the extra responsibility given to him. Before a mentor is appointed, a leader needs to satisfy himself or herself that the appointed mentor shares the values of the leader and the organisation.

Mentor what?

What does a mentor impart? Anything and everything of relevance and value in both a career and personal sense. To this end it is not unusual to have mentors who are experts at particular issues and who fill that role while those issues are addressed. But it is generally desirable to have the same mentor throughout the training period.

It is not the intent of the authors to become apologists for *Situational Leadership 2,* but if one takes the modus operandi of *SL2,* which deals generally with the skills needed for the job and translates it to other areas, we can see that we have a complete picture of mentoring.

The leader, or the leader's representative as mentor depending on the level, will introduce the newcomer to the organisation's culture, the accepted and established procedures and the regulations. The mentor will explain the performance standards expected by the boss and help in the first few projects. He or she will help to introduce social contacts in the work environment. He or she will help with personal and work-related objectives and even in establishing career goals and expectations. Altogether the mentor will help the recently-joined worker or follower towards the process of self-mastery, which we will cover in the next chapter.

Mentoring requires enormous trust on one hand and no small sacrifice on the other. Both roles require the building of character, because one has to trust in the character of another as well as their competence.

It is also incumbent on a leader to develop a subordinate's character at the same time as developing their competence. Hopefully we have given some reasons why and some suggestions how. The next chapter relates to the building of one's character as a leader.

She was a great mentor she taught me all about penalty rates, overtime, sick leave, pay rates, sexual harassment, discrimination, shopping places, lunch spots, introduced me to the shop steward, and told me how to contact the IR tribunal. Next month I'm going to start learning about my job

Key concepts

- Development includes; formation, training, discipline, reward and punishment.
- Responsibility for worker's skill development for the task lies with the leader.
- Workers need not only competence in skills but motivation and confidence. The leader is responsible for creating the right environment for skill, confidence and motivation to develop.
- All of the above can be assisted greatly by the use of an adequate performance appraisal and review system.
- When procedures are automatic, agreed and understood there can still be great challenge and freedom of action.
- One of the aims of subordinate development must be to equate personal ambition with achieving work goals, that is, *career progress equals achieving the goals of the task and job.*
- Personal habits and life will clearly relate to work habits.
- Personal development of subordinates must therefore be very important to a leader.
- Recognition of one's own and subordinates' limitations is essential.
- Understanding when and how to use praise and reprimand is essential.
- Know when to let people 'go'.
- A good leader will encourage formal and informal mentoring systems.

CHAPTER 10
Tenth Precept

Know yourself!

Before we can begin to know and understand others—a prerequisite for any leader—it is essential for us to know and understand ourselves. Commensurate with this is the necessity to accept ourselves as we really are. Sometimes this may be difficult; there may be aspects of our personality or even character that we may not like. While it may be possible to change some character traits, it is not possible to 'change' personality.

Who we are is what we are.

This doesn't mean that having found out who we are, we cannot change. We can modify our behaviour deliberately, or—as was mentioned earlier—change the paradigm we are living in. The most important thing to recognise, however, is that leadership doesn't depend on being an introvert or an extravert (something some motivationists may have difficulty with), or having a sense of humour (although in some cases it might help). Being a leader means being true to who we are. Followers will very quickly see through a fraud or someone who doesn't know who they are.

It is no coincidence that the concept of self-knowledge is generations old and, indeed, the quotation 'Know thyself' was inscribed at the site of the Delphic oracle in ancient Greece. We learned in previous chapters that followers' trust of a leader is based on both competence and character. Essentially, this chapter is about character, and the timelessness of this quality is demonstrated in a quotation from Shakespeare's *Hamlet* in a short piece of advice Pollonius gave to his son Laertes as he was about to depart the country for foreign lands:

> *And these few precepts in thy memory*
> *Look thou character. Give thy thoughts no tongue,*
> *Nor any unproportioned thought his act.*
> *Be thou familiar but by no means vulgar.*
> *Beware*
> *Of entrance to a quarrel; but, being in,*
> *Bear't that th'opposed may beware of thee.*
> *Give every man thy ear, but few thy voice,*
> *Take each man's censure but reserve thy*
> *judgement.*
> *This above all—to thine own self be true,*
> *And it must follow, as the night the day,*
> *Thou can'st not be false to any man.*
>
> *(Extract of Pollonius's advice to Laertes—Hamlet, Act I, Scene 3)*

Every word of the quotation is as valid today as it was four hundred years ago and in fact is surprisingly apt for today's generation.

FINDING THE REAL PERSON

Pollonius's lecture is a real lesson in life, as was much of Shakespeare's work. 'Develop strength of character, keep your own counsel, think before acting, develop the common touch but never lose your dignity, don't pick fights but stick to your guns, take advice but don't give it, seek to understand others, accept criticism but don't offer it, finally— know yourself and live by your principles.' The most important piece of advice and one that is strongly stressed is to be true to yourself. To do that you need to know who that self is.

In the Introduction we spoke of the '*does*', now we speak of the '*is*'. Both sum up the concept that no matter how accomplished and successful a person may be, who he or she '*is*' is just as important as what he or she does or has done.

Quite often in our more introspective moments many of us dwell on those things about ourselves that we are not happy with. Often, of course, they are not obvious to others and we learn to live with them. But sometimes others see them only too readily when we either don't or refuse to see them ourselves.

In recent times there seems to have been an increase in people's desire to gain a better insight into themselves. All sorts of self-development programs began to appear in the last few decades, especially in the 1970s. Many of these programs suggested that the real problem with relationships lay in people not coming to grips with their own selves so that in a marriage, for instance, there were two lies living together. People even began taking a renewed interest in such old theories as the Hippocratic personality styles.

One such development suggests that from childhood we learn to behave in ways that will make us more acceptable to others and enable us to get our way. This pattern of behaviour becomes a mask that we wear all the time, even when it is inappropriate or we don't feel like who we are supposed to be. An American called John Powell, who was an expert in the human relationship field, wrote a series of books on just that theme. Though the books had a religious flavour, the psychological reasoning was undeniable. One such reasoning suggests that we hide the real self because it's 'all I've got and you may not like it'. So we go on trying to be someone else.[1]

But the truth will come out. Everyone's mask or predominant behaviour is more likely to be an exaggerated caricature of who we are. The real person is hidden behind this behavioural mask, and often stays there without ever emerging. The mask might represent who they are most of the time. We are all aware of the duck comparison: calm as can be on the surface and paddling like mad underneath.

For instance, if I am a fairly competent and confident person I will tend to behave like that all the time, even when I'm feeling anything but confident under the surface. That behaviour is fine as long as I recognise it and am prepared to let go at crucial times. The revelation would surely be a sign of confidence in a confidant(e) and would lead to great trust.

SELF-CONTROL

The first thing that recognising a mask will teach us is that we can decide to act in a certain way despite how we are feeling at any particular time. Now, if you look at the positive side of that, it is very liberating. We no longer have to be victims of our emotions. You may feel bad, as we said in a previous chapter, but you can recognise it and take a rational decision not to be dictated to by those feelings. A lot of positive thinking is based on that concept.

*Of course I know who the real me is. If I'm **NOT** really me then I'm having great fun with somebody else's wife.*

This also represents a first step on the way to taking control of yourself and being prepared to readily change or modify behaviour. The real problem can lie in an environment when someone adopts an inappropriate behaviour to cover up an inadequacy—like someone who becomes a bully to cover up a basic insecurity. Robert E. Lee said, 'I cannot trust a man to control others who cannot control himself'. And to control yourself, you must have a good idea of who you are.

> The first step in self-control is self-recognition.

Self-recognition would also clearly put someone in charge of his or her own destiny. If we learn to subordinate an impulse or a feeling to a seemingly predetermined set of accepted behaviours or values then in many things we can really become our own masters. But even more than that, we present to any follower a model of consistent behaviour —consistent because it's an accurate reflection of who we are.

Knowing and controlling who we are is a very necessary step in the leadership process. If you recall our chapter on vision, you will remember that we alluded to an idea that often it is not a leader's vision that brings them to grief but their distorted view of current reality, where they actually are right now practically, and in this case, psychologically. In other words they are starting from the wrong place!

PERSONAL CURRENT REALITY

This idea of current reality is as important in a personal sense as it is in a corporate sense. If we are living a lie at this time then we have a distorted view of current reality. We cannot hope to reach our destination if we are starting at the wrong place. We may fool ourselves for a short time and we may fool others for a longer time, but sooner or later either the truth will out or we will find our vision beyond our capacity to reach.

Peter: This was brought home very forcefully to me when as a twenty-one-year-old I had my first real position of leadership.

My platoon of thirty men was doing its regular physical fitness tests and one of the tortures devised by our masters was that each person had to climb a fifteen foot rope, traverse another horizontal rope for thirty feet and descend at the other end. Failure to do so could lead to physical downgrading and loss of promotional opportunity. It was one of the less important skills a soldier needed. Some very good fit soldiers who were somewhat unco-ordinated couldn't do it.

One of these was one of my best junior leaders. After many tries over a number of days I called him aside and said that I did not think that he would ever make it, but between the pair of us we could overlook it and fiddle the results.

That disappointed him because he knew that I would never be able to forget that we cheated and he would never be able to live with that knowledge. That it was an unimportant exercise was irrelevant. He then suggested that if I really wanted to help him I would go down to the ropes with him and teach him and practise him in the proper technique on the quiet, after work each evening.

We went each evening and on Saturday mornings for about three weeks until he was successful. Then he called all his section together and made them watch while he did it. It's obviously something that has stuck with me all my life. Years later as a company sergeant major he was decorated for great bravery at the Battle of Long Tan in South Vietnam. Tragically he was killed some months later.

What has always impressed itself on me was how well he knew himself, how much integrity he had and how well he had summed me up. What I have since understood is that that man was firmly secured to his own current reality, at least in that environment. He knew that if he wanted to get where he was going he would have to start from the right place and that meant not living a lie. Since then I have always tried to distinguish between the best way or the quickest way and the right way. The right way includes starting at the right place.

How do we begin to get people to understand themselves? To start with we have to encourage people to understand that there is nothing bad about who they are; the morality or judgment is only applicable to what they *do* with who they are. As well as that, people should also understand that others will sooner or later spot them for what they are, if they are living a lie.

Not only do we need to clarify our starting point, we also have to be clear about the fuel we use. That fuel is our value system. We can also live a lie in our value system. And a value is more than an ideal. We must be *acting* upon a value if we claim to espouse it as a value. For instance, if someone claims to value helping the poor and homeless but never lifts a finger to do so then that espoused value is really only an ideal and the person involved is indulging in self-delusion or wishful thinking. They too are distorting current reality.

A value must be something that is lived out. How often do we see such a gulf between espoused behaviour and actual behaviour? How often do we hear our own leaders mouthing platitudes about family values when their own family life suffers incessantly as a result of their own ambition, or they do nothing to further those values when they have the opportunity to do so? Fortunately, or unfortunately for so many of our so-called leaders, the vast majority of people can see that the emperor has no clothes.

TO SEE OURSELVES AS OTHERS SEE US

A good leader has the duty to help subordinates in this sometimes difficult area. A leader will often see only one side of a subordinate and that will often be the mask that brings approbation and prospects of advancement from the leader. The subordinates themselves will often present another somewhat different side to their subordinates in turn.

Peter: Someone I once worked for used to get people to write their own formal appraisal. This happened many years ago when the idea of formal appraisals was not widely accepted throughout industry. We used to have to line up once a year for our 'annual adverse', as we called them.

Once they had written their own appraisal he would produce one of his own for comparison. In most instances it was far more flattering than the one the person had prepared on themselves.

This man had a remarkable theory for those days—to the effect that what we saw in ourselves was most likely to be closer to reality but more to the point, it was what followers also probably saw. It was his way of teaching us to lead rather than focus on impressing our superiors. Whether or not his method was right, there is little doubt that our followers will see us for what we really are rather than what we purport to be.

How often have we found it difficult to reconcile senior management's view of our immediate superior or manager? Senior management often don't seem to be aware of the reality and they only see the side presented to them. Moreover, because senior management no doubt looks to management skills rather than leadership skills it becomes evident that there is a considerable gap in opinion.

A follower may have a better idea of who a person really is than a leader will.

> There is an old adage that says, 'There are many ways to impress the boss, but only one way to impress the troops'.

This means that a leader must know subordinates at all levels and have their confidence. However, this doesn't mean spying, it means communicating—and we have already said that this is primarily done with the ears!

If ever anything really needed creating and properly validating it is a system that caters for 'peer' and 'follower' (360°) review as well as self-appraisal. The difficulty is how to *successfully* make the process of peer and follower review non-threatening. Elections of leaders is one way, but that process is open to abuse. There are some successful systems that have evolved from a process that ensures that everybody develops and owns it, and it is essentially used as a tool for self-knowledge and development rather than judgment and promotion. The redoubtable Ricardo Semler records some interesting subordinate–peer review procedures, but they may not work for everyone.[2]

There are a number of commercial tools available that offer considerable assistance and insight into ourselves and which, when used properly, can help to create a greater understanding of differences in personality and a more sensitive sense of acceptance in peers and subordinates. The fundamental difficulty with all of these is that they tend to put people in boxes and there are so many borderline cases.

People often find themselves categorised by type such that certain behaviours are expected of particular types of people. Often challenges are removed because they might demand behaviours that 'those sort of people can't respond to'. Smart people can also fool others into categorising them incorrectly and so others expect a certain behaviour.

TYPE AND TEMPERAMENT ASSESSMENT

Any sort of assessment has primary value for the person being assessed, and should only be used by others as a guide to help the person under assessment to know themselves. When we spoke of teamwork in Chapter 6 we mentioned the value of differences between people in creating an innovative team. The differences are of value only when they are known and appreciated, which hasn't always been the case.

Peter: I suppose I have done over twenty psychological tests in my career, the first being a simple intelligence test when I was thirteen and applied for a Government scholarship to higher secondary school. In most cases I either got to the next step or got selected for the position.

> *In all that time I have never received feedback on my test results, or have even as much as been told what sort of person I showed up to be on the tests. That seems to me to be a fatal flaw in the system of psychological testing—until the arrival of the self-administered tests of recent times. Of what earthly good is a personality profile if it is so confidential we aren't allowed to see it, let alone use it?*

However, everyone appears to fit some mould, even if it is often hard to identify. People have recognised these moulds for centuries. We mentioned earlier the old Hippocratic personality types and most people are also familiar with the alchemists' 'humours', which suggested that people were either *phlegmatic, sanguine, choleric* or *melancholic*. It's surprising how accurate they were. These days the most popular commercially available indicators are the Myers-Briggs Type Indicator (MBTI)™ systems and their derivatives.

Many of these systems lead us to a better understanding of our own temperament and the way we prefer to process information in a psychological sense. They give us a better, though far from perfect, understanding of the way we are likely to react in certain circumstances and, almost as important, they point out to us the way that others prefer to act. If properly understood, they at once tend to make us more tolerant of others and able to assess and use their strengths while avoiding our own weaknesses. The preferences are generally based on Jungian psychology.

It is not appropriate here to go into the area of personality types other than to deal with the effects a type will have on leadership styles and possible teamwork. What should be said, however, is that aspiring leaders today should avail themselves of one or other of the instruments for both themselves and their work group.

While the MBTI talks of sixteen different types, Charles Handy, the British organisational guru, informally speaks of four different types of people: the *captain*, the *administrator*, the *driver*, and the *expert*.[3] Imaginative people can find rough parallels with the four 'humours' mentioned above. US psychologist David Keirsey seems to have settled on *rationalist, guardian, artisan,* and *idealist* respectively for the same types, although he too originally named them from ancient Greek mythology.[4]

In brief, the *rationalist* is generally a creative, innovative and objective thinker; the *guardian* a commonsensical, ordered and decisive person; the *artisan* is also commonsensical, a down-to-earth action person who is flexible and open-minded; while the *idealist* is a deep-feeling creative person with a firm vision based on ideals. Good leaders come from any one of these temperaments, and though you will no doubt see a little of yourself in each, one of them will be predominantly you.

LEADERSHIP STYLES AND TYPE

If we go through just some of the precepts we have suggested throughout this book as indicative of good leadership and lay them against the temperament preferences that people have, we may find, somewhat disturbingly, that there really are such things as born leaders, or at least people born with a type preference and, more especially, a temperament that makes it easier for them to develop the characteristics of the better leader. It doesn't mean that others are precluded, just that, as we said in the Introduction, some need to work at some areas harder than others. For instance:

Accountability—guardians are more likely to be responsible than artisans.

Vision—rationalists and idealists are more likely to be able to articulate a vision than other types.

Procedures and *decisions*—guardians are more likely to be able to handle these, while *goals* and *planning* are certainly the strength of the rationalists.

Initiative and *delegation* will be an artisan strength, while *participative management* and *concern for followers* will be a strength of the *idealist*.

Similarly, rationalists will solve complex problems while artisans are likely to be great troubleshooters. And so on!

Types of people can also be further broken down from temperament according to whether people are introverted or extraverted. Introverts are more likely to understand themselves than extraverts because they will tend to be more introspective, while extraverts are more likely to be at ease with followers (e.g. MBWA), and more likely to operate with an open door policy. Introverts are more likely to communicate on paper.

It follows from the foregoing, which is by no means exhaustive, that the concept of contingency leadership has great validity. Some people are men and women of action, others of thought and planning, others of care and compassion. If you are caught in a plane crash in a jungle, chances are it will be an artisan who will get you out. If you are building a skyscraper then maybe turn to a rationalist to lead the project

planning team. If you are establishing a welfare agency then include at
least one idealist in the leadership team; in fact, it was probably the
idealist's idea in the first place.

> *Although crossovers are very useful, the clearest vision of the future
> comes only from an intuitive, the most realistic practicality only from a
> sensing type, the most incisive analysis only from a thinker, and the most
> skilful handling of people only from a feeling type.*
>
> *(As quoted in 'Gifts Differing'.)*[5]

The good news is, it doesn't matter what you are. The danger comes
when someone assumes that one is better than another and pretends to
be someone else without understanding what it means. For instance,
many of the great motivational salespeople these days equate extraversion with leadership and expect that any leader has to be articulate,
up-front and even humorous. Nothing could be further from the truth.
Admittedly, a leader needs to be able to communicate, but not everyone
will communicate the same way.

> Extraversion is not a prerequisite for communication!

On the other hand, it is necessary for leaders, however appointed and
type-caste, to understand that they need to develop those underdevel-
oped preferences in themselves where they are needed in a leadership
role. So an artisan needs to develop a sense of vision and an idealist
needs to develop a sense of realism and so on. It is not good enough to
hide behind a preference and say 'that's just me, you'll have to cop it'.
But at least understanding these things in oneself and others is half the
battle. We must recognise our strengths and our weaknesses, and this
process can certainly help us.

Type and temperament also have nothing to do with intelligence,
integrity, experience, environment, values and so on, all of which have
a profound effect on our leadership capability. Similarly, if someone is a

certain type then it should be accepted that, *all else being equal,* that is how they should be allowed to operate. Our *value* system is what will tell us whether we should modify our preferred method of operating. If there is no need to change our preferred style, then we shouldn't do so.

We need to reiterate that these types are indicators only and some people can be very marginal in one or another. But the theory does help in fitting people to various types of task. The greatest value is in recognising that one set of characteristics may be no better than another. When you go into an office some people are neat and organised and very methodical at doing things, others are untidy and seem to be haphazard. The truth is that many people can probably do a dozen things at once and no matter how many time management courses you send them on, they don't seem to change.

In the same way, how often have you seen someone with no sense of humour trying to tell a joke during a presentation, because they've been told that's the right way to do it? It might be—for someone with an outgoing sense of humour. It could be a disaster for someone with no sense of humour.

If you don't know who you are, find out!

Incidentally, extraversion and humour are in no way connected. There are as many unfunny extraverts as there are humorous introverts. To coin a phrase: 'Humour is a funny thing'. A real sense of humour is demonstrated when someone has a sense of the ridiculous and can laugh at themselves with or without others. It is not an offence in a leader to be lacking in humour as long as a leader can learn not to take himself or herself too seriously.

The great thing about a sense of humour is that it can be a groundbreaker if it is used sensibly. Have you ever noticed that laughter has no accent? You can identify the laughter of children, the laughter of men and the laughter of women—that's all, generally. But it doesn't mean that everyone laughs at the same things or has the same sense of humour, and any attempt to change that generally leads to blank stares and misunderstanding.

> Good leaders will take everything seriously except themselves.

Another misconception is to equate personality type with the ability to form relationships, be they fleeting or permanent. Personality type has to do with preference or orientation, not with observed behaviour. I could become a world-class speaker and an accomplished diplomat with all the social and political contact that requires, but I might prefer to be at home in my study reading philosophy or poetry. I have simply learned to adjust my behaviour to the situation.

It's when the personality type takes over and *dictates* behaviour that problems occur. We've all met the extravert who can't shut up. Eventually he or she drives people to distraction. However, there are plenty of extraverts who have modified their behaviour—in fact most people learn, otherwise there could be no real social interaction. Not only do people learn to adjust their own behaviour, but by recognising preferences in subordinates it is easier to make allowances and adjust expectations of their behaviour as well.

> The ability to recognise people's personality preferences is a great asset in a leader.

OTHER PSYCHOLOGICAL NEEDS

Having learned to recognise type and temperament in ourselves and followers or subordinates we have to be careful that we don't box them in as well. No doubt we have all heard of the old song, 'Little Boxes'; the key phrase is *And they all get put in boxes and they all come out the same!*

There is a myriad of other boxes that people can fall into, and they include such things as the personal psychological needs that individuals have in relation to their jobs. These are quite different to type and temperament and will have an equally profound effect on how you and your subordinates relate and perform. They are summarised very well in Robert Benfari's book *Understanding Your Management Style*.[6] Libraries of books have been written about them. What it does help to do is give you an idea of the complexity of styles and compulsive but modifiable behaviours that exist in people.

Interestingly, in studies that have been done in the United States, the predominance of the various characteristics are the same for both men and women. Women are just as likely to have a need for *aggression* as men, both are just as likely to have a need for *affiliation* and men are just as likely to have a need to play mother (*nurturance*) as women and just as likely to need *succorance* and so on.[7] Conventional wisdom would seem to have us believe otherwise.

> Personal psychological needs that people have in relation to their jobs are essentially the same for men and women.

That understanding has implications for leadership in the future as more women move into positions of leadership. We are all led to

believe that women are more affiliative, more nurturing, more participative altogether. Well, perhaps they are. Then again, maybe what we
are seeing is women demonstrating learned behaviour when they show
those characteristics, which means that if the behaviours are desirable
men can also learn them. And that does have enormous implications.
We'll leave that question to the psychologists and social scientists.

When we spoke earlier of people wearing masks, the masks they
wear are often really a combination of the needs we have just seen. For
instance, a leader who has a tendency towards *affiliation*, which is a
need for companionship and affirmation from others, will tend to show
that affiliative need even when it is quite inappropriate. The importance of recognising limitations can easily be seen in this context.
Imagine a fire chief with strong affiliative needs consulting with peers
before taking action—while Rome burns! There will often be times
when leaders have to put aside psychological needs to adopt more
appropriate behaviour quite inconsistent with their style.

What you see is very rarely what you get!

One of the benefits of finding our masks in this way is learning to accept
our feelings. For many it is an immensely liberating revelation. What
follows then becomes an exercise of looking at how we *do* live our lives
followed by a picture of how we *could* live our lives. Thus we can create
a personal vision. If we see what our lives are like now and we are truthful with ourselves we then have an accurate view of personal current
reality. The gap between our *vision* and *current reality* forms the healthy
creative tension mentioned by Senge.[8] This gap analysis helps people to
recognise where they have to change their behaviour.

A NEW LEADERSHIP?

What does all this mean to us? Primarily it gives us an idea that we
should take steps to learn more about ourselves, both formally and
informally. It is incumbent upon aspiring leaders to learn who they are
in order to determine their weaknesses as they are seen and as they
affect others and—most importantly—to do something about them.
With all this talk of change, are we really talking about a new style of

leadership? No, we aren't. When one reads of the leadership of some of history's great leaders we are seeing a mirror of the behaviours about which we are talking. So what we are suggesting is that it is not new leadership but new leaders that are needed.

If we believe that the best way to lead is through PowerSharing, then there is a fundamental change called for in the style of most people when it comes to managerial personality and leadership. The old industrial confrontational model is no longer relevant but it still persists because people know no better.

However, the best leadership has always been a process of PowerSharing. If one looks at the great movements of history within the context of the time, one sees leaders of the calibre of Buddha, Christ, Mohammed, even down to Ghandi in our own day, all of whom led from the position of serving. PowerSharing leadership is not new; we simply need more PowerSharing leaders.

What emerges most clearly from the preceding discussion is the clear message that no matter how hard a leader may try to change someone, that change must come from within the person and the only way to ensure that is to motivate that someone to want to change. And to do that they must recognise who they are and bring about change themselves. There has to be positive motivation—not motivation from fear of the consequences or a desire to ambition, because as soon as the threat of any sanction is removed the undesirable behaviour is likely to return.

There is no point in expecting that a behaviour can be turned on and off at will. Sooner or later our actual behaviour will become our espoused behaviour rather than the other way around. It's no good suggesting that when the time comes we can change, because who and what we are will have dried and set. The time to commence changing is now!

We know not of the future, and cannot plan for it much. But we can hold our spirits and our bodies so pure and high . . . that we can determine and know what manner of men we will be whenever the hour strikes, that calls to noble action . . . no man becomes suddenly different from his habit and cherished thought.

Joshua Chamberlain 1863

CHARACTER

It will be noticed in all our references to type, temperament and style that we avoided suggesting what might be regarded as rights or wrongs. However, something prompted that young NCO all those years ago to recognise that there was something wrong in the suggestion his platoon commander had made, no matter how convenient and sensible it sounded. This was determined by his value system.

Despite all the characteristics we have spoken of here, we haven't seen one which matches Shakespeare's 'Look thou character?' In all of the things we have examined, we have seen our orientation, our effect on others, our needs and so on, but we have not identified anything among them which could be regarded as moral or immoral, ethical or unethical. What helps us to determine the *best way*, the *quickest way* and the *right way*?

The best or quickest way may not always be the right way.

What is it that often takes competent or well-trained people down the path of expediency? These are the things one ponders on in times of contemplation. There is some advice we can give, but the choice must ultimately rest with each individual—and you may not always like what you read.

BECOMING A NEW LEADER

What we are looking for is a plan as to how we can rearrange our personal lives to become a mirror of exemplary PowerSharing leadership. This involves examining our values and determining if they match our ideals, establishing our vision based on our ideals, finding our current reality based on our values and then, over time, changing that current reality and the values upon which it is based to align with our ideals and our vision. Simple! And this must have to do with setting personal goals, which are based upon something we may or may not have learned in our early development.

Phase 1

Determine your values. What are the things you value most in life: family, freedom, pleasure, money, service, work? Most people would no doubt opt for the first—family—and then, even so, many behave as though the family is the last thing they care for. Establishing your underlying values doesn't mean that other things aren't important and that they may not assume top priority at times.

We mentioned earlier, and we must stress again, that a value must be freely chosen and acted upon in your life. If it is not being acted upon it can hardly be claimed to be of value. Most people seem to cope with about seven or eight values that provide their personal engine with fuel.

What is the underlying ethic behind these values? Remember, leadership is a people game and if the things that matter most to you are money or pleasure, for example, then maybe leadership isn't for you. Remember, a value is an active ingredient in your life. Do your values match your ideals? If your values are all self-centred and have little concern for others within them, then you are going to have difficulty with a PowerSharing environment.

Set your life vision and goals. All the management by objectives and time management experts have been saying this for years. And remember— if you are a rationalist or an idealist you may find this concept easier than a guardian or artisan would.

Setting goals involves picturing or imagining what you want to be doing at the end of a certain period: where you want to be living; whether you will be comfortable or wealthy; whether you have travelled; where you will travel; how successful you will be. If the goals you are setting do not conform to the values you claim to have guiding you, then you need to do some rethinking either about your values or your goals. For instance, it is no good imagining yourself as wealthy in ten years time if the pursuit of wealth or the urge to work and succeed are not among your values.

It's important to set far goals and remember to set goals in every facet of life. Often people forget that work is only one aspect of life.

Establish current reality. This may not be a process that you can do quickly, because current reality includes an honest appraisal of who you are as well as where you are. Remember, if you start from the wrong place you may be disqualified and your life goals or vision will be an illusion.

Current reality requires scrupulousness about who you are and what your values are. If one of your values is a happy family and in examining current reality you find you are working till 10 pm five nights a week, then your current reality must reflect that. Similarly, if you regard yourself as a compassionate, dispassionate human being, and then indiscriminately fire people you don't like and so on, then you do not have a truthful picture of current reality. Or if you have a vision of making a million dollars in the next five years and you are currently on social security and unqualified, then that is a very serious impediment to your vision or goal.

Determine who you are. Try and establish your basic personality attitude and the other characteristics as well. What is the mask you wear most of the time? Are you satisfied that those close to you and those you work with see the real you most of the time, 'warts and all'. If not, why not? How can you be sure they can't see right through you anyway, even if you aren't exposing the real you?

Find a role model. This doesn't mean just one role model for everything; no two people could be that alike anyway. And it doesn't necessarily mean selecting Albert Schweitzer. It could mean selecting your mother for a role model as a parent, a neighbour as a role model for community service and someone else as a career role model. The important thing is to have someone in each area who *matches your values in that area* and whose goal achievements you admire. Mother Teresa would not be a good role model for a rationalist with a goal of wealth within ten years!

Phase 1—determine values, establish current reality, set goals, determine who you really are, find a role model(s).

Phase 2

Set yearly and weekly or monthly personal goals. We could call phase 1 the strategic planning stage. We are now getting onto the tactical phase, putting the master plan into operation as it were. We start to do this by planning yearly, monthly and weekly goals. These goals cover all aspects of our lives and they don't have to be mind-boggling. It's fairly easy to break yearly goals down into bite-sized monthly pieces, and the weekly goals simply become a program of work. These goals can be as simple as finishing one chapter of a book each week and so on.

Indulge in some introspection each day. This is really underdone. Everyone needs private space and time to be alone. Some people meditate, and it is finding an increasing number of adherents and is very beneficial for some people. However you achieve it, time is still needed for reflection each day. Things are so frenetic today that we tend to look upon reflection as a luxury and people who indulge in it as lazy or in some way abnormal. Whenever anyone says that they haven't got time to scratch themselves, then they are going to have an awful itch by the end of their lives.

Regularly examine your results against your goals. This isn't a daily requirement but probably needs to happen monthly and yearly. The daily requirement is to use the above time each day simply to review the day and see how things went and whether you could have done things differently or better.

Examine your leadership. Examine what you have done each day in relation to your style of management and leadership. The important thing is how that style has impacted on others, and how it has impacted in relation to others' styles, be they colleagues, team members or superiors. What have your team members had to cope with? Do people respect you and co-operate; are they loyal and do they share your goals and vision?

> Phase 2—set yearly, weekly and monthly goals, reflect each day, examine results against goals, examine your leadership.

Phase 3

Determine the gaps between you and your ideal. This means finding the gap between you and your role model and matching your vision, ideals and values in Phase 1, and your results against your goals in Phase 2. The difference between your vision and current reality, between you and your role model, and between your ideals and current values, are all part of that healthy *creative tension*. It is this creative tension which helps to provide you with the energy you need to temporarily mark time, press on or change.

Determine the changes needed. What do you need to change about yourself? How do people get to see the real you? What behaviour do you need to change? Do you need a change in attitude? Are you in the right paradigm? Do you need to revisit your values? Unfortunately, changing behaviour is not all that easy, even for those who want to change. There are many who don't want to change and many don't even know they should be changing.

Stephen Covey speaks about changing paradigms in relation to behaviour.[9] Let us look at an example. If you cycle to work you tend to be very critical of motor vehicle traffic because the drivers are selfish and careless and their cars pollute the atmosphere. On the other hand, when you drive to work you tend to be very critical of cyclists because they are hard to see, they slow the traffic and they make assumptions about car drivers. All these attitudes are very recognisable and natural. In fact, the cyclist is in one paradigm and the driver is in another and they both have different perceptions of the same reality.

However, if you cycle to work for two days a week and drive for three, then you will soon be able to see things from both points of view and you will be a more aware cyclist and a more safety and cycle conscious driver, because you have changed the paradigm you are in and you have developed a dual perception of the reality. Behaviourists differ in their opinions about whether changing behaviour will eventually change attitude. That's where the phrase *learning to bite one's tongue* is useful. That's a change of behaviour without a change of attitude or paradigm. But when all is said and done, is it better to have really changed your attitude, or to have an exceedingly painful and scarred tongue?

The conflict between an attitude or paradigm and an expected behaviour is the cause of a lot of stress. It is best by far to change your paradigm, but it may not always be the ethical thing to do because your values may be in conflict with an accepted prevailing social attitude. In which case you may have to put up with a sore tongue!

Change! There are no short cuts here. Nobody else can do this for you; it's something only you can do. There are some ways of making it easier, like taking it a little at a time, but in the end it's like giving up smoking—you have to want to do it. Convince yourself of the benefits, review the benefits at the end of each month, and see how much better you feel, see how differently other people respond to you. Record the benefits, tell other people about them so that it becomes harder to backslide.

Phase 3—Where is the gap? What changes are needed? Change!!

Phase 4

Never stop the above. Continuous improvement is just as valid on a personal basis as it is organisationally. We should never stop trying to change or improve our behaviour. We should never stop examining our motives. We should never stop trying to eradicate inappropriate attitudes or behaviour.

Phase 4—Repeat!

PERSONAL AMBITION

We have mentioned ambition before and suggested in Chapter 2 that it shouldn't be confused with vision. Perhaps here we should explain our differences in view. A vision is other-focused, it is something that leads us, providing that healthy elastic *creative tension*. We see ambition as a driving force. Our vision is based on our ideals or ideal values; ambition is based on values that are more self-centred and may not even be necessarily sound values. After all, our values may not necessarily be altruistic.

For instance, the CEO (person A) of a small energy provider may have a vision of a single organisation providing all the electrical power needs for a particular state. That person may work towards that, consistently bearing in mind that there are competing organisations and views, and executives whose views need to be taken into account, but all the while focusing on the fact that by amalgamating he or she can provide better service and cheaper power to the community. Another person, B, from another like organisation, may have exactly the same vision, which is based on the same principles, but at the same time have the ambition to be the chairman or chief executive of the final powerful organisation.

Neither vision is wrong and nor is the ambition of person B wrong, but person A's vision is based on values which are different to person B's and it is those differences in values that determine B's ambition. What is certain is that the way B goes about the task will be different to the way A does. A's modus operandi is likely to be less oriented to power per se and more oriented towards PowerSharing.

While we should never lose touch with our values and principles, even if it means retaining unpopular attitudes, we must nevertheless continually reassess our values. This is something a lot of people seem to disregard. With the plethora of social changes going on it is almost a given that on a regular basis we are expected to change our behaviour. Often people are called upon to change their attitude to one thing or another—and in time values can change or erode.

Sometimes an attitude change becomes expedient and it has even been known for the imposition of law to change people's attitudes. While in most cases the change is sensible and necessary, it is not invariably so. A good leader should not change his or her attitude to suit the prevailing social trend simply because it is a trend. A good leader's attitude will be shaped by his or her value systems, not by social trends. Hence one needs to distinguish between the personal ambition for success and the timelessness of a vision. A vision based on the right values will always point to the *right way*.

In many ways, in recent years for instance, we have replaced some of our moral values with economic values. We could even coin a new replacement word—*dorrals!*

Few stories ever written have as profound a statement to make about self-knowledge, self-control, self-acceptance, vision, ambition and values as Oscar Wilde's famous book The Picture of Dorian Gray.
The story concerns the life of a very personable young man whose portrait was painted during the innocence of his youth. Over the

years Dorian's very attractions become his downfall as he lives a life of hedonism, immorality and dissolution. Strangely, he retains his beauty, but year by year the portrait ages. He alone visits it year after year and observes the lines of cynicism, disillusion, age and the effects of an evil way of life take their toll on the portrait until it becomes a picture of a vile old man.

Eventually the mouth of the portrait assumes the crooked curve of the hypocrite and Dorian can bear it no longer. He tries to destroy the portrait in a rage and falls dead in the attempt. When his reprobate friends call the next day they find the corpse of an ugly old man lying on the floor beneath a beautiful picture of their friend Dorian just as they had left him the day before.

It's possible, of course, to postpone knowing oneself and just keep turning the other way. The beauty of the story is that the truth will out—as we mentioned earlier—and who we are and our behaviour is being somewhere recorded and will sooner or later be visited upon us.

In an earlier chapter we mentioned the necessity of setting an example, and we warned against expecting from followers what we are not able or not willing to give ourselves. We see it demonstrated daily in all walks of life by many leaders. Many, unfortunately, live by the adage *'Do as I say not as I do'* and what's more, they do it brazenly.

In the penultimate scene of the book we just mentioned, Dorian eventually decides to destroy the picture—and of course himself—because he observes in the picture, among all the other wicked signs, the ultimate curled lip of the hypocrite.

Everyone is understanding enough of people who genuinely espouse a form of behaviour and then can't live up to it themselves even though they try. That's in the nature of human weakness, and to err is human. Hypocrisy is the patent and blatant disregard for the principles one supposedly espouses. That becomes the ultimate crime and a hypocrite is possibly the ultimately anathematised person in history, such that legends in condemnation of him or her exist in just about every culture. There may be no more public hypocrisy today than in the past but fortunately, or unfortunately, it seems more evident. That situation creates a lot of cynicism, which in itself is a problem because it leads to mistrust.

PERSONAL COMMITMENT

Cynicism is not just disbelief, it is the loss of faith in any form of belief and an assumption that people are motivated entirely by selfishness.

A good leader with a good vision can give or return meaning to a program and a sense of innocence to followers. He or she needs to be proud of that vision and not be afraid to publicly espouse it. He or she needs to be able to passionately believe in it and be seen to do so. If one is not prepared to publicly proclaim it then it may not be a worthy vision or one may not be a worthy leader. If it is less than a worthy vision then this is where the truth will out.

For very much the same reason, we tend to be suspicious of enthusiastic people. We see them as pushy or naive. But enthusiasm doesn't mean that; enthusiasm is the wholehearted adoption of a vision or a chosen course of action. It overtakes people. Shy and quiet people are capable of being just as enthusiastic as are gregarious people. A quiet person will have the same intensity of feeling as will someone who is outgoing.

Enthusiasm, whether quiet or gregarious, will be a measure of a leader's commitment.

> Enthusiasm is the wholehearted adoption of a vision or a chosen course of action.

It is to be hoped that people don't think that what has been said is too tall an order, because following the concepts, being aware of the issues at stake, and taking steps to continuously improve oneself, are surely the essence of self-mastery. If anyone finds the concept too difficult, then leadership as we have been espousing it is not for them.

It is an appropriate point here to draw to a close the last of the ten precepts and to sum up. The concepts contained in this chapter are at once a result of years of experience and of general and particular reading. Self-knowledge is vital to leadership. That it appears last is no indication of its lack of importance for the PowerSharing leader; indeed, it is of fundamental importance to any person and to any successful relationship between people. It is also fundamental to change, and bringing about both personal and organisational change is part of the vocation of a leader.

Key concepts

- What a person *is*, is just as important as what a person *does*.
- People have a responsibility to act in accordance with who they are.
- The *right* way is better than the *quickest* way or the *best* way.
- Everyone behaves from time to time in a manner which conceals who they really are.
- People can learn to behave in a manner contrary to the way they feel.
- The above concepts begin to form the basis of self-control.
- No one knows a person better than himself or herself.
- Follower and peer judgment are likely to be closer to the real person than is judgment by a leader, because of the mask we show to superiors.
- Personality types are indications of a preferred means of processing information.
- Aspiring leaders should try to determine their type and temperament and management style.
- People can modify their behaviour patterns despite their orientation in personality.
- Every leader should be driven by a set of fundamental values.
- We must ascertain values, set goals, find role models, reflect and change continuously.
- Followers reserve special contempt for hypocrisy.
- We should develop an enthusiasm about our leadership.

CHAPTER 11

Epilogue

VISIONARIES AND REALISTS

The late twentieth century has seen a maturing of leadership in a variety of environments and an almost universal acceptance that the old authoritarian ways are no longer appropriate. And yet at a time of obvious change we don't seem to have caught up with what a re-assessment of leadership entails. Everything else has become scientific and it seems to be assumed that leadership can also be so treated. However, the essence of leadership is an understanding of people, who nevertheless seem to be the first and most consistent casualties in recent managerial 'advances', particularly under the banner of economic rationalism.

As we said at the beginning of this book, every advance made in this world has been as a result of human endeavour. Leadership and human endeavour are interdependent, but despite increases in knowledge and understanding in a management sense, why is it that followers are still crying out for leadership in so many fields: politically, culturally, spiritually, economically and socially? Why is it that people are not producing to their optimum capacity? Have we forgotten—or perhaps never understood—what real leadership is?

From every side and from many sources we are being assailed by experts declaiming that their latest theory is the solution. We are being consistently told that the old ways are gone forever and yet it seems that in real terms, workers and certainly people at the margins, are comparatively worse off, at least in Western society, than they have been for many years. The gap between the haves and have-nots seems to be widening appreciably. Does this mean that there is a crisis in leadership?

Is it possible that there is something cyclical about leadership type? John Adair seems to think so.[1] In his view, various types of leadership have arrived and lasted for various lengths of time according to the prevailing ethos of the day—imperial, church, military, social, scientific and so on. That has happened over many centuries.

What have we today?—economic rationalism. So many of today's leaders are the rationalists—intuitive creative thinkers; brilliant, visionary, theoretical—who focus on the future rather than current reality and whose only concern for people is how they can conveniently place them in the most appropriate box to suit their theories. Pitted against these are the idealists, the creative, people-oriented types, the social engineers with great concern for people, great vision and great compassion but with sometimes little commonsense understanding. In past generations they may have found themselves in the church or in hands-on helping positions. Today they are educated and are in positions of authority and planning. Then there are the myriad of academics of both types, all anxious to publish their vision and theories and have the world follow the latest trend.

However, the world is a sensing world and it is the artisans and the guardians who have to make things happen. They have little time for theories or academia, and because the visionaries are less able to make things happen and the realists can't be bothered with possibility thinking, there is a distrust between the two. So you have a tension between the visionaries and the realists, which most of the time is less than creative. Only good leadership can bring the two together.

> It has been said that rationalists start wars, guardians run them, artisans win them and idealists set up the peace process in time for the rationalists to come out of hiding and start again.

Because the vast majority of people neither own nor share these visions, they are often blamed because they didn't get behind the latest trend wholeheartedly enough. Very few visionary leaders some of whom are well-known to us, will admit to having a vision that can only be shared by a fraction of the population. But if the vision cannot be shared, how can the power be shared? Alternatively, do the leaders share the current reality of the followers? Is this a cause of the crisis?

DEFINITION REVISITED

Let us revisit our definition:

Leadership is the art of consistently influencing or directing people towards the achievement of a clear, common goal—in such a way as to engender loyalty, respect and willing co-operation.

Everything we do in leadership must be directed towards the principles contained in that definition. In examining your own performance are you able to conscientiously answer in the affirmative to those concepts?

Is your leadership consistent?

Do you genuinely try to influence, and where necessary direct?

Are you afraid to direct? If so, why?

Is it because your followers do not respect you?

Is your goal a shared and clear goal?

Do you have the same view of reality as your followers?

Have you and your organisation earned the loyalty of your followers?

Do they willingly co-operate because they respect you and share your vision or is the co-operation less than willing but based on fear?

Do you continually study your art or do you simply keep up with the latest scientific management trends?

Do you genuinely like your followers and respect them? Are you afraid of them?

What we have tried to do in this book is to give you some insights as to how you can positively answer most of those questions by understanding the concepts of PowerSharing.

A FUTURE OF PARADOX

There are a number of ironies, if not paradoxes, in what is emerging in modern leadership. The first is that the growing emphasis on PowerSharing should emerge from both industrial management and the military concept of *directive control*, which is very similar.

Secondly, many management theorists such as Tom Peters are predicting a future where flexibility is going to be paramount because of the pace of change and the ever-increasing degree of uncertainty which exists.[2] Because the future is crowding in so fast, there is a growing call to move away from the constraints of the confined strategic planning of the past into a period of industrial *opportunism*, for want of a better word. This means that whatever way we plan for the future we can only guess at it because of the pace of change. We must, therefore, have extremely flexible plans and extremely imaginative and visionary visions!

Clearly, what is developing is an environment that is not unlike the *friction of war* familiar to all students of military history or those experienced in combat. Once combat is joined, all planning is up for grabs; just make sure you have your vision on straight!

> The only thing that we can be sure about in the future is that people will be just as important tomorrow as they are today; all the more reason to invest our future in people rather than things.

Third, we in the West are very egalitarian and we are very conscious of individual rights. We rarely espouse the submerging of individuality to the common good but we expect people to operate in teams with the same degree of acceptance as people to whom such acceptance is part of a national ethos. We wish to be competitive internationally but we are becoming suspicious of competition. We want our children to succeed, and to stand out in their work, but we want them to be primarily team members. All the messages our youngsters are getting are mixed.

The ultimate irony is that studies done as late as the 1970s indicate that in an environment of danger or even uncertainty, such as organisations could now be facing economically, there was a decided preference among the workers for *defined autocratic* leadership. Yet we seem to be heading for a period of participative leadership at a time when the environment and the workers may well be seeking a more directive and autocratic style because of the uncertainty of the future.

At the same time, economic imperatives seem to be driving all decisions at the organisational level. What we are getting is lip-service to good leadership when times are good and a total abdication of leadership when times are bad—at precisely the time that good leadership is necessary.

English philosopher Roger Scruton suggests that a good society is one which shows concern and respect for generations other than its own. Presumably this means concern for future generations and respect for past generations.

Interestingly, a definition that 'a leader is a good steward of the enterprise's future', (and one with which we do not fully concur), is featured in the watershed Australian publication 'Enterprising Nation'.[3] The definition would carry more weight if it had also added the concept of concern for the past.

It is that past from which we have carried forward many of the values we now seem to be determined to discard. And we seem to be doing so without in any way considering the effect on the future.

THE PAST

Fortunately the future and the past need not be mutually exclusive. But there are some pitfalls that may be ahead if aspiring leaders aren't conscious of the contradictions that are likely to arise. One of the issues relates to the perceived difference in the role of the leader, arising from our past. It is our contention that leadership hasn't changed; nor has the definition. What has changed is management, the techniques of application and the growth in information. Our forebears were just as wise as we are, they simply had less data and ergo less information.

Just how far have we come? There are significant moves throughout the West to address the fundamentals of ethical leadership. Everywhere, management gurus and experts are extolling the virtues of the 'new leader'. If we look at what they are saying about teamwork and consultation and the importance of people, one could be forgiven for being cynical. There seems to be 'many a slip twixt the cup and the lip'. If we revisit a quotation that we used in the Introduction, one thing becomes obvious:

A leader is best when people barely know that he exists, not so good when people obey and acclaim him, worst when they despise him. Fail to honour people they fail to honour you! But of a good leader who talks little; when his work is done, his aim fulfilled—they will all say, 'We did this ourselves!'.

Lao-Tzu (c. 600 BC)

There is no such thing as new leadership. There are managers discovering leadership for the first time and assuming that it is new.

A NEW DEMOCRACY?

Are we to assume that nothing about leadership is new? Not at all. Just as the political systems of the world have evolved to where, hopefully, democracy of some sort is the preferred form of government of most developed countries, we have a similar development in industry and the workplace. But the development is certainly not universal and nor is it even necessarily agreed universally.

A democratic workplace suggests not only that people have some say in their own work conditions and the direction of an organisation, but that they also have some formal means of having a say in the selection of their workplace leaders. This is theoretically possible in large public companies where workers can be shareholders and can exercise a vote no matter how small an influence that vote may hold. Small shareholder dissatisfaction has certainly brought about leadership change in recent Australian experience.

Even some small and medium-sized organisations offer some degree of ownership to workers, as do other organisations that offer director-ships and partnerships to better performing managers and so on. But these can only marginally affect leader selection when the majority of shares are in the hands of one person or a family or group of like-minded people. Where this occurs, as it does in a majority of small and medium businesses, the only way to convince the majority shareholders or own-ers that PowerSharing makes sense is to prove that power for its own sake is transitory and that PowerSharing will provide a better economic performance—as a result of greater and more enthusiastic worker input.

Ironically, many small and medium-sized owner-managed busi-nesses are autocratic by definition but decidedly non-authoritarian in operation. They are run as mini-democracies, but because of the own-ership issue can never be democracies by definition.

Authoritarian means having respect for authority. An authoritarian person will be very conscious of the need to defer to the authority of others as well as expecting that others will in turn defer to his or her authority. Generally speaking, he or she believes in this in preference to individual freedom of judgment or action. We should add that cer-tain personality types value freedom more than others, while others value order and so on. Guardians, for instance, value regulation, order and decision and are generally more likely to be authoritarian.

Again, contrary to received conventional wisdom, studies have shown that women are more likely to be authoritarian than men. Many of the summaries of these studies are outlined in the now dated but very entertaining and relevant book by Norman Dixon, *On the Psychology of Military Incompetence*.[4]

On the other hand, *autocratic* means unlimited power in the hands of one person over others. Conventional wisdom would suggest that men are more likely to be autocratic than women. That perception could be related to numbers in positions of authority. In the previous chapter we saw that not only certain personality types like power or control but that there was unlikely to be any difference between men and women.

The issue of ownership also must fundamentally affect whether a person will tend to autocracy. If a person is the sole owner of a medium-sized business he or she would be very tempted to behave autocratically and many would believe that such is their right. Nevertheless, if the business is successful there is also a sound argument to suggest that this success is likely to be just as much due to the efforts of the workers as it is to the investment of the owner.

By definition, autocracy is the antithesis of PowerSharing and consequently is undesirable leadership. This is not to say that ownership is undesirable but that an owner-leader needs to be doubly vigilant of any tendency to concentrate power.

> An authoritarian believes in submission to authority, however that authority is constituted. Autocracy is the concentration of total power and authority in the hands of one person.

POWERSHARING IS NOT COLLEGIAL

There is a study that shows, at least in a military sense, that decisions made of a collegial nature are more likely to be wrong than decisions made by one person. In the mid-1970s a study of the four worst military disasters in recent US history indicated that the decisions taken were all taken by committee and not by one person.[5] PowerSharing doesn't suggest that decisions need to be collegial but *that they are made at the appropriate level* by the appropriate person or persons and that the responsibility lies at the level where the decision was made, without in any way diminishing the responsibility of the person ultimately responsible.

The most recent and outstanding success of the American army since World War II, Operation 'Desert Storm', was observed to be run as a PowerSharing operation by Norman Schwarzkopf. This doesn't mean he commanded by committee, but he did allow his subordinates, many of whom were from Allied armies, considerable freedom of action within an overall directive. The irony is that he had supreme and total position power at his point of impact and though he constantly communicated with Bush and Powell, there was no interference and he could distribute his own authority as he wished. He could have acted as the ultimate autocrat. For months afterwards there was a rash of material in US management and business journals extolling the virtues of 'Desert Storm' and the leadership philosophy it was based upon.

> *That the concept of PowerSharing has been used so successfully in war says that we may have reached the high-point in leadership philosophy. Since leadership was first studied, we have seen the development of the qualities, functional, contingency, situational, styles and powerSharing approaches.*
>
> *In the same period, management theory has covered such issues as styles, MBO, TQM, quality circles, continuous improvement, team based organisations and a host of other sub-sets.*
>
> *We've gone from personnel to HR and back again. We have psych tested, Myers-Briggsed and personality tested. We have decentralised, flattened, downsized, right-sized and we have workshopped and been facilitated ad nauseam.*
>
> *We have visioned, missioned, strategically planned, annually planned, business planned and budgeted year after year.*
>
> *Many of these concepts dovetail, but many are mutually exclusive. As one concept after another has been launched, we have looked to it being a panacea. But alas, it has not become so. Only one thing has remained constant—people—and the need for them to be skilled sufficiently to undertake a task. And it will be people who will ensure that the next step we take is a success.*
>
> *PowerSharing will not be a panacea but it does recognise the absolute primacy of people and leadership.*

People should recognise that a democratic leader can be very authoritarian and an autocratic leader can be decidedly unauthoritarian and there are examples of both in the world today.

> PowerSharing is non-authoritarian, and non-autocratic but not collegial.

In a PowerSharing organisation all planning and operational power is shared, but discussion finishes when the decision on a course of action is taken. At this point all are required to play their part. *This doesn't mean, of course, that if new information is gleaned or new factors emerge there is not consultation or freedom of action.* Such flexibility is the essence of PowerSharing.

PRECEPTS REVISITED

It is now time to revisit our precepts of practical leadership that, if wisely followed, will ultimately lead to the leadership we have called PowerSharing. They have been worded a little differently to make the PowerSharing aspect clearer.

1. *Acceptance of ultimate responsibility*

Regardless of how much you delegate or how much power you push down or share, or how much authority you divest to followers, everything that happens in your sphere of activity and the ultimate outcome at your point of impact is your responsibility, no matter how long or short a time you have held the leadership position. Ignorance is no excuse, nor are incompetent followers.

2. *Imparting the vision*

This is a fundamental concept of PowerSharing. First, you must have a vision or grand design and then you must make sure that even down to the most newly-joined junior worker everyone is not only aware of, but shares that vision.

Your vision is a product of the business you are in. You cannot push power down if people don't know why they are getting the power. Nor can they exercise it if there are unnecessary constraints upon them.

Norman Dixon records a quotation from Nelson that encapsulates an understanding of the visionary aspects of PowerSharing. Nelson was the least authoritarian of men and had a healthy disrespect for blind obedience. Who could fail but to follow him? He was reported to have said to the Duke of Clarence:

> *To serve my king, and to destroy the French*, I consider as the great order of all, from which all little ones spring; and if one of these little ones militate against it (for who can tell exactly at a distance?), I go back and obey the great order and **Object**. (emphasis added)[6]

Nelson could hardly have motivated his sailors with, 'to contribute to the wealth of the country'.

If anyone doubts that vision is the fundamental of leadership consider this: Leadership by definition requires followers; a goal reached without followers is not a leadership goal. While it may be exemplary, it is not leadership. When others follow the same or a similar path, then the example becomes leadership.

When one has a vision of one's own, it is exemplary; when others take up the same vision, it is leadership. One of the paradoxes is that a person can be a loner during their lifetime and become a leader after their death. The espousal of their vision by others has made the person a leader. Often the leader then becomes a posthumous hero or heroine.

Imparting the vision also implies that followers understand the mission and desired outcomes. Every follower or worker must be able to self-select objectives, goals or targets that will produce his or her own desired outcomes and that will contribute to the vision in the most effective way. They must be alert for continuous improvement. To do this, every intention you have must be clearly communicated to all. But to reach a goal you must establish a plan or pathway. It's no good having a great vision without a plan to get there.

3. *Adequate procedures*

Both yourself and your followers must have very clear procedures that speed decision making. This includes procedures relating to decision making and planning. These procedures do not constrain people; rather, they give an enormous amount of flexibility because there is no need to on-refer. This enables followers to make their own decisions within well-established parameters, even if this means disobeying previously issued directives or directions. Is any further evidence needed of the right and duty to selective disobedience, even at the ultimate cost of a mistake, than the quotation from Nelson above?

4. *Delegation and freedom from interference*

Keep out of the way. Don't keep a dog and bark yourself. Nobody better knows what they have to do in a PowerSharing environment than a trained follower. They'll let you know if they need you. By the same token, you must let them know that they don't need you. Remember— no questions only answers; no problems only solutions. Commensurate with this delegation is:

Full allocation of resources. If you are unwilling or unable to allocate resources and authority downwards then forget about PowerSharing leadership. This requires a step in the dark and almost a leap of faith. If you haven't the authority to allocate resources then take a risk, or forget about PowerSharing.

5. *Concern for followers*

People are the first and last resource and nothing in a leadership sense is ever achieved without them. If an endeavour requires more than one person, then the environment for leadership exists. The extent to which others are motivated will be the major determinant of the success or otherwise of the endeavour, notwithstanding other forms of support and assistance.

6. *Teamwork*

Everyone must work together. To the extent that someone tends to or wants to operate outside the team or dictate to the team then their position must be considered to be in jeopardy. This doesn't mean that there should be no team leader but that everyone's input is as important as everyone else's. Two plus two is greater than four.

7. *Influence the environment*

A leader must at all times know where followers are at!—without interfering. There could be many dependent or peripheral activities that need to be adjusted. Even so, accurate decisions can only be made on the basis of up-to-date information. It is not only information about followers that a leader must be in touch with, but up-to-date information on processes and progress towards objectives and external influences and factors.

8. *Identification with followers*

A leader needs to remain part of the team, which includes followers. It is more important to demonstrate empathy downwards rather than upwards. A leader must share the good and bad times and never try to find a scapegoat. Isolation from followers leads to only imaginary successes.

9. *Continuous training and development of followers*

If you expect your organisation to run like a well-oiled machine then you must oil it. This means training and developing followers in life issues as well as career matters. However, ultimately it is in your organisation that you want the results to occur. This requires investment and continual training and preparation of people in the expectations of your own organisation as well as outside development. The leader is more than a manager, he or she is a teacher, mentor and role model at every level.

10. *Awareness of your own limitations*

The advice once given to young leaders was: 'take everything seriously except yourself!' This contains a wealth of truth—because to be able to laugh at yourself you must know who you are. Even more so, you must know your followers, because they will know you, and their followers will know if you don't know them! It may sound strange, but in the ultimate, *the way a leader is judged can only ever be on the number and quality of genuine followers.* It is followers who make a leader's plan successful. If a leader ever achieved anything on his or her own, then he or she had no followers in that instance, and therefore he or she was not a leader.

> Leadership, by definition, requires followers; a goal reached without followers is not a leadership goal.

CONCLUSION

In this regard, there is one last point to make that often escapes the proponents of the so-called new leadership and that is this: in all the necessary thrust towards consultation, participation and teamwork, one must not automatically assume that peers or other team members are right. They are just as likely to be wrong—especially when it comes to communication—as you are. They are not infallible and there is still a place for enlightened direction, as long as outcomes are discussed and clear. It will help followers as much as leaders.

> Lead, follow or get out of the way.

For this reason it's unwise to attempt commitment to PowerSharing, which may involve such things as peer review, informally and without warning. It's also unwise to attempt it in a new or unstable environment. Stabilise the environment and let people genuinely get to know you and you them. PowerSharing is not something that you can have a piece of—it is a total philosophy.

Seeking the opinions and input of followers is essential and easy. Assessing the value of those inputs is difficult. Therefore let the team evaluate all those inputs prior to making a decision.

Even if you do everything right, things will go wrong. Followers aren't going to be perfect no matter how well a leader performs—and Murphy's Law is bound to intervene. That's why leadership is so challenging. Hopefully it will be made significantly easier by adherence to the principles of PowerSharing.

As was mentioned in the Introduction, this book was not designed to be an academic work. We hope it has been easy to read and even if you aren't an avid reader that you have been able to complete it in the course of a few boring train journeys from the outer suburbs to work and back. Perhaps it may also have helped you to sleep for a few nights.

The book represents the combined leadership experience of two people spanning in excess of sixty years and covering such diverse problems as the heat of battle, the convulsions of consulting, the traumas of career change, the vagaries of working with part-time or voluntary boards of directors, serving on boards of management and taking leadership roles in the community.

What we hope is obvious is that we have given some thought to the things we have done over the years and have at least tried to examine the reasons why we have done them, why some succeeded and some failed. We can both attest to the fact that you never stop learning and you must continue to live an examined life.

Finally, a leader is only a leader if there are followers. We both have had genuine followers at some periods of our lives. Only these people will ever be able to decide if we have been good or indifferent or poor leaders. Insofar as we place ourselves in their hands, that's the only way we can know. Generally speaking our fellow men and women are tolerant, compassionate, humorous, willing and trustworthy and to the extent that they aren't, then poor leadership must bear a good portion of the blame.

The final fifty

This questionnaire poses fifty questions. The questions represent a broad summary of the main thrust of 'So Now You're a Leader'. You should try to answer them as truthfully as possible. This means you and your circumstances should be grounded in current reality and your answers should reflect that reality. The questionnaire claims no statistical validity, nor is it a test, but it could be a helpful inventory for you and your workplace.

	Yes	No
1. Do you accept that you are ultimately responsible for the sum of the outcomes of your subordinates' work?	☐	☐
2. Is your vision understood and shared by your followers?	☐	☐
3. Are you aware of your subordinates' visions?	☐	☐
4. Do your followers know your values?	☐	☐
5. Do you know your followers' values?	☐	☐
6. Are your values in harmony with those of your followers?	☐	☐
7. Do you always keep your aim in mind while implementing your plan?	☐	☐
8. Do your subordinates always have a clear aim?	☐	☐

	Yes	No
9. Have you facilitated your subordinates prioritising activities in accordance with your aims?	☐	☐
10. Do you trust your followers?	☐	☐
11. Do you look for opportunities to demonstrate to your new subordinates that they have your trust?	☐	☐
12. Do all your subordinates trust you?	☐	☐
13. Do you differentiate between delegation and assigning tasks?	☐	☐
14. Do your followers receive full authority and resources for delegated responsibilities?	☐	☐
15. Do you check on outcome rather than process?	☐	☐
16. Do your subordinates understand that when they are given a job they are getting the whole job?	☐	☐
17. Do you let your subordinates do it their own way?	☐	☐
18. Does your organisation see people as more important than human resources?	☐	☐
19. Do your followers recognise your obligations to them?	☐	☐
20. Is line management ultimately responsible for people matters in your organisation?	☐	☐
21. Do you reward teams ahead of individuals?	☐	☐
22. Do your teams share more than a simple work task?	☐	☐

	Yes	No
23. Is loyalty important in your organisation?	☐	☐
24. Do you primarily direct your loyalty downwards?	☐	☐
25. Does your organisation or the work group you lead, function effectively for an extended period in your absence?	☐	☐
26. Do you have an open door policy?	☐	☐
27. Are you aware of the latest rumours in your workplace?	☐	☐
28. Are your followers open and truthful with you informally?	☐	☐
29. Are your subordinates confident about telling you what you don't want to hear?	☐	☐
30. Would your followers see you as consistent?	☐	☐
31. Do you have favourites among your followers?	☐	☐
32. Do you ensure that your favourites don't have privileges ahead of other?	☐	☐
33. Do you ensure that there is no division between those you particularly like and others?	☐	☐
34. Are your privileges based on your need to perform?	☐	☐
35. Do you encourage your subordinates to have personal career goals?	☐	☐
36. Does your organisation have a policy for personal/individual development?	☐	☐

	Yes	No
37. Are you aware of the social and recreational activities of your followers?	☐	☐
38. Do your followers have a funny story about you?	☐	☐
39. Do subordinates share their humour with you?	☐	☐
40. Despite humour, do your subordinates treat you seriously?	☐	☐
41. Do you have a process for recognising outstanding performance or achievement?	☐	☐
42. Do you try to mask your stresses and moods?	☐	☐
43. Do you know and accept your own strengths and weaknesses?	☐	☐
44. Do you actively seek to 'know' yourself?	☐	☐
45. Do you actively seek to better yourself?	☐	☐
46. Do you actively seek to know and better your subordinates?	☐	☐
47. Do people seek advice from you for other than work-related situations?	☐	☐
48. Do you put yourself in the background to promote your subordinates?	☐	☐
49. Does your organisation function along PowerSharing principles?	☐	☐
50. Are you prepared to share your answers to these questions with your subordinates?	☐	☐

If you find that you have answered 'yes' to all fifty questions, please contact us. Lois Lane would love to meet you.

While it would be unreasonable to expect anyone to answer 'yes' to all fifty questions, it is not unreasonable for anyone in a leadership position to aim for just that. If you answered yes to more than forty ask your subordinates to validate your perceptions (anonymously?). However many you answered positively you should be prepared to use the questionnaire at least as a guide to the organisational health in your workplace.

Endnotes

Introduction

1. Adair, John 1990, *Not Bosses But Leaders,* Kogan Page, London.
2. ibid.
3. Hersey, Paul 1984, *The Situational Leader*, University Associates, Escondido, California.
4. Fiedler, F. & Chemers, M. 1984, *Increasing Leadership in Action*, John Wiley & Sons, New York.

Chapter 1

1. Carlzon, Jan 1987, *Moments of Truth. New Strategies for Today's Customer-driven Economy*, Harper & Row, New York.

Chapter 2

1. Mant, Alistair 1983, *Leaders We Deserve*, Martin Robertson, Oxford.
2. Semler, Ricardo 1994, *Maverick!*, Arrow edition, London.
3. Senge, Peter M. 1992, *The Fifth Discipline*, Random House, Sydney.
4. International workplace survey as quoted in *The New Leaders* (Bi-monthly) March–April 1995, Sterling and Stone, San Francisco.
5. Senge, Peter M. 1992, *The Fifth Discipline*, Random House, Sydney.
6. ibid.
7. De Pree, Max 1989, *Leadership is an Art*, Australian Business Library, Melbourne.
8. Bennis, Warren 1976, *The Unconscious Conspiracy—Why Leaders Can't Lead*, Amacom, New York.

Chapter 3

1. Covey, Stephen 1989, *The Seven Habits of Highly Effective People*, The Business Library, Melbourne.

Chapter 4

1. Covey, Stephen, 1989, *The Seven Habits of Highly Effective People*, The Business Library, Melbourne.
2. Bennis, Warren 1976, *The Unconscious Conspiracy—Why Leaders Can't Lead*, Amacom, New York.
3. *Fort Hood Leadership Study* US Army CATA Ft Leavenworth Kansas 1986.
4. ibid.

Chapter 5

1. Albrecht, Karl 1990, *Service Within—Solving the Middle Management Leadership Crisis*, Dow Jones Irwin, Homewood, Illinois.

Chapter 6

1. Senge, Peter M. 1992, *The Fifth Discipline*, Random House, Sydney.
2. Gullett, Henry (Joe) 1978, *Not As A Duty Only*, Melbourne University Press, Melbourne. This quotation is probably the finest description of an infantry battalion ever seen by the authors, both of whom have been privileged to command one during their careers. It captures nothing of the organisation or management involved in such a command but it totally captures the spirit and energy without which all the command and leadership are as nothing. Joe Gullett would qualify in the first few pages of any book written about famous Australians.
3. Covey, Stephen 1989, *The Seven Habits Of Highly Effective People*, The Business Library, Melbourne.
4. ibid.
5. Semler, Ricardo 1994, *Maverick!*, Arrow Edition, London.
6. Wavell, Lord A.P. As quoted in Connell, John 1964, *Wavell, Soldier and Scholar,* Collins, London. Wavell was a wonderful trainer of men and a classical scholar and poet of no mean talent. He died in 1950 before he had the opportunity to blow his own trumpet in manuscript as many other famous generals did. Then again, his character was such that he may well not have done so even had the opportunity arisen.

Chapter 8

1. Mant, Alistair 1983, *Leaders We Deserve*, Martin Robertson, Oxford.
2. Williams, John 1981, *So Ends This Day*, Globe Press, Melbourne.
3. Covey, Stephen 1989, *The Seven Habits Of Highly Effective People*, The Business Library, Melbourne.
4. Williams, John op. cit.

Chapter 9

1. Hersey, Paul 1984, *The Situational Leader*, University Associates, Escondido, California.

Chapter 10

1. Powell, John 1969, *Why Am I Afraid to Tell You Who I Am*, Argus Communications, Illinois.
2. Semler, Ricardo 1994, *Maverick!*, Arrow Edition, London.
3. Handy, Charles 1990, *Inside Organisations*, BBC Books, London.
4. Keirsey, David & Bates, Marilyn 1978, *Please Understand Me*, Prometheus Nemesis, Del Mar, California.
5. Briggs-Myers Isabel with Myers, Peter B. 1980, *Gifts Differing*, Davies Black, (1995 edition), Palo Alto, California.
6. Benfari, Robert & Knox, Jean 1991, *Understanding Your Management Style*, D C Heath & Company, Lexington, Massachusetts.
7. ibid.
8. Senge, Peter M. 1992, *The Fifth Discipline*, Random House, Sydney.
9. Covey, Stephen 1989, *The Seven Habits Of Highly Effective People*, The Business Library, Melbourne.

Chapter 11

1. Adair, John 1990, *Not Bosses But Leaders*, Kogan Page, London.
2. Peters, Tom 1988, *Thriving on Chaos*, MacMillan, London.
3. The Report of The Industry Task Force on Leadership and Management Skills, 1995, *Enterprising Nation*, Australian Government Publishing Service, Canberra.
4. Dixon, Norman F. 1976, *On the Psychology of Military Incompetence*, Pimlico edition, London.
5. ibid.
6. ibid (As quoted in the above).

Bibliography

Adair, John 1988, *Developing Leaders—The Ten Key Principles*, McGraw-Hill, Maidenhead, Berkshire.

Adair, John 1990, *Not Bosses But Leaders*, Kogan Page, London.

Albrecht, Karl 1990, *Service Within—Solving the Middle Management Leadership Crisis*, Dow Jones Irwin, Homewood, Illinois.

Benfari, Robert, PhD (with Jean Knox) 1991, *Understanding Your Management Style,* D C Heath & Co, Lexington, Massachusetts.

Bennis, Warren 1976, *The Unconscious Conspiracy—Why Leaders Can't Lead*, Amacom, New York.

Bennis, Warren 1985, *Leaders—The Strategies for Taking Charge*, Harper & Row, New York.

Bennis, Warren 1993, *An Invented Life—Reflections on Leadership and Change,* Addison Wesley Publishing Co, Reading, Massachusetts.

Blanchard, Kenneth, Zigarmi, Patricia & Zigarmi, Drea 1990, *Leadership and the One Minute Manager*, Fontana Collins, London.

Briggs-Myers, Isabel with Myers, Peter B. 1995, *Gifts Differing*, Davies Black (1995 edition), Palo Alto, California.

Cabrera James C. & Albrecht Charles F. Jr. 1995, *The Lifetime Career Manager*, Adams Publishing, Holbrook, Massachusetts.

Carlzon, Jan 1987, *Moments of Truth*, Harper & Row, New York.

Cohen, C. 1990, *The Art of the Leader*, Prentice Hall, New Jersey.

Covey, Stephen 1989, *The Seven Habits of Highly Effective People*, The Business Library, Melbourne.

Covey, Stephen 1992, *Principle Centered Leadership*, Simon & Schuster, London.

De Pree, Max 1989, *Leadership is an Art,* Australian Business Library, Melbourne.

Dixon, Norman F. 1976, *On The Psychology of Military Incompetence*, Pimlico Edition 1994, London.

Fiedler, F. & Chemers, Martin M. 1984, *Increasing Leadership in Action—The Leader Match Concept*, John Wiley & Sons, New York.

Gullett, Henry 1978, *Not As A Duty Only*, Melbourne University Press, Melbourne.

Handy, Charles 1989, *The Age of Unreason*, Arrow Books, London.

Handy, Charles 1990, *Inside Organisations*, BBC Books, London.

Hersey, Paul 1984 *The Situational Leader*, University Associates, Escondido, California.

Keirsey, David & Bates, Marilyn 1978, *Please Understand Me*, Prometheus Nemesis, Del Mar, California.

Limerick, David and Cunnington, Bert 1993, *Managing The New Organisation*, Business and Professional Publishing, Chatswood, NSW.

Mant, Alistair 1982, *Leaders We Deserve*, Martin & Robertson, Oxford.

Peters, Tom & Waterman, Robert H. Jr 1990, *In Search of Excellence*, Harper Collins, Sydney.

Peters, Tom 1988, *Thriving On Chaos*, MacMillan, London.

Peters, Tom 1989, *Liberation Management*, MacMillan, London.

Semler, Ricardo 1994, *Maverick!*, Arrow Edition, London.

Senge, Peter M. 1992, *The Fifth Discipline*, Random House, Sydney.

Tichy, Noel M. & Devanna, Mary Anne 1986, *The Transformational Leader*, John Wiley & Sons, New York.

Report of the Industry Task Force on Leadership and Management Skills 1995, *Enterprising Nation*, Australian Government Publishing Service, Canberra.

US Army CATA, 1986, *Fort Hood Leadership Study*, Ft Leavenworth, Kansas.

Index